EVERYTHING
WAS POSSIBLE

EVERYTHING WAS POSSIBLE

The Birth of the Musical

FOLLIES

BY

TED CHAPIN

Alfred A. Knopf  New York   2003

THIS IS A BORZOI BOOK
PUBLISHED BY ALFRED A. KNOPF

Library of Congress Cataloging-in-Publication Data

Chapin, Ted.
Everything was possible : the birth of the musical Follies /
Theodore S. Chapin.
p.   cm.
ISBN 0-375-41328-6 (alk. paper)
1. Sondheim, Stephen. Follies.   2. Chapin, Theodore S.   I. Title.

ML410.S6872C53 2003
792.6'42—dc21   2002043291

Manufactured in the United States of America
First Edition

To the gentlemen and ladies of *Follies*, 1971

Life was fun, but oh, so intense.
Everything was possible and nothing made sense
Back there when one of the major events
Was waiting for the girls upstairs.

—from "Waiting for the Girls Upstairs"

Contents

Foreword

More than three decades after its premiere, *Follies* remains the most elusive of landmark Broadway musicals. Set at a reunion of onetime Follies performers on the eve of the destruction of their old theater, it is a show for which the word "problematic" could have been coined. Its theatricality is lavish but its mood is downbeat. Its storytelling plays tricks with time that are poetic to its fans but disorienting gimmickry to less sympathetic onlookers. The principal characters are narcissistic, unpleasant, and prone to onstage nervous breakdowns. Yet the Stephen Sondheim songs they sing are now classics of the musical-theater repertoire, full of heart even when they delineate arid, disappointed lives.

From the start, critics have been divided about *Follies*, passionately pro or con but rarely on the fence. The original production, though running well over a year at the Winter Garden, lost its entire investment. Major revivals in London (1987) and New York (2001) were also commercial failures. Each of them used revised versions of the original James Goldman book, and to this day there is no agreement as to what constitutes the "definitive" text. In each rendition, *Follies* draws new adherents, but also new detractors. Is it really a great musical, or merely the greatest of all cult musicals, the most fabulous of self-indulgent failures? Or might it be still unfinished, awaiting the perfect script revision, the radical new staging no one has yet thought of? Could one stroke of luck finally make the whole elaborate edifice fall into place as triumphantly as the Follies scenery descends in the fabled "Loveland" sequence?

In the pages to come, Ted Chapin doesn't try to answer these unanswerable questions, which is one of many reasons his memoir is so illu-

minating. He really does take us all the way back in time to 1971 when he was a twenty-year-old college student hired as a production assistant—i.e., a gofer—by the director Harold Prince. *Follies* was not a legend yet; it was another big new Broadway musical in a day when every season still boasted a number of big new Broadway musicals. Sondheim, Prince, and Prince's codirector, Michael Bennett, were rising young Turks and not yet the theatrical establishment they would become. Working from the detailed diary entries he kept at the time, Chapin resists superimposing the future of his characters and their project onto their past. He simply wants to tell us in real time how the show was put together from earliest conception to opening night (a story that is anything but simple). While he saw nearly everything and seems to have forgotten nothing, he never pours on the retrospective sentimentality that warps most backstage stories and those of Broadway musicals in particular. Nor does he gild his account with all the critical and cultist filigree that has attended *Follies* ever since. If there has ever been an account of the creation of a major Broadway production as complete, candid and apocrypha-free as this one, I have not found it.

What Chapin couldn't know in 1971 is that he was capturing not just the assembling of one particular show but a representative example of a dying breed. Everything was still possible on Broadway, but just barely; nothing in *Follies* made economic sense. Original new musicals with 27 musicians in the pit, 140 lavish costumes, and casts of 50 would soon be abandoned by the commercial theater. (Bennett's subsequent hit, the 1975 *A Chorus Line*, was developed Off Broadway and was the antithesis of *Follies* in scale.) And while certain chapters in the *Follies* story are eternal—the chaotic rehearsals, the clashing temperaments, the opening night party clouded by mixed reviews—much of the production process that Chapin charts here was already on the brink of extinction. He was an eyewitness to the last gasp of a low-tech Broadway, where script changes still had to be laboriously mimeographed (rather than Xeroxed, word-processed, faxed, or e-mailed), where orchestra parts were still copied by hand, where weak singing voices could not yet be rescued by body mikes, and where unfathomably complex scenic and lighting effects were not yet guided by computer. Toss in a company as eccentric as it was large—with a vividly drawn cast ranging from insecure B-list Hollywood stars and ancient Broadway hands to neophyte Vegas showgirls—and you have a

poignant snapshot of a showbiz civilization as distant from our time as 1971 was from the heyday of the Ziegfeld Follies.

Like Ted Chapin, I was also a minor college-age footnote to the *Follies* story (due to circumstances he'll explain), but we would not meet each other until many years later. Once we did, I came to admire him for his management of the Rodgers & Hammerstein Organization but never imagined that he might also have been a first-class journalist. Then again, his account of what he saw in 1971, written from the deep perspective of an observer who is now the same age or older than many of the principals in his narrative, cannot accurately be called journalism. It is history, and everyone who loves the musical theater will be the wiser for it.

—Frank Rich
February 2003

Follies *incarnate: Showgirl Ursula Maschmeyer in her beaded black-and-white costume—when the curtain rose, she was the only figure onstage.*

Introduction

". . . At Least I Was There"

It is fall 2001. I am standing on the stage of the Colonial Theatre in Boston. A total renovation has recently been completed, timed to coincide with the theater's one hundredth birthday, and the owners are throwing a party to celebrate. As president of the Rodgers & Hammerstein Organization, I have been invited to represent the contributions of Richard Rodgers and Oscar Hammerstein II, many of whose shows played at the Colonial on their way to Broadway. Their first joint effort, originally titled *Away We Go!*, was being performed on this very stage while, out in the lobby, the decision was being made to rename it *Oklahoma!* That's the kind of rich history that has been chronicled in a sumptuous new photograph-filled book, whose author is circulating through the crowd. There is a lot of mingling, sipping wine, and munching from the tables of food laid out around the stage.

I walk to the footlights, peering out at the empty auditorium. The cherubs adorning the front of the balconies, the frescoes on the ceiling, and the chandeliers are now gleaming. There is a gentle, elegant sweep to the rows and rows of newly upholstered seats, and over to the sides are the boxes, one on top of another, grand and ornate. Looking down to the orchestra pit, now covered, I think of the songs that were first played there, songs that have become famous.

My mind is on someone specific. A young man, who stood on this stage long before tonight. I can almost see him, that twenty-year-old, who found a way to observe rehearsals and the out-of-town period of a show he hoped—he knew—would be thrilling. Focused enough to keep a diary, he was enthusiastic and green; he kept his eyes and ears open to everything that was going on around him. Naive, but eager to please, he adored every minute.

Introduction

I am thinking of myself, age twenty, the gofer on *Follies*.

It's been thirty years since I was in this theater, but in many ways it feels like yesterday. While the cocktail festivities continue on the stage, I wander surreptitiously up the back stairs to the dressing rooms, all of them now locked, down to the darkness below stage, and through the pass door into the paneled foyer of the men's lounge. I climb up to the rear of the second balcony—not easy, since a separation of patron entrances was part of the initial design—and look down on the stage framed by the golden proscenium arch. It's all just as I remembered it. Nothing seems to have changed.

I get back down in time for the formal part of the celebration. A small platform with a microphone has been set up, downstage center, facing upstage. When introduced, I thank the hosts of the party for the meticulous restoration job they have done. I reiterate how important the Colonial Theatre was to the careers of Richard Rodgers and Oscar Hammerstein II, and to the history of American musical theater. I mention *Follies*, the Stephen Sondheim, James Goldman, Harold Prince, and Michael Bennett musical that played in the theater for four intense weeks during the winter of 1971. Acknowledging that I played a small role in that show's Colonial Theatre life, I tell the guests that the spot on which I am standing is where a song was first introduced to the world, an out-of-town replacement that soon became one of the staples of the Stephen Sondheim repertoire: "I'm Still Here." There is a bit of an "ooh" from the crowd. I conclude my remarks and go back to mingling. One stagehand, now in uncharacteristic suit and tie, tells me he has fond memories of *Follies*. He's proud of the many years he has put in working at the theater.

Follies is about the past, revisited, embraced, rejected, relived, denied. It is really about the effects the past has on the present and the future. Here I am, standing on this stage, thinking about that young man from the past and welcoming him into the present. I am back in 1971, with all those talented artists struggling to get their show right, with all those actors hoping this would be the one show that would do it for them. In the course of research for this book, I found that twenty-year-old in photographs, many of which I had no knowledge existed. He looks very young, he has too much hair, and his clothes have a decidedly collegiate look. I found him in one shot, seated among the entire creative staff, legal pad in hand, taking notes for Hal Prince (see page 110). What was he thinking at that precise moment?

What was he staring at so intently? Damned if I can remember. There's another shot in which everyone is laughing. At what? I realize he knew then, as I know now, that *Follies* would have happened without him. Its fate would have been the same. But his being there at the beginning has given me this gift today: the opportunity to get this all down on paper.

In the credits at the back of the Playbill for the original Broadway production of *Follies*, I am listed as "Production Assistant." That means "gofer"—the low man on the theatrical totem pole who runs all the errands and does whatever the management asks him to do: go for this, go for that . . . Hence the name. At the time, I was a junior at Connecticut College, which had recently gone coed. I had spent the fall on an experimental off-campus theater program and wasn't anxious to go straight back to school. The *Follies* rehearsal period neatly paralleled the second semester, and I felt I could probably sell the college on allowing me to make a credit-worthy independent study of observing the creation of an intriguing new American musical. In order to graduate on time, I would need to get two courses' worth of credit, so I agreed to keep a journal that I would fashion into a report. It was 1970; colleges then were somewhat in turmoil anyway, and they tended to welcome creative independent studies initiated by students. Thanks to one particularly sympathetic registrar, a holdover from the days of Connecticut College for Women with a twinkle in her eye for show business, my request was accepted. I hadn't yet quite gotten Harold Prince to agree to let me observe the rehearsals.

My fall semester's experience had been extraordinary. I was part of a group, and a motley group we were, of thirty undergraduates from all over the country participating in the inaugural semester of the National Theater Institute at the Eugene O'Neill Theater Center in Waterford, Connecticut. It was designed as an intensive program in which students would have nothing but theater thrown at them all day long, seven days a week. Courses were taught by professional theater practitioners in all kinds of disciplines; we had to take every one, regardless of what we thought our ultimate career goal might be. We designed sets; we studied acting. We put on kimonos and practiced Japanese theater techniques. Someone from Joseph Chaikin's innovative Open Theater had us twist into athletic clumps. The two design teachers, David Hays and Fred Voelpel, were working on a new Broadway-bound musical entitled *Two by Two*, so we piled into a bus

and went to see a dress rehearsal at the Shubert Theater in New Haven. We came to New York for a week to see shows and meet with actors, directors, and producers—including Hal Prince and Michael Bennett. Friday afternoons were set aside for puppetry, since Margo and Rufus Rose, the originators of *Howdy Doody*, lived nearby. For them we suffered through a series of visiting puppeteers who attempted to teach us what one referred to as "the most basic of all art forms because there is nothing between the creator and his art." We were, however, won over the day a gangly, soft-spoken Jim Henson arrived with a duffel bag full of his creations for a new children's television show that had just gone on the air. They were the Muppets from *Sesame Street* and he simply told us: "These are my friends." We were enthralled. Somehow going straight back to an undergraduate collegiate program of directing and acting in one-act plays at a college that didn't have a theater department and only a 2,000-seat proscenium auditorium known mostly for the American Dance Festival felt like an inevitable letdown. Working on *Follies*, I imagined, would provide a great decompression chamber. And I promised the college that I would gear up for a senior year in which I would stay on campus and do all the right things.

I had become a big fan of three of the creative artists who were collaborating on *Follies*: composer-lyricist Stephen Sondheim, producer-director Harold Prince, and choreographer-director Michael Bennett. I was staggered by their work on *Company*, the musical they had all produced the season before and which I had seen at an early preview matinee. Everything about the show struck me as new, vital, interesting, bold, contemporary—and wildly exciting. It told a story in a nonlinear way that still made logical sense. The characters and the relationships were modern and understandable. Something about it made me feel for the very first time that a musical could really be a serious work of contemporary theater. I couldn't quite explain why, but it made a connection for me both emotionally and intellectually as no other show had. I knew I wanted to be around the people who were creating this kind of theater. I had talked my way into attending the recording session of the original cast album of *Company*—an event captured brilliantly on film by D. A. Pennebaker (if you focus over Hal Prince's shoulder to the wavy hair and the plaid sport jacket in the background, you can see me lurking). I was just hell-bent determined to be part of their world. I

hungered for the opportunity to watch them work. I knew that *Follies* was their next project. And I wanted to be there.

I was lucky in one important respect. My father, Schuyler Chapin, had made his professional career in the arts, from concert management through running the classical division of Columbia Records, to general manager of the Metropolitan Opera, eventually becoming New York City Commissioner for Cultural Affairs. In him, I had a resource to be used—carefully—to help make connections. He had helped me get my first job as a production assistant in 1967, when I was sixteen. It was on the original production of Peter Ustinov's antiwar play *The Unknown Soldier and His Wife*, which was produced as part of Lincoln Center's Festival '67, one of the projects that fell under his general responsibilities as vice president for programming for Lincoln Center. The show was produced by Broadway's Alexander H. Cohen, whom I met at a family dinner. "So which one of you is coming to work for me?" he had asked. I piped up. He told me to write to his assistant, which I did, and became the production assistant, at seventy-five dollars per week. Originally only the gofer, when the rehearsals moved into the Vivian Beaumont Theater, I became the assistant to the director, John Dexter, as well. Dexter was a brilliant, demanding, and acerbic Englishman— just trying to keep on his good side was a task unto itself. A *New York Times* profile appeared at the time titled: "The Geometry of Pleasing Mr. Dexter."

A slightly rumpled figure hung around the theater during rehearsals, sitting in the auditorium, coming and going as he pleased. He didn't say much; he just sat there, unobtrusively, watching. He was Stephen Sondheim. Dexter was scheduled to direct Sondheim's new musical, *The Girls Upstairs*, which was to be produced the following season. They had worked together once before on *Do I Hear a Waltz?* an unhappy collaboration of a musical based on the Arthur Laurents play *The Time of the Cuckoo* with music by Richard Rodgers. But Dexter had been signed for the new show, and he invited Sondheim to hang around. Dexter described *The Girls Upstairs* as "a brilliant study in nostalgia with a breathtaking score." This was 1967, when Stephen Sondheim was known primarily as a lyricist, having written the words to Leonard Bernstein's music in *West Side Story* and to Jule Styne's music in *Gypsy*, both of which, of course, were big hits. He had then written both words and music for *A Funny Thing Happened on the Way*

to the Forum, which, though successful, failed to gain him recognition as a composer. His contribution wasn't even nominated for a Tony Award. The prevailing opinion in the theater community was that his music wasn't up to his lyrics, which were acknowledged to be brilliant. But he persevered, and his next effort was words and music for *Anyone Can Whistle*, an innovative, original story dealing with the question of insanity, which lasted only nine performances. It did have a champion, however, in Goddard Lieberson, president of Columbia Records, who felt so strongly about the show that he made an original cast album on the day after the show closed. The failure of *Anyone Can Whistle* threatened the future for Sondheim the composer. But after *Do I Hear a Waltz?* he swore he would never write only lyrics again. According to Dexter, *The Girls Upstairs* would show the world once and for all that Sondheim was as good a theater composer as anyone.

The Girls Upstairs had its genesis when Sondheim approached James Goldman about writing a musical together. Sondheim had read Goldman's play *They Might Be Giants* and felt he would be a good collaborator. Goldman had been contemplating a play about a reunion, and that led to discussions about a musical centered on a high school reunion. The focus shifted to ex–Ziegfeld Follies girls when an article about a gathering of Ziegfeld alumnae appeared in the *New York Times*. Inspired as well by the actual tearing down of the Ziegfeld Theater in 1966, the show they began to write told the story of a group of ex–Follies girls attending a party in the "Follies" theater the night before it was to be torn down. It evolved into a murder mystery, more of a "who'll do it," than a "who done it," as old jealousies among two ex–Follies girls and their husbands came to the surface. Finding a producer took several years, and in the interim Sondheim and Goldman collaborated on a television adaptation of a John Collier story titled *Evening Primrose* for ABC-Stage '67, a bold one-season series of original musicals created especially for television. In June of 1967 *The Girls Upstairs* was scheduled for the coming Broadway season, to be produced by David Merrick and Leland Hayward. The plan ultimately fell through, and a year later the show found its way into the hands of Stuart Ostrow, an innovative producer who was making something of a specialty of producing oddball musicals. He announced *The Girls Upstairs* for the 1969–70 season and hired Joseph Hardy to direct, fresh from Off-Broadway's successful *You're a Good Man, Charlie Brown*. At one point both *The Girls Upstairs* and *Company* were

Harold Prince: Producer, codirector.

scheduled to open in the same season. But the Ostrow production plan also fell through.

Harold Prince knew about *The Girls Upstairs*. He and Sondheim had been friends for years. He was a very active producer, having been responsible for several important hits, including *West Side Story*, *The Pajama Game*, and *Fiorello!* with partners, and then, on his own, *A Funny Thing Happened on the Way to the Forum* and *Fiddler on the Roof*. But as Sondheim wanted to be a composer, Prince wanted to be a director. When the opportunity arose to take over a musical in trouble entitled *A Family Affair*, written by John Kander and the brothers

Goldman, William and James, he jumped. Unfortunately, he wasn't able to turn it around. His next venture as a director was *She Loves Me*, a chamber musical by Jerry Bock, Sheldon Harnick, and Joe Masteroff, which he was also producing. Although not a financial success, it did garner a loyal following, but the direction was hardly mentioned in the reviews. He was then hired to direct *Baker Street*, a large musical based on Sherlock Holmes stories produced by Alexander H. Cohen. Cohen was known for extravagant spectacles (mostly bad), interesting theater pieces imported from England (mostly good), and an extraordinary and tasteful series of comic evenings with conveniently late curtains under the banner of "The Nine O'Clock Theater." For *Baker Street* he had hired the legendary director Joshua Logan, but when Logan left the project, Cohen approached Prince. Although Prince initially saw the show as a moderately sized musical, Cohen wanted it to be an extravaganza. I saw *Baker Street* during its pre-Broadway tryout and loved every minute, including its jubilee parade of marionettes devised by Bil Baird. When it came to Broadway, Cohen did everything imaginable to convince New Yorkers that it was the biggest hit of all time. He plastered Manhattan with billboards, some painted on blank sides of buildings never painted before or since, a couple of which remained well into the 1980s. The marquee of the theater had color photographs of his three stars—Fritz Weaver, Inga Swenson, and Martin Gabel—appearing, alternately, as reflections in a huge Victorian looking glass. He even played an extra performance one week, thus allowing him to claim in an ad that the show had achieved "the largest gross for a week of performances in Broadway history." The fact that there had been an extra performance was never mentioned. As it would turn out, *Baker Street* didn't set the world on fire, and it didn't do much for Hal Prince's career as a director. It looked as if the best producer for him to work with was himself. And that's what happened with *Cabaret*.

When I saw *Cabaret*, I was floored. Among other things, it was really interestingly directed. The theater community noticed and began to take Prince seriously in that role. The show was a marvel—a musical that really had something to say and said it in a dramatic and stylish way not normally associated with musicals at the time. The show was set in a cabaret—mostly—or was the theater itself a cabaret? It featured a bizarre emcee who charmed us and then turned on us. The creepiness of the milieu matched the creepiness of the story, in which multiple realities existed at the same time. The score was influ-

enced by the popular German music of the 1930s, and the cast even included Lotte Lenya, whose style and persona were so keenly linked to the era and its sound. She was singing new songs written in the style of her late husband, Kurt Weill. It felt authentic, it was theatrical, it was compelling, and it was brilliant. The same team followed the success of *Cabaret* with a less interesting musical adaptation of *Zorba the Greek*, titled *Zorbá*.

The *New York Times* reported in the spring of 1969 that Prince would produce and direct a new musical titled *Threes*, based on several short plays by George Furth about a bachelor and his married friends. The score would be by Stephen Sondheim, the man who had originally sent Furth's plays to Prince. The *Times* piece spoke of a new-style show, and who knew what that would mean? Prince and Sondheim had certainly worked together before, but never as director and composer. Few knew at the time that their friendship actually went back twenty years, to the opening night of *South Pacific*, when they met for the first time, Prince having come as a guest of the Richard Rodgers family and Sondheim having come with his Doylestown family friends Oscar and Dorothy Hammerstein. It proved to be a pivotal event for the two young enthusiasts who obviously shared a passion for the musical theater and wanted to be part of Broadway. They had remained friends through the years and had been working toward collaborating at what they both wanted most to do. This new show sounded as if it might be the right project.

Indeed it was. *Threes* became *Company*. Its premiere in April 1970 was greeted with the kinds of intelligent cheers reserved for something truly new and exciting. Some carped that the show was antimarriage and didn't add up to much, but for those of us who flipped, it was a moment for rejoicing. Suddenly there seemed to be an interesting future for the musical theater. As Richard Rodgers observed toward the end of his autobiography when asked where the musical theater is heading, "One night a show opens and suddenly there's a whole new concept." That's what *Company* felt like. Prince and Sondheim were suddenly a collaborative team to reckon with. Their own individual talents were singled out, but something about their collaboration made people feel the American musical theater had been set on a path to the future.

No one knew it at the time, but, in fact, Prince had agreed to produce *The Girls Upstairs* next if Sondheim would agree to write *Com-*

pany. That was actually the only way he could get Sondheim to agree to do *Company.* So on the Sunday following the opening of *Company,* the News of the Rialto column in the *New York Times* was titled "It's Those 'Girls' Again" and contained the news that the show would be "available early next spring following rehearsals in December or January."

The important third member of the *Company* team was its young choreographer Michael Bennett. Bennett had been quietly working his way up through the ranks, from dancing in Broadway choruses to dancing in the youthful television series *Hullabaloo,* and then to choreographing Broadway musicals. He had done four so far, and had received Tony nominations for them all. *Promises, Promises* had been the one for which he was the most noticed. His energetic dances matched the spirit of a show written by the then enormously successful pop songwriting team of Burt Bacharach and Hal David. I enjoyed *Promises, Promises,* but it didn't feel special to me. So I was unprepared for my reaction to his contribution to *Company.* I had never seen anything quite like it. With a cast made up almost entirely of non-dancers (his muse, Donna McKechnie, was the only bona fide dancer in the group), he managed to keep a fluidity to the movement in and around Boris Aronson's multileveled steel and chrome set so there was no discernible seam between dance and other stage movement. His use of standard dance steps performed by non-dancing actors felt appropriate, dramatic, and almost political. Case in point: during "Side by Side," a song about having a partner, there was one section in which each married couple did a little time step, in turn—first the husband, then the wife. The couples were lined up across the stage, and alternated—first from extreme stage right, the next one from extreme stage left, working to the lead character, Bobby, who was in the center. When his turn came, he did the husband half and then pointed to where his wife should be, and there were simply four empty counts of nothing. It was funny, it seemed to come out of nowhere, and it was totally appropriate. The audience wasn't prepared for it, yet it told us everything we needed to know about how single and alone that character was, especially as the rest of the company continued to dance cheerily on with their partners beside them while Bobby just stared at the empty spot on the stage.

Once I knew that the same team would be doing another show, I wanted to be there, so I wrote Hal Prince a formal letter asking if I

could observe the rehearsal period of *Follies*. I had met him through my parents as well as having seen him during the week when the National Theater Institute had come to New York. One of the shows we saw was *Company*, and afterward we all went back to George White's apartment to meet with both Hal and Michael Bennett. Hal wrote back, urging me to meet with his trusted associate and right hand, Ruth Mitchell, who didn't seem overly thrilled with the notion. After some gentle coaxing, I was given the green light, but I was told that I would have to be Ruth Mitchell's general assistant as well. I was soon to learn that two other people had also been given permission to observe rehearsals—a young playwright named Carole Wright, who had won an established position of "observer" through the New Dramatists, and Larry Cohen, the New York–based theater critic for the *Hollywood Reporter.* He was planning to write a book about the making of a musical. Carole didn't appear to be too interested in the process and stayed close to Jim Goldman on the rare occasions when she was around. Cohen came and went, and he and I became friends. He started out knowing no one, but as the rehearsal period progressed he established a friendship with Michael Bennett. When he realized that would give him a bias were he to follow through on his plans to write a book, he abandoned his project. He and Michael remained friends and colleagues after *Follies*. I've stayed in touch with him through the years. He has become a respected screenwriter, and we worked together when he wrote the teleplay for the ABC-TV version of Rodgers and Hammerstein's *South Pacific.*

And so I became part of the *Follies* family. For the most part, I was made to feel welcome. Any new show in rehearsal becomes a family, if a forced one, and the *Follies* family was pretty good. Some reached out to me more than others did, but I never felt like an intruder or an outsider. Some in the company knew that I was making notes and keeping a journal, others did not. Justine Johnston, elected the Equity deputy, asked me early on if I was writing a novel. One of the actors, Fred Kelly, brother of Gene Kelly, offered observations from time to time for "that journal of yours." But for the most part, I was just the gofer to everyone. Conversation was spirited and gossipy in some quarters, while in others discretion was strictly maintained. I tended to be more interested in the creative staff and the principal actors, but that was at least partly because the chorus tended to stick together.

Introduction

What I wrote in my journal was only what I actually saw and heard. Some of what went on behind closed doors filtered out to the rest of us; some of it will never be known. My adventures took me away from rehearsals a fair amount, but there was always something to learn from the task at hand. I loved the experience of watching the show as it grew, changed, and emerged. Whenever I didn't have a specific task, I would sit in on rehearsals. There were usually three different ones happening simultaneously—dance, music, and dialogue—and I couldn't be in three places at one time. I had to choose. I grew to love the show and came to have my own opinions about the changes that were being made. Sometimes I questioned a choice, and, confused, would jump to the conclusion that someone didn't know what he or she was doing. Perspective is hard to come by when you are in the trenches. I grew to respect some of the artists more than others. Some people were kind; some were downright mean. Some observed strict hierarchical lines and wouldn't speak to those they deemed on a level below theirs. Mostly, everyone was extremely professional. Obvious tensions caused some appalling behavior. I watched people become totally stymied. I overheard conversations I thought were insulting, and yet I believed they were all in the interests of saving time and cutting through to the best idea. I watched collaboration at work, and wondered whether there were any fixed rules to the process. I saw good work being done; I saw some work I thought embarrassing. The constant was the show and getting every element coordinated to be ready for the curtain to rise for the first paying audience on Saturday, February 20, 1971, in Boston. That is, of course, one of the magic aspects of the theater— hate or love your collaborators, no one can avoid the fact that everything and everybody must be ready at the same time. That curtain will go up, no matter what. By the time the show opened in New York, I wasn't sure whether *Follies* was brilliant or flawed, or both. I knew elements were brilliant—of that there was no doubt. And I was hooked. I was also having the most magical experience of my life. "God-damnedest hours that I ever spent," as one lyric goes.

The summer following my *Follies* semester I ended up in San Francisco working on a doomed production of Leonard Bernstein's *Candide*. Several of us in the company rented a large house in San Rafael. One of the game rooms had a table large enough for me to

spread out all my notes and attempt to fashion my report for the English Department at Connecticut College. It took the better part of the summer, and even after about 120 typed pages I still hadn't quite made it to opening night on Broadway. I had never before attempted any piece of writing that long, and nothing in my schooling had taught me to make the choices needed to fashion a working journal into readable form. It was a daunting task. I took my best guesses as to how much background information and opinion to include. My paper was titled "Bargains, Buddy," from a line spoken by Phyllis, the acerbic and sophisticated character played by Alexis Smith. It seemed a good assessment of the collaborative process I observed. Luckily, I was granted the course credit I needed and did graduate on time.

My experience would have been a whole lot less interesting had the show not become *Follies*. *Follies* is now considered a legend, a cult, and a landmark. At the time, we were all just hoping for a good old-fashioned smash hit. My guess is that Hal Prince was counting on the show-business grandeur of a production linked even tangentially with the Follies of old to appeal to a larger audience than he had been able to find with *Company*. The initial publicity was extensive; in addition to the usual preopening interviews with cast members, articles and color photo spreads appeared in publications ranging from fashion magazines to technical theater journals. Both *Time* and *Newsweek* were planning to do cover stories on the show. Because of the surprise success of a revival of the 1920s musical *No, No, Nanette*, starring Ruby Keeler, the press looked at *Follies* as further proof that nostalgia was the theme of the 1970–71 Broadway season.

When the show opened, both out of town and in New York, the reviews were split down the middle. Passions were in full force on both ends of the spectrum. Those who didn't like it were cruel and dismissive. Those who liked it used words like "thrilling," "sumptuous," "groundbreaking," and "dazzling"—its champions have been loud from the very beginning. Those who loved the show went back to see it time and time again. Early on, fans kept up vigils of letter-writing and commentaries in the press. *New York* magazine even featured it in one of its literary competitions: readers were instructed to come up with an alternate origin for the famous Dickens quote "It was the best of times, it was the worst of times." The winning entry was, "And what did you think of *Follies*?"

Maybe part of its enduring interest is precisely that it can't be

pinned down. At its core it is about something that keeps changing in each of us. Reconciling who we thought we were then, who we are now, what we hoped for then and what we're stuck with now are not simple matters. They begin to tell us what *Follies* is all about. Sondheim, Prince, Bennett, and Jim Goldman were at high points in their careers. In fact, all members of the creative staff, including the designers, arrangers, and orchestrator, were at the peak of their talents. *Follies* solidified the Prince-Sondheim collaboration and they became recognized as two of this country's great theater artists.

So why this book now? First, I think there is a great story to tell. The putting together of a new American musical is something that remains intriguing. As people have grilled me about specifics over the years, I realized there is an abiding fascination with this particular show. Frank Rich, who figures in this story later on, asked about the number of performances in which Alexis Smith omitted singing her character's signature song "Could I Leave You?" during the Boston run. Others have asked what specific members of the company were like. There have even been some persistent myths that I've been happy to help debunk.

Second, having observed what it was like to be a collaborative artist, I have nothing but admiration for the artists who created *Follies* in 1971. I discovered they were all people with foibles—which shouldn't have been a surprise, though to a wide-eyed potential groupie, it was. Watching them work hard to create something a little different from anything that had come before was seductive. At every stage there was someone on the creative staff who was miserable. Hal Prince hated the early rehearsals before everybody knew their lines. James Goldman hated going out of town. Steve Sondheim had so much to do that he seemed to be in a perpetual state of distress. And there was tension built into the team: Michael Bennett and Harold Prince were billed as codirectors, something neither of them relished but which both realized was the right thing for this particular show. Each man knew that he needed the other, although I think they were reluctant to admit it. In addition, everybody hated opening nights.

Third, once I decided to give this book a try, I was struck by something I hadn't realized. While reviewing my daily notes and diaries, I found many direct quotes. In addition to the notes I kept during the day, I also sat down at home each night and typed out three or four expanded pages of what I had seen and heard. There were many actual

quotes that I had culled from the day's activities. To discover Michael Bennett's fear of growing old expressed in a comment in which he all but predicted that he would be dead by the time he was forty-five was chilling. Stephen Sondheim's precise instructions to performers about how to deliver his material were illuminating. Hal Prince's energized comments provided almost a running commentary on the proceedings. James Goldman was decidedly taciturn, but his few comments were choice. And many members of the cast made wonderfully appropriate wisecracks and observations. All direct quotes come from my notes.

One final thought. In some ways, writing this book now is betraying confidences. I wasn't just "a fly on the wall"—I had tasks to perform and had conversations with people that weren't meant for publication. Sometimes when I contemplated this book I wondered if there wasn't something a little voyeuristic about the whole exercise. But I kept coming back to the idea that I had witnessed something unique and important. I saw the agony of artists at work. I saw a lot of disparate, almost warring, elements merge together to become a show. Everyone wanted *Follies* to succeed, whatever the cost. That, I realized, is what putting a musical together is all about.

EVERYTHING
WAS POSSIBLE

1

"... Walking Off My Tired Feet"

Over the New Year's weekend (1971) I got a phone call from production stage manager Fritz Holt. He asked whether I could show up at the studio at ten A.M. on Sunday, January 3rd. I didn't think rehearsals were to begin for another week, but since I was just hanging around at home, I agreed. The show was rehearsing at the American Theater Lab, which filled the entire second floor of a two-story building on West Nineteenth Street, just off Seventh Avenue, above a tire shop. It had been created for Jerome Robbins, one of America's most talented choreographers and directors, who wanted to experiment with a European-style workshop. The experiment didn't work, but it left a workable space in which Harold Prince liked to rehearse his shows. The quarters were spare, but more than adequate: one large rehearsal room big enough to represent an entire Broadway stage; a second room half its size, large enough for dance rehearsals; and a third one even smaller, for music. Support facilities included a couple of offices in the front, changing rooms in the back, and a commons room with some slightly ratty sofas and chairs.

Few people were around when I arrived. As I came up the stairs I heard a piano and a number of feet thumping a steady rhythm. I reported to the first open door I came to—the production stage managers' office, where Fritz Holt greeted me as "our production assis-

3

tant." First day, first defeat—or so I thought. "Production assistant" is the theater euphemism for "gofer," and that's not what this experience was supposed to be. Sure, I had done it twice before, and enjoyed it both times. But this was to be different; even though I had agreed to be a general assistant to Ruth Mitchell, this time I simply wanted to observe the process. That's also how I had sold it to Connecticut College, which was giving me credit for observing a show being assembled. I hadn't proposed an independent study of fetching coffee and sandwiches. The journal I agreed to keep would show an observer's objective eye, not the musings of an errand boy, so when I heard myself referred to as the "production assistant," my heart sank. But in short order I realized I was wrong. While I still had plenty of time to observe, being the gofer gave me a real position, albeit a minor one, within the company. It also, frankly, gave me things to do, and as the weeks went on, I ended up with some pretty responsible tasks, including maintaining up-to-date scripts with all the constantly changing dialogue and lyrics. I was made to feel a part of the experience, and felt accepted by the company in a way I might not have been had I just been watching. And being the gofer gave me license to wander into rehearsals without people feeling as if a stranger were in their midst. It provided a great position from which to observe the goings-on.

Fritz introduced me to the two other stage managers: first assistant and dance captain George Martin, a lithe and tidy, well-groomed gray-haired dancer who seemed a model of efficiency and discretion; and second assistant John Grigas, an ex-dancer, somewhat older, stern faced, and with a caustic quip for every situation. Clearly not a man to cross. His first words to me were: "We want you to go out and get us some coffee." So I pulled out my pad, took the orders, and out I went. If a job is worth doing, I figured, it's worth doing well—and I had learned during my first gofer experience that in New York, "regular" coffee means coffee with milk and sugar, not "regular" as in plain. There is no such thing as plain—black means black, regular means regular, and those who prefer regular are sorely disappointed to open a cardboard cup and find black liquid inside. I'd made that mistake.

A musical as large as *Follies* needed its three stage managers. Fritz Holt, as production stage manager, was ultimately the boss of the stage and everything behind the curtain. It was his responsibility to schedule the overall rehearsal period and to coordinate all technical aspects of the production. He was also the liaison with the shops—costume,

props, scenery—and with all the other support personnel who were contributing to the show. During the rehearsals, he would stay with Hal in the large room whenever possible, marking down the blocking and scene shifts in his master script. It would become the map by which the show would be run once in the theater, and since he would be responsible for all understudy and brush-up rehearsals, his script needed to be up to date and accurate. George Martin, as dance captain, would stay with Michael, and he would notate the dances, both as a reminder of what had happened in prior rehearsals as well as to create a choreographic map for the whole show. John Grigas was stationed in the office, and so became the conduit for company problems and concerns. He was also assigned the small acting role of a chauffeur. Once the show got assembled onstage, Fritz would call the show from the stage managers' desk on stage right, George would man his desk on stage left, and John would float backstage and assist any performer who needed guidance or a helping hand.

During rehearsals, the stage managers were clearly in charge of logistics. Schedules were their responsibility, not only of who would be using which room, but who would be needed for what rehearsal. As I was shown around, each room's use was described to me. Today the midsized rehearsal room was Michael Bennett's domain, as evidenced by the sounds of dance rehearsals already in progress. The music room was empty, with only a piano and a couple of chairs placed about. When we got to the large rehearsal room, John said, ". . . and this is where Mr. Prince will be working, so always check first with Fritz before coming in here." I was shown where I should park myself in the common hallway while waiting for tasks, always making myself available, never in anyone's way, but near the bulletin board and the pay phone. "Get yourself a clipboard and always be poised for action," he said. The whole place looked organized, and the stage managers' office was most organized of all—desk, typewriter, phone, cups of pens and pencils, stacks of current scripts, neat piles of music, etc. There was also a two-drawer filing cabinet. "This is where Mr. Prince keeps his stuff," John said, and then, pointing to the lower drawer, ". . . and this is where he keeps his Courvoisier." (It wasn't Courvoisier; it was Fernet-Branca, a digestif that had been recommended to Hal as a cure for his anxiety-prone gut, or what he referred to as "JBS—Jewish Boy Stomach." Once he found out it contained alcohol, he stopped having it around.)

Through the wall I heard a piano playing one particular section of one song over and over while several voices sang, repeatedly: "Mirror, mirror, on the wall, who's the saddest gal in town?" The dancers were working with Michael Bennett and his longtime assistant Bob Avian. John Berkman, the dance-music arranger, was at the keyboard. Paul Gemignani, the show's percussionist, was at the trap set. "Who's That Woman?" was being created. More on that later.

Harold Prince arrived at noon. He greeted me warmly and said that the day before, he had turned to his ever-present associate Ruth Mitchell—called Ruthie by one and all—and said: "Where's Ted? Get him down here now, for God's sake. We can always keep him busy!" The place seemed far too empty for Hal; he was anxious to get rehearsals going. He wandered around, trying to find things to do. Walking into the empty large rehearsal room, the one I had been told would be his, he said, "I just want to *start*! Give me some actors, *please*!" Outlines of the intricately tiered set had been taped out on the floor; it passed his inspection. By week's end there would be movable platforms approximating the levels of the set, but for now the traditional masking tape would have to do. Back in the stage managers' office, he pulled out a transparency of the poster for the show and proudly taped it to the window, declaring it to be "the best poster I have ever had." Colorful and striking, it had been created by David Byrd, a longhaired young artist whose distinctive style was first noticed in his psychedelic posters for the Fillmore East—sometimes called "nouveau art nouveau." He had walked into Hal's office one day and said, "I want to do posters for you." Hal said, "Sure," and luckily his initial take on *Follies* led to this artwork, which both Hal and the advertising agency felt was the best idea presented. Its focal point was a face, bold, austere, and stony, with droopy and prominent eyelids—presumably a woman—looking up and out, wearing the rest of the poster, including the bold lettering proclaiming the title of the show, as if it were a headdress. (A stark black-and-white photograph of Marlene Dietrich was said to be an inspiration.) Running from her lower right cheek, across her face and continuing up past her left eye up through the "E" of "FOLLIES" was a long, widening crack. Something was clearly amiss in the image of this American icon. The colors were very strong, with shades of orange in the space below where all the credits would ultimately go, a border of orange, pink, blue, and midnight blue at the top with nighttime stars shining through. It seemed appropriate, yet very strong. (A

few months later, the producer of *Godspell* looked out his office window at the Winter Garden marquee and told David Byrd, "Make me a poster like that," which he did. Byrd's *Godspell* poster was stylistically similar.)

With only one dance number actually in rehearsal, Hal didn't know what to do. He tried to get in touch with anyone he could find via phone. First was Florence Klotz, the costume designer. "Where is she? She could be designing a costume now and could bring a sketch down at the end of the day!" Because it was Sunday, there was no one at his office in Rockefeller Center to tell him what the box office grosses had been for the week just ended for his other two shows then running on Broadway: *Fiddler on the Roof* ("it did $29,000 for the first two performances, so I hope we did over $70,000 for the week") and *Company*. He called Stephen Sondheim: "I'm having a nervous breakdown. I'm down here with nothing to do and I've lost all enthusiasm for the show."

Then Ruthie, his calming influence, arrived. A former stage manager, she had worked with Hal for years and knew him better than anyone. Sensing his restlessness, she told me, "Wait until next week when everyone is here. It's easier when everyone is working. This week is just piddling around." In fact, there was a lot of piddling around to do in this final week before the full company rehearsals began.

O nce Hal Prince took on *The Girls Upstairs* it became *Follies*. Although he had said offhandedly that the first title sounded to him like "a bunch of hookers," the change to *Follies* was profound. He wasn't sure that a murder-mystery musical would work, and wasn't interested in finding out. But he was intrigued by the psychology of a reunion of old chorus dancers, and loved the play on the word "follies"; in addition to the obvious Ziegfeld Follies connection, he was intrigued by the notion of a "folly," something frivolous and silly, as well as the madness inherent in the French word *folie*. Operating, as it was, on many different levels, the show was the kind of musical that interested Prince, the director. He found inspiration in a black-and-white photograph he saw in a book about old movie palaces, which had originally appeared, albeit in a slightly different pose, in full color in the 1960 election-day issue of *Life* magazine, with the caption: "Swan Song for a Famous Theater." The photograph was of Gloria Swanson standing amidst the rubble of the half-demolished grand foyer of the Roxy The-

ater, looking upward, with her arms outstretched, dressed in black, but dressed to the nines—"gowned in a Jean Louis sheath, a feathery boa, and $170,000 in jewels"—and standing on a steel I beam. Her glamour stood in stark contrast to the surroundings. What's left of the Roxy Theater looks as if it must have been spectacular, with elements of the gold filigree still gleaming, although everything is half destroyed and beyond repair, with broken concrete, dangling wires, and bricks strewn about. Swanson, who had starred in *The Love of Sunya*, the movie that had opened the Roxy thirty-three years earlier, looks triumphant. Or is she pleading for something? Clearly it's too late to stop the wrecking ball. Is she somehow embodying show business from the viewpoint of someone with a glamorous past dealing with the harsh realities of the present? Is this a show-business precursor to Greenpeace? Whatever its true meaning, it is an extraordinary photograph, filled with romance, heartbreak, glamour, pathos, and drama. It was, Hal felt, a key to what he wanted the show to be about. It provided him with a tool to use with his collaborators as they reinvented *Follies* from the elements of *The Girls Upstairs*.

Hal decided he wanted to use ghost figures. Some would be ghosts from the Follies of the past, reminiscent of the grandeur of the Ziegfeld showgirls, who would haunt the shadows of the present, almost as part of the scenery. But he also wanted specific ghost characters to portray many of the principal characters as they were back then. The present-day characters would not necessarily be aware of their ghost counterparts, although they might be. He challenged Steve, Jim, and Michael to come up with ways to make the two realities play off each other. Characters and their ghosts could exist side by side, and conversations could take place that were part present and part past. Ghosts could act out what the present-day characters are remembering—sometimes accurately, sometimes not. Present-day characters could try to go back in time to change the outcome of what happened, and so on. Michael had the thought that the ghosts haunting the theater would move very slowly, drifting throughout in their own rhythm as lurking memories. He was conjuring ideas for "Who's That Woman?" a musical number in which the various possibilities of past and present would play off each other. And it was his idea that all ghosts would be dressed in black and white—characters as well as showgirls. All characters in the present would be in full color.

Originally, the plan was that at the penultimate moment, the girls,

led by Sally, would put together a realistic show for their husbands and the party guests. During rehearsals for their show, history would repeat itself as Sally and Ben would run off to Weissmann's upstairs office together to relive a moment of youthful indiscretion, creating a scene in a slightly surreal time warp. This was in some ways the apotheosis of an idea that Sondheim had dealt with at the end of the first act of *Anyone Can Whistle* where reality and fantasy merged in the song "Simple." As *Follies* transformed, the idea of the girls' doing a show remained, but Hal liked the idea of making it surreal. A Follies, if you will, in which the entertainments resonated with the characters, where ghosts and present-day characters would break through time boundaries and turn on each other or comment on each other. It would be a reenactment of a Follies from days gone by—but with a twist. Whoever was to sing "Losing My Mind," for example, would be doing just that. And each of the four lead characters would have a turn. This was clearly exciting and innovative, but one problem continued to haunt everyone: Once we're in this surreal follies, how do we get out and get back to reality? No one yet had the answers, and as a result, several songs for the show, including most of those needed for this still-developing sequence, had yet to be written. In fact, the last page of the script that would be handed out on the first day of rehearsal read: STILL TO BE WRITTEN.

And the cast wasn't complete. John McMartin had been cast just days before, since the original actor hired for the role of Ben, Jon Cypher, had backed out after participating in a reading of the script around a table in November. His performance had been lackluster, and something about the role troubled him. The role of his younger counterpart wasn't filled either. And no one had been successful in finding an older ballroom-dancing couple to provide the modern-day versions of Vincent and Vanessa, a specialty couple whose bolero was to be a choreographic highlight of the show.

There were last-minute changes, additions, and deletions being made to the designs for scenery and costumes. All the designers were eager to hear what the Follies sequence would contain so that they could begin. For them, time was ticking away, as all new designs would have to be approved and budgeted before they could be handed over to the shops. The closer to opening night, the less time there is, the more overtime might be needed, and therefore the more things would cost. I also soon discovered that the whole production was way overbudget

already. That at least partly explained why I was asked to be the gofer: the budget didn't allow for a paid position, and I was free labor.

The dancing ensemble was already hard at work. It's customary with a large musical for the dancers to begin ahead of the full company, so they had been called in on Saturday. When a break was called, the six men and eight women dancers emerged, and I was introduced. This was a friendly group—friendlier than other companies I had been around. When introduced to Michael, I reminded him that we had met a few months earlier at George White's apartment, with the students from the National Theater Institute. "Oh," he said, "I don't remember much about that evening—I was too drunk."

The four leading actors had been called in a week early as well. To the Broadway community, they were a surprising group, names with some recognition factor but without strong theater associations. Of the four, two had never appeared on Broadway, one had appeared only once (and that had been many years before), and one was familiar with the territory. They were all eager to get a head start on learning their songs, and Michael was anxious to see how much choreography they were going to be able to master, especially the women, since he already had a notion for "Who's That Woman?" that would require some fairly extensive dancing from all the leading ladies. They were supposed to have been good dancers at one point in their lives, but they were now "of a certain age." Some of the cameo parts had been cast with actors in their sixties and seventies, but the leads were only supposed to be thirty years past their dancing days. And they had to carry the show. Calling them in a week early would also help them feel comfortable with each other. They all arrived after lunch.

Alexis Smith and Gene Nelson had flown in from California. Although they were well known in Hollywood circles, starring on Broadway was a new experience for them both. Alexis, who would play Phyllis, had only appeared in summer-stock productions of musicals. Her career had been mostly in Hollywood, where she had been plucked by Warner Brothers directly from college in 1940 to play leading ladies in what ended up being a series of B-grade movies. They changed her first name from Gladys to Alexis, and cast her opposite many of Hollywood's most romantic leading men—Errol Flynn, Cary Grant, Clark Gable. She often made a good impression in clearly secondary productions. Among her best films were 1945's *Conflict*, which she nearly stole away from Humphrey Bogart and Sydney Greenstreet,

1954's *The Sleeping Tiger*, directed by Joseph Losey, and *Night and Day*, in which she played Mrs. Cole Porter. She was clearly intelligent and was often called upon to play "disarming schemers and beguiling opportunists." She had remained comparatively inactive during the 1960s, preferring the role of wife to Craig Stevens, who was enjoying success as the lead in the television series *Peter Gunn*. They had toured together in various theater productions, most recently with *Cactus Flower*. Looking quite smashing at forty-nine, she stood tall in red knickers, white shirt, and a blue sweater wrapped around her shoulders. She had an infectious, good-natured cackle of a laugh that could be heard echoing down the hall. Her straightforward manner was very helpful, if at times a bit harsh. When I asked if she wanted some coffee, for example, she replied: "I'm not a coffee drinker, so you never have to ask me again." She was, however, always grateful and gracious when I did bring her what she wanted—buttermilk. I was told that at her first audition, she looked less than glamorous, but before her second she was put in the hands of Ruthie Mitchell and the show's hair designer, Joe Tubens, who turned her into the movie star she had been in the 1950s. She also worked with David Craig, the guru of singing coaches for nonsinging actors. His magic was such that he was able to instill the kind of confidence that ultimately led her to win a Tony for her role in *Follies*. Although she gave off the aura of not caring profusely about her career, she was determined to be in this show and had worked tirelessly to get the part. It would prove to be the highlight of her later career.

Gene Nelson was very friendly. He had been an athletic actor-dancer in Hollywood musicals of the 1950s, originally a figure skater, best known for his role as Will Parker in the film of *Oklahoma!* His other dance films had titles like *She's Working Her Way Through College*, *Painting the Clouds with Sunshine*, and *Three Sailors and a Girl*. Anticipating the end of his dancing career, he began to direct both feature films and television, including two Elvis Presley movies and a slew of television series. After changing his birth name from Eugene Berg, he appeared briefly on Broadway in the 1940s before moving west. When his name came up for *Follies*, Michael immediately remembered him as the best dancer in all those Hollywood musicals. He was quick and cheerful, always with a handshake at the ready, like a really nice and honest salesman. His character, Buddy, was in fact a traveling salesman, so he and Buddy were a neat fit. His usual attire was a light-blue sweatshirt, light-gray slacks, and white loafers. Our conversations rarely

Dorothy Collins and Gene Nelson—a publicity shot.

amounted to much more than "Hi there, Teddy boy," but he was pleasant and open. He was clearly psyched for this experience, if a little nervous, looking trim and fit. He asked if it was okay for him to come in an hour early each day to warm up before rehearsal. He and Alexis compared Hollywood notes. He rattled off the guest list of a going-away party that had been thrown for him: ". . . oh, Donna Reed was there, and Tony Quinn and his wife came over . . ." The other Hollywood creature in the cast, Yvonne De Carlo, was a featured player who would show up with the rest of the company the following Saturday.

The other two principals were from the East Coast. Dorothy Collins was known primarily as a singer and for her appearances on television's *Your Hit Parade* and *Candid Camera*. She had been spending a lot of time performing in the summer and winter stock circuits,

mostly in musicals. Both Steve Sondheim and Hal Prince had Dorothy in mind for Sally. Sondheim saw her play Leona opposite her husband, Ron Holgate, in a production of *Do I Hear a Waltz?* when she became his one and only choice for the role. Hal had auditioned her for the lead in *She Loves Me* and agonized between her and Barbara Cook, whom he ultimately hired. He knew he wanted to work with Dorothy at some point. *Follies* was the perfect project. She had begun her singing career at fourteen, when she changed her name from Marjorie Chandler and became "one of the finest vocalists of her era." She made numerous appearances on various television shows, where she showed a flair for comedy. Petite and cheerful at forty-four, she was full of nervous energy, and very much the den mother. On occasion, she would bring in apples for everyone from a farm in New Jersey near her home. *Follies* was a really big deal for her, and she was an immediate favorite with the creative staff. John McMartin, a Broadway regular who first came to prominence in *Sweet Charity*, was extremely professional. Taciturn and shy, he was quiet to a fault. His demeanor never changed, although there was a twinkle when he smiled. He was such a late addition to the cast that three weeks earlier an ad had run in the Sunday *Boston Herald Traveler* for the engagement at the Colonial Theatre with Jon Cypher's name in the credits.

Harold Hastings, the production's musical director, arrived after lunch as well. At this point in the process, his main responsibility was to teach the songs to the actors. But as the director of the musical aspects of the production, he was kind of the stage manager for all things musical. A bespectacled, silver-haired somewhat patrician figure with one curiously wandering eye, he didn't fit anyone's cliché of a Broadway musical director or conductor. He looked and acted like a banker in shirtsleeves. He had been in charge of the music for the Harold Prince musicals for years, starting with *The Pajama Game* in 1954, with the exception, for some reason, of *Fiddler on the Roof.* He was remarkable in his calm, soothing manner, which built confidence in all types of performers—actors, singers, dancers, old salts, young whippersnappers. He commanded respect. Until everyone learned what they had to learn, his patience knew no bounds, but once they were supposed to know their stuff, he could be rather sharp. As rehearsals progressed, he helped the performers deliver the material in a way acceptable to the composer, the director, and the choreographer. He also had to coordinate all the musical aspects of the production: the

dance and vocal arrangements, the orchestrations, the music copyists, and, finally, the musicians in the orchestra and the onstage band. He had a couple of rehearsal pianists to help, beginning with David Baker, a fairly well-known composer and arranger in his own right. It's interesting that musicians are willing to help their comrades without concern for perceived position of hierarchy, provided, however, that the "gig" interests them.

Hal Hastings took over the smallest room. Because there were only a few people hanging around, he would come and find his next victim as if he were a doctor calling a patient in from the waiting room— "Next!" Alexis was ushered in first to learn "Losing My Mind," a Helen Morgan–like torch song that was one of the first songs finished for the Follies sequence. Sondheim's original idea was that it would be a double torch song, sung by both Sally and Phyllis, who would start at either end of a chorus line, slowly working their way toward the middle. Everyone in the chorus would have masks of Ben, since he was the object of both women's affection. That idea was discarded in favor of a Jerome Kern–like song for Sally to sing while seated on a swing that would swing out over the audience. That left "Losing My Mind" for Phyllis alone, but another song—"The World's Full of Girls"—was being played around with for her as well. Giving "Losing My Mind" to the character of Phyllis was to emerge as a mistake before too long, but Alexis struggled her way through. At one point she turned to Hal Hastings and said, "Are you helping me here? Aren't you playing a little something extra for me—like the tune?" By the end of the day, all four principals had been taken through "Waiting for the Girls Upstairs," one of the first songs written for the show.

The Follies sequence that ends the show was still in a formative stage. Following the words "STILL TO BE WRITTEN" on the last page of the script was this description: "What follows is a capsule Follies—costume parades, comedy routines, specialty acts—traditional and accurate in all ways but one. Sets, costumes, music, movement; all this is faithful to the past. What's different and unusual about it is the content, what it's all about."

The idea was clear: the four lead characters—two ex–Follies girls and their then stage-door Johnnies (now husbands)—having been pushed past the emotional breaking point by the realization of the bleakness of their present lives, perform a modern-day "Follies." They would, in essence, become performers in a fantasy Follies whose con-

tent was inspired by everything the entire play was about—traditions from the old days, psychological realizations from the events of the play itself, disappointments about the present, hopes from the past, lies listened to, lies ignored. It would be almost hallucinatory, and the transition into it would involve some kind of breakdown. Then the audience would see a version of what some of them had expected they were going to see for the whole evening, based on the title. Or at least that was the thinking.

But the Follies sequence was nowhere near completed, nor was its shape determined. It would clearly have songs. In fact, Steve had finished one the day before, "You're Gonna Love Tomorrow," played it for the creative staff, and everyone had liked it except Hal. But more songs had to be written. (There were still five songs for this sequence that hadn't been started—"Love Will See Us Through," "Buddy's Blues," "Uptown, Downtown," "Live, Laugh, Love," and "The Story of Lucy and Jessie," a Boston replacement.) Since the Ziegfeld Follies also contained sketches and routines, the inclusion of such material was being contemplated and discussed at length in phone calls and in conversations behind closed doors. Gene Nelson's character, Buddy, the traveling salesman, might do his "turn" in the form of a Will Rogers–style comedy monologue. Librettist James Goldman, a tall regal-looking man with horn-rimmed glasses and a distinguished gray-flecked beard, had come to the rehearsal hall to discuss this. I was called into the room and given a task: go to the New York Public Library and research jokes. Goldman sat there while Hal went over what he wanted me to find—"Old jokes about family life . . . the guy lives in Phoenix, so there should be stuff about Arizona . . . the West . . . unhappy suburban life . . . the country club . . . the washing . . . sex . . . budgets . . . the bucolic life . . ." and so on. Goldman remembered a joke book from his childhood, *Through Missouri on a Mule* by Joe Miller. (It turned out to be full of racist humor.) Hal wanted me to find an actual Will Rogers monologue so he could examine its shape. And he didn't want me to edit anything: "Even if it's a Milton Berle joke, don't throw it out." Goldman sat there silently, puffing away at a cigarette. After a pause, he smiled and said: "The only reason you're doing this is because I cannot write jokes."

The next morning I was on the way to the library's main branch on Forty-second Street when I ran into playwright John Guare on the subway. His play *The House of Blue Leaves* was in rehearsal for its world

premiere production at the Truck and Warehouse Theater on East Fourth Street. He was a friend of Prince and Sondheim and was a big fan of *Follies*. He told me which other branches of the New York Public Library were likely to be helpful and gave me John Lahr's telephone number, saying that he was very knowledgeable about vaudeville, having recently completed a biography of his father, Bert Lahr. I spent most of the day gathering a whole bunch of corny jokes, writing them down on a yellow legal pad. (This was before libraries had accessible photocopying machines.) I went to rehearsal, gave them to Hal who checked off the ones he was interested in, then went home, typed out a list, and brought it down to Goldman's house on West Eleventh Street. I shoved the papers under his door. A nine-page version of a monologue for Buddy was presented to Hal a few days later, went into his master script, and was never heard of again. Buddy ended up with a song, "Buddy's Blues" (or, as it was alternately titled, "The God-Why-Don't-You-Love-Me-Oh-You-Do-I'll-See-You-Later Blues"), in which he drove a toy car between two girls impersonating Sally, his wife at home, and Margie, his mistress on the road. Initially, the two girls were played by men in drag.

Michael Bennett and Bob Avian continued working with the dancers through the week. From what I could see, it looked as if the main body of the complicated dances had been worked out ahead of time, but the choreography would change as the steps were being taught. The constant seemed to be "Who's That Woman?"—partly, I realized, because Michael wanted his dancers to know the routines when the principal actors arrived. He knew it would be helpful for the "old broads" to have all the dancers available to help them go over the steps. And was he ever proved right!

Watching Michael work was a lesson in collaboration. He usually sat in front of the wall of mirrors facing the dancers, with Bob Avian dancing the principal's role. Bob would demonstrate the steps. Then Michael would get an idea. He'd jump up and work it out, extending or modifying it, all the while watching himself in the mirrors. Then he would sit down and watch Bob execute it again. Other dancers in the ensemble would throw in ideas as well, but a clear hierarchy started to become apparent. Some had clearly worked with Michael before. Two were his assistants, Graciela Daniele and Mary Jane Houdina. Daniele, who has gone on to have a distinguished career as a choreographer and director, was more "upscale," both in person and in dancing style. Gor-

Michael Bennett working out a step.

geous, slightly exotic, and often wearing a colored scarf around her head, she was not intimidated by Bennett in the least. He relied on her for lyrical steps, and as rehearsals progressed he put her in charge of many of the older members of the company who needed hand-holding. She would also dance the role of Young Vanessa in the ballroom-dance specialty "Bolero d'Amour." Mary Jane, who had known about Michael since they both grew up in Buffalo, was clearly the tap-dance assistant who provided different tap steps. She was a no-nonsense gal, also not

intimidated by Michael. When tap steps were being created, she often stood right by Bob's side. Clearly, the final decisions were always Michael's, but he accepted ideas freely.

I watched them working on "The World's Full of Boys," an idea for a Follies song. I was amazed at how Michael took clichéd dance steps and placed them in a context in which they felt fresh and made dramatic sense. The song was a can-can (it ended up in the movie *Stavisky*, where it sounded like a French dance hall tune) that began with Phyllis and the male dancers. She describes how she wants to go on the prowl: "The world's full of boys who are waiting to be kissed. Oops! There's one I missed . . ." Bennett had the men dance into a "V" shape with Phyllis at the pivot point down front. Once she has found the boys, and they are in proper formation, she sings about continuing her search. "And then, and when, I've kissed them all and satisfied my yen . . ." Bennett had Phyllis simply leave her "boys" in their "V" and saunter away at an angle. Simple, but you got the point that she was never satisfied, that no set formation would ever appease her. She would always go off to find something more interesting. It was appropriate and creative—and surprising.

Work was also done on "Loveland," the transition song into the Follies sequence, which was soon to be alternatively referred to as Loveland. It sounded like one of those grandiose Ziegfeld showgirl numbers, as much about introducing costumes and scenery as it was a song—"A Pretty Girl Is Like a Melody," that kind of thing—and its introduction was the same as "Beautiful Girls," the first song in the show, also reminiscent of a specific Ziegfeldian style. Even though no one was quite sure how the leading characters would get onto the stage for "Loveland," it was clear that they would be center stage when the song began and would be surrounded by Follies people, played by the members of the ensemble. The song "Loveland" was also the device that moved the show from the present to the hallucinatory past, from the party event of the play into the fantasy world—not yet determined or designed—of the splintering minds of our lead characters. There was a lot of planned swirling around and posturing à la Ziegfeld. At key moments, six tall showgirls in outrageous themed costumes would be presented, accompanied by platitudes spoken by individual men in the ensemble. Even in the rehearsal room, it looked thrilling. Michael said to his dancers: "My work grows, and often as something is growing I will change large sections, so be prepared."

Florence Klotz, the costume designer, brought sketches for Hal and Michael to approve. For "Loveland" her new idea was a cloudlike base for each of the showgirls, which would roll on. Hal quickly dismissed the idea; since the whole set was a series of raked levels, he explained, the idea of a base rolling on with a person standing on it was out. (Rumor had it the Vegas showgirls might be asked to go topless—it never happened.) She also had a series of sketches for the principals. "These sketches are good, Flossie," said Hal, "but the only problem is that they have got to be related." "They are," she said. Hal then brought Michael to look through the sketches with him. "There are some I like very much and there are others I hate." Michael agreed. The ones that they both didn't like were never seen again. After Klotz left, Hal said, "The costumes are the best I've ever had for any of my shows." Clearly expensive, they were a large reason *Follies* was over budget. Word began to circulate around the rehearsal hall that the original budget of $700,000 was now looking more like $800,000. No wonder Hal seemed agitated.

Although most of the show would take place in the present and at a party, it was the aura of the Follies that was most intriguing. Any show set within earshot of Ziegfeld demands a certain kind of opulence. If you have showgirls, they have to wear showgirl costumes, and they'd better be spectacular. Since *Follies* made thinly disguised Ziegfeld references, there was a lot of research available. Books and magazines had photographs of the very shows used for inspiration, and many of the showgirl costumes ended up exact copies of specific dresses. Of course the art of stage costuming lies in assimilating research and creating a unique vision. The task of costuming *Follies* was given to a seemingly unlikely candidate. Every era on Broadway seems to have a reigning designer who does the shows with the flamboyant costumes, and they tend to win Tony Awards; examples include Alvin Colt, Freddy Wittop, Theoni V. Aldredge, Willa Kim, and William Ivey Long. Florence Klotz wasn't yet one of them, but to be fair, she had never been given an opportunity to show what she was capable of. *Follies* was to provide her entree into that group, and she was to win the first of her many Tony Awards for the show. She was also part of the Harold Prince family, having designed a few of his productions. She was also Ruthie's life partner.

Her costumes for the chorus in "Loveland" were Dresden milk-maids and their lads, in pastel pinks and yellows with lots of gold trimming and big white shoes. Three Las Vegas showgirls, each six feet tall, had been cast specifically for this moment, and they, along with the three tallest dancers from the ensemble, would wear enormous, pastel "love-themed" costumes with tall headdresses. These showgirl dresses ended up being so large that they couldn't be moved around backstage at either the Colonial Theatre in Boston or the Winter Garden in New York, so they had to be dead hung from the fly floor in the extreme corners backstage, three to a side. Each performer would have the skirt lowered onto her just before her entrance—which she had to make sideways.

The palette for the costumes for the entire show was carefully chosen. Black and white were for the ghost figures. The Follies sequence began in pastels and worked up through bright colors to fire-engine red. By the end, every member of the chorus was in red—top hat, jacket, trousers, and shoes—with white vests, ties, and shirts or blouses. Ben, who had the final *Follies* number, was entirely in formal whites—tails, hat, cane. The men's modern-day clothing, always a challenge to designers, was in subdued dark colors. Everything, including all the men's suits, was color. The only people wearing black in the present were the players in the stage band who wore tuxedoes. The women's present-day costumes were as stylistically diverse as their colors.

Of course the costumes had to complement the palette of the scenery. When Hal Prince found the photograph of Gloria Swanson standing in the rubble of the Roxy Theater, he took it to Boris Aronson, the seventy-year-old scenic designer with whom he had worked on his last four shows. Aronson was having something of a renaissance under Prince. Following a long and varied career, he had found something new and imaginative in his decadent and theatrically twisted scenery for *Cabaret*. He then came up with the ultramodern, chrome, glass and shiny-black urban environment of *Company*, which was so modern and new that many felt it had to be the work of a young artist. It was simply Boris Aronson being inspired. Independently, he had also seen the Swanson photograph, and when he heard Hal describe a show that took place in an empty theater, he was excited. "An empty stage is a gold mine, a concept that really fascinates me," he was quoted as saying in *The Theatre Art of Boris Aronson* (by Frank Rich and Lisa Aronson)—"a chance for Cubism of the highest order—and not just for the

sake of abstraction, but based on something real." He drew a preliminary, atmospheric sketch for the *Follies* set that captured the essence of the photograph, adding a broken catwalk above, abstract pieces of ripped scenery hovering in space, staircases leading nowhere, pieces missing from the proscenium arch, and a main stage area that looked as if things had been simply left behind. Ghostly figures, including one far upstage that looked just like Gloria Swanson, lurked in the shadows. The set became refined in each successive drawing, but it never lost the impression of that first sketch. It looked less like a theater being torn down than a theater that had just been neglected for a very long time. Nothing was entirely intact—walls were crumbling, remnants of old drops hung down, piles of bricks and rubble were strewn about. And despite the existence of the original color photograph of the Roxy Theater, in which the gold filigree and the red brick were as striking as Gloria Swanson's black evening attire, for Prince and Aronson, this was the black-and-white version. Everything in Aronson's design had lost its color. Of course, it was actually shades of gray, black, and white, but the impression was of shadow, and empty space. We were never shown how far the wrecker's ball had gone until the final image of the show, in the early morning following the party. There was also no furniture; although the event of the play was a party, only a buffet table would ever make its way onto the set. Whenever anyone sat, it was on some piece of the set.

In its simplest form, the set was a series of three square, raised platforms rising to the rear of the stage in angled perspective, with a corner facing the audience. Each angle was different, giving a sense of false perspective, and they were all floating on a flat-black floor, which was itself raked. Skeletal units, which also looked as if they were crumbling, were stationed offstage right and left, three on each side. They moved in tracks in the floor, on the diagonal. These units, made of structural steel and pipe, included pieces of crumbling walls, staircases (some functional, some not), piles of rubble, and various planks making areas in which small scenes could take place. One series of planks formed an area large enough to accommodate a piano, bass, and drums for the onstage party band. When these units were pulled offstage, the stage looked vast, black, and empty; when they were pulled onstage, the emptiness of the space closed in and shifted, so that scenes could appear to be more intimate. Cleverly disguised within one stage-left unit was a series of levels that created a rubble-strewn staircase used for

*The basic Aronson set during rehearsal at Feller's Scenic Studio,
Michael Bennett in the center.*

the grand Follies-style entrance of all the ex–Follies girls at the top of
the show during "Beautiful Girls." As the aged tenor sang "Hats off,
here they come, those beautiful girls," they each made a grand
entrance at the top of the stairs and promenaded down. To the audience, it looked like variously shaped older women dressed in a motley
assortment of fancy party dresses walking through a junk pile. To
them, it was gliding once again down the staircase of their youth. It
was a moment that captured the essence of *Follies*. And it was only the
first song of the evening.

Even though the Follies sequence was still being conceived and
written, Aronson had already come up with some ideas. That there
would be such a sequence was known, as was the fact that it would be
reminiscent of the old Ziegfeld Follies. The main set was far too big
and "constructed" to be moved out of the way, so the challenge was to
take over the space effortlessly. The ingenuity was extraordinary:

Aronson had designed two pie-shaped small stair units—three steps each—that were hidden underneath the main platforms and which, when pivoted out, joined the top two platforms to make one big, if slightly abstract, round staircase. Then from the flies would come Follies drops, inspired by paper doilies, valentine cards, and certain Fragonard paintings. They would be bright—white with red hearts and cherubic scenes painted in cameos—and their round openings would get larger with each downstage drop, creating an iris of doilies. In front would be a richly textured sky-blue tab curtain. The appearance of all this color was meant to be startling, and it would be. And all the drops hung only over the center portion of the stage with no masking, so the ghostly sides of the stage were never obscured. It was magic.

Aronson's presence was felt during the week, though he was in contact only via telephone. Hal had made a decision to lower the entire set, and his designer was not pleased. Originally the set was to begin three inches above stage level, and when Hal realized just how high that would make everything else, he decided to have the basic raked floor start at stage level. Fritz Holt, in his position as production stage manager, was on the phone for an hour and a half discussing this with Aronson. The producer was making decisions about his set that tampered with his artistic vision and he wanted his set left alone. Hal had already explained how nervous he felt the actors, especially the older ones, would be with the multiple levels of the set. Lowering everything would at least mitigate the problem to some degree. In addition, Hal and Michael were a little annoyed at Boris because they had gone to see his new production of *Fidelio* at the Metropolitan Opera, and when the curtain went up they had turned to each other and said: "Oh, my God, it's the set for *Follies.*" There were similarities, to be sure, but no one else ever expressed a similar concern.

I was sent to Aronson's apartment to pick up some drawings. He lived in an old ten-story apartment building just off Central Park West. Through the ornate iron door of the building I could see one of those old-style elevators built in a cage, with an open staircase wrapped around. Finding the bell was a challenge—it was carefully hidden in a gargoyle rosette. As the elevator descended, a mass of cables hanging down the middle of the cage moved, in both directions, it seemed. The operator looked as if he belonged on an old steamboat, especially when he thrust the lever all the way to one side of the engine-room-style telegraph. As we arrived at the proper floor, he opened the door, then

pointed, saying, "Aronson is there." He waited while I rang the door-bell. Numerous locks were turned, and a serious-looking red-haired woman opened the door—slightly. When I explained why I was there she smiled and through the partly opened door handed me a carefully wrapped roll of tracing paper with the words "Follies—Stage Manager" written on it. "Be careful that it does not fall out," she said. Later on I found out that this was Lisa, Boris's wife and assistant. As she closed the door, I noticed Boris himself lurking quietly in the shadows behind her, and then I heard the locks turned once again.

In the middle of the week Michael flew to Cleveland for the opening of the tour of *Coco*, a musical that he had choreographed starring Katharine Hepburn as the couturiere Coco Chanel. Rather than have everyone just go over what had already been staged, he left the choreography in Bob's hands for more work on "The World's Full of Boys." When he returned, the first thing was to show him what had been done in his absence. The work was fine, but the song was cut shortly thereafter.

Auditions were held on Tuesday, first for the older ballroom-dancing couple. This was hard. It does seem to be the only process that works, but auditioning is ruthless. When it involves older performers, there is an added melancholy. Who wants to reject someone the age of his parents or grandparents? Still, everyone in the theater understands the rules: if you want the part, you have to audition. Couple number one is introduced to Michael. They say how thrilled they are to meet him, what good things they've heard about him, etc. He thanks them graciously. Then he asks: "What do you have for me?" "Oh, anything you want—tango, merengue, fox-trot." "I would just like to see you move, so anything would be fine." The couple go over to the pianist, hand him some music and mutter a few words, then wander to the center of the room and begin. They move about the floor, doing a series of routines, but their faces show no emotion. When they finish, Michael says: "Thanks very much. We will let you know when we decide." And suddenly the feeling of disappointment in the room is palpable. They know what that line means. They haven't made it. They leave as quickly as possible. If it doesn't go well and you get the "thank you," it's best to beat a hasty retreat. No one wants to engage in conversation. The next couple is ushered in. "How tall are you?" Michael asks. "Five-eleven." "We are looking for dancers over six feet." The woman pipes up: "Do I have to be six feet, too?" The man suggests: "We could

go on the stretching machine every day." They do their routine. "Thank you." The woman goes over to Hal, who is not looking thrilled, and introduces herself as the friend of a friend of his. The name doesn't register. "Well, she doesn't even know I was coming down to audition for you. Won't she be surprised?" Hal smiles. Several other couples come in; none gets selected.

Then come the three finalists for the role of Young Ben. Sondheim is summoned from a conference with the music department. The first candidate is brought in. All three young men have been screened by Hal's in-house casting director, the respected actress Joanna Merlin. The first two seem lightweight—one wears a floppy bow tie, the other has a bouffant hairstyle. Neither is of much interest. But the third, Kurt Peterson, is a distinct possibility. He reads some scenes with a stage manager and everyone seems pleased. John McMartin is summoned to see what they would look like together, since they would be playing the same person at different ages. "Well," said Hal, "it looks as if over the years the nose has changed shape a little bit, but we can play with some putty." John asks if he could hear him sing. "Oh, yes, fine, okay, by all means." Kurt chats with the pianist, then his large voice fills the room with "Lonely Town," from *On the Town*, and everyone is pleased. He stands there, smiling, with his hands in his pea coat, looking somewhat sheepish. When asked how old he is he says: "Twenty-two, twenty-three in February," to which Hal replies, "No. Didn't hear that. You're twenty-two." Kurt seems somewhat dumbstruck. "Well," says Hal, "I hope to see you . . . in rehearsal!" "Ah, really, thank you very much." Then Kurt beats his own hasty retreat. As he leaves, a toothbrush falls from his pocket. The atmosphere this time is decidedly upbeat. A good and successful audition can energize a room. The truth is that everyone in the room wants every audition to be great. It's just that so few are. Kurt Peterson is hired to play Young Ben.

The four principals were taught their signature song, "Waiting for the Girls Upstairs." Michael began to rough out some staging, with Hal sitting close by. It was the first time I had seen them together. Their relationship seemed carefully crafted. They had clearly enjoyed working together on *Company*, a joyous experience for everyone. Michael had his sights set on directing, and he was looking for the right opportunity. Hal was in transition, clearly preferring the artistic challenge of directing to the business drudgery of producing, and he wasn't about to hand the direction of this show over to anyone else. Michael knew that

the fluid nature of the show would require him to do a lot more than just create isolated dances, so he saw it as an opportunity to move one step closer to directing. Both men realized that this show would be important to their careers, so they had agreed on the almost unprecedented notion of codirecting. Basically Michael was responsible for all the dances and the movement, which in *Follies* was a prominent part of the direction. Hal directed and staged the book scenes, which were, by nature, episodic and short; very few were traditional in structure, and they tended to involve ghost figures and crowd movement in addition to dialogue. But, to the credit of these two artists, the end result looked seamless. The actions of these first few days, however, were indicative of how things would progress: Michael was using every second of the time allotted to him, while Hal would work with any actors who were free on any scene in which they were involved. (Hal seemed to have a lot of time on his hands.) "Waiting for the Girls Upstairs" was a song that landed right between both men's responsibilities, and it was Sondheim's favorite song. He made it known that he wanted to see how it was to be staged as soon as it was on its feet. By week's end, enough of it had been blocked out for him to be summoned for a run-through. He was pleased, but afterward he called a brief meeting out of earshot of the actors to explain just what liberties he would allow within the melody and rhythms—and which ones he would not.

As the week went on, preparations for the first day of full company rehearsals took focus. The scripts had been prepared by Studio Duplicating, a firm that specialized in scripts for Broadway shows. Everyone used them, and their style was distinctive. The process was by mimeograph, in which each page had to be typed onto a stencil that would then be placed on the drum of the printing machine, inked, and printed, copy by copy, on $8\frac{1}{2}$" × 11" paper with two holes on the left-hand margin. The process was repeated for each page, and then the collated scripts would be bound in specially coated covers fixed with little brass screws. The covers were distinctive; no other copying establishment had them. And they were available in a vast array of colors. *Follies'* was orange, but there had already been earlier versions in green, red, and light blue. The title was embossed in the center in a single, no-nonsense typeface. Because the mimeograph process was time-consuming, once rehearsals began it would become my responsibility to type out individual pages with changes and make enough copies to go to those who needed them. I would make copies either by

placing multiple carbon sets in the typewriter (I worked up to being able to do ten at one time) or by using the new machine at the Prince office made by the Xerox company. This dry copying system was fairly new, and it was slow. It would, however, be the preferred route if large numbers of copies were needed.

Saturday would be the official first day of rehearsal. A whole lot of people would be showing up. In addition to the entire cast, people who would be working on the show over the next few months would also be attending—designers, musical staff, press agents, and assistants from the office—as well as some friends. Part social event, part actual work, the first day of rehearsal has an almost ritual feel to it. Everyone would gather in the large rehearsal room, which would be arranged with several tables pushed together in the middle surrounded by as many chairs as we could find. Around the periphery would be additional chairs, even crates and boxes, to accommodate everyone. A high table on casters was positioned so that the model of the set could be viewed by everyone. The piano was pulled out of the corner so Sondheim could play the songs. Following general introductions, the script would be read through. Then the work would begin.

On Friday, I helped the stage managers prepare. The week—not to mention the years—of preparation was coming to an end. *Follies* was about to begin in earnest. Several songs were still not written, the Follies sequence wasn't fully formed, and there was no ballroom-dance couple. But on Saturday, at ten A.M., a motley assortment of people with a variety of different talents would converge for the first time in the service of the collaboration that would result in *Follies*.

2

"Hats Off, Here They Come, Those Beautiful Girls"

IN THE REHEARSAL STUDIO, THE FIRST WEEK, JANUARY 9–15

Since I had been asked to help open up, I made certain I was there on time. In fact, I was the first to arrive. The three stage managers followed shortly. There was work enough for all four of us: lights on, tables and chairs checked, scripts and music collated for all the actors, and so on. Although the day marked the official beginning of rehearsals, there was a decidedly social aspect to the morning's activities. I had no idea exactly who was going to show up, only that it was to be quite a crowd.

The next to arrive was Terry Marone, the official from the union for actors and stage managers, Actors' Equity Association. She was a fixture on the first day of rehearsal for all Broadway shows. A former singer and dancer, she was responsible for making certain all the proper union paperwork was completed, including contracts, insurance, and pension and welfare forms. Any performers who weren't members had to join, and she was to take them through the process; the three Las Vegas showgirls were likely candidates. And once all Equity members were assembled, she had to read the rules and regulations out loud. As Terry unloaded her papers and laid out her forms on a table in the hall, John Grigas hovered, helping her get organized. The forms were complicated, and as he separated the different forms into neat piles, he muttered, "Some of these actors are really very

dense. I'm sorry to have to say it, but I've been in this business for a long time." Terry, in her capacity as a union administrator, said, "I have also been in this business for a long time, but I can't talk about it anymore."

I posted a couple of messages on the callboard. From George Furth, author of the book of *Company*: "The next thing is the best thing. Good luck with the next thing. *Follies* is beautiful. Warmly, with love, George Furth." A letter from Louis Botto, an old-line theater journalist who was hoping to do a piece on Hal for *Look* magazine: "Dear Harold Prince: Thank you for letting me read *Follies*. It is to the American musical what *Virginia Woolf* was to the American drama. It takes its form one step further than *Company*, and higher praise I cannot bestow."

The actors started arriving around nine-thirty. And they were quite a group. Mary McCarty, a zaftig woman somewhere in her fifties, had

The supporting players in a publicity pose on the first day of rehearsal: Mary McCarty, Ethel Shutta, Michael Bartlett, Fifi D'Orsay, Ethel Barrymore Colt.

made a splash in 1949's *Miss Liberty*, but hadn't been on Broadway since *Bless You All* in 1950. Her career had included a lot of nightclub work, and she had recently opened her own "Eastside niterie," appropriately named MaryMary. She would play Stella Deems, who would lead the group of old Follies girls in "Who's That Woman?" Hers was a secondary character, but her backup dancers would include every woman listed above her in the show's program. This number would prove to be a highlight. Fifi D'Orsay was to play Solange LaFitte, the Follies' resident French person. She had been calling all week to check on this or that, so often that Hal stopped taking her calls, always happening to be unfortunately unavailable. She arrived fully made-up, a librarian's chain hanging from her eyeglasses, in a sweater, plaid pants, and a pageboy hat, and she talked a mile a minute in her heavily French-accented English, greeting everyone with " 'Allo, babee" and calling everyone "chickie-poo." Turns out she was from Montreal and had never been to France, but never mind. She was a bundle of nerves. And then there was Ethel Shutta, at seventy-four the oldest member of the cast, who trudged up the stairs, solid, standing firm in her sensible orthopedic shoes. When she was hired, she wrote a four-page thank-you letter to casting director Joanna Merlin, telling her how happy she was to be cast, since she had been sure her career was over. She was the one holdover from one of the show's previous incarnations, having been cast by Stuart Ostrow when he held the option, and had written to Hal when she heard that he had the show. "You won't have heard of me," she began, but what she didn't know was that when Hal was eight, he had stood in line at his school with all the other boys to get the autograph of one classmate's mother, who, they said, had been a Follies girl. The classmate was Georgie Olsen, and his mother was Ethel Shutta. Michael Bartlett was to play Roscoe, the old tenor who serenades everyone with the opening song, "Beautiful Girls." He looked as old as Ethel did, and seemed a little bewildered, his eyesight less than perfect. But his silver-white hair and mature girth gave him an aura of faded grandeur. Ethel Barrymore Colt, a member of the famous theatrical family, was always gracious, although she looked as if she had ventured a little farther downtown than she was used to. Somewhat out of her element, she stayed pretty quiet. Gene Kelly's younger brother, Fred, who had been running a dancing school in New Jersey, played a small role. He, too, was a quiet figure, keeping to himself most of the time. Sheila Smith, Broadway's stalwart leading lady standby, most

recently for Angela Lansbury in *Mame*, had her own part this time but was also called on to cover the leading women. Low-voiced, dark-haired, and slim, she had the poise of a dancer and the look of someone who had seen it all. Justine Johnston, a full-figured character actress with an operatic voice, would play Heidi Schiller, a singer from Vienna, who, years ago, had had a waltz written specially for her. She would shortly be elected Equity deputy for the company, with the responsibility of seeing to it that management behaved and that rehearsals were run by the rulebook. As rehearsals progressed, she could be seen glancing at the watch she wore permanently around her neck. Justine wasn't someone to tangle with.

The rest of the company was full of good New York character actors—among them Dick Latessa, Helon Blount, Charles Welch, Dortha Duckworth, and John J. Martin. Of course, the dancers looked great—young, slim, attractive, alert, and cheerful; they seemed to be a source of limitless energy and stamina. When the first casting call went out, bona fide ex–Follies ladies showed up, looking nothing like their old photographs which they presented as current. Few could actually act.

While looking for something in the stage managers' office, I found a list of actors who had been considered for the show. The task was to find old Hollywood stars, regardless of whether they could sing. Among the men: Van Johnson, E. G. Marshall, Peter Lawford, Jim Backus, Howard Keel, Craig Stevens, Jack Albertson, John Raitt, Don Ameche, and Ray Middleton. And the women: Rhonda Fleming, Joan Bennett, Kitty Carlisle, Barbara Cook, Gloria DeHaven, and Jane Wyman. So Alexis Smith, Gene Nelson, and Dorothy Collins fit right in, as did the woman who was about to make a somewhat grand entrance.

Working her way up the stairs, wrapped in fur, wearing a black wig and teardrop-shaped sunglasses, and carrying a small suitcase covered in fabric of brightly colored flowers, came Yvonne De Carlo. Of all the actors in the show, she was considered to have the best "name" because of her recent television experience as Lily, the mother in *The Munsters*, a ghoulish family situation comedy created somewhat as a humorous twist on Charles Addams's cartoons and characters (who had their own series called *The Addams Family*). Arriving in Hollywood in 1940 from Canada with a pushy mother, Peggy Yvonne Middleton yearned for a career in the movies, which happened once she changed her name to something more exotic-sounding. Taking her mother's maiden name,

Direct from Hollywood, in all her glamour: Yvonne De Carlo.

De Carlo, she landed the title role in an audience-pleaser titled *Salome, Where She Danced.* She had found her niche, and continued to portray harem gals and dance hall gals, mostly with a fair amount of flesh showing. As Leonard Maltin put it rather succinctly, "her starring roles didn't usually require much in the way of emoting, but she gamely rose to the occasion when something more than looking beautiful was required." *The Munsters* had become a camp favorite, and Yvonne De Carlo quite embodied the spirit of the show, driving around Hollywood in a car outfitted like a hearse. New York's autograph hounds, a scruffy group of men who followed celebrities around town, didn't take long to find out where *Follies* was rehearsing, and although they often toted movie magazines with photographs of Alexis and Gene, and even Dorothy and Ethel Shutta, Yvonne was the catch. Her daily outfits rarely changed and the dark glasses were standard attire when she ven-

tured out into the real world. After a while she even mustered a sense of humor about herself, reporting that a cab-driver, looking in his rearview mirror, had remarked, "Hey, lady, why do you wear those sunglasses? What do you think you are, a movie star?" She was playing only a featured role, Carlotta Campion, but it was being beefed up for her. Although she had "also starring" billing, right below the title, her name was equal in size to the four principals, and she had the line all to herself. Before long, nicknames were established for the stars of the show: "the big four" for Alexis, Gene, Dorothy, and John, and "the big one" for Yvonne. Make no mistake about it, until she sat down at the table and became one of the gang, she was our resident movie star. After she had greeted everyone and had settled herself in, I handed her a script. She looked around and remarked, "Hey, this is some classy joint."

She was also aware that there were photographers in the room. Martha Swope, reigning photographer for both ballet and theater, was on hand, snapping both candid shots of everyone gathering and milling about and a few posed shots to be used for promotional purposes until production shots of the finished show could be taken later on.

The creative staff—Hal, Steve, Michael, and Jim—arrived and huddled quietly in the stage managers' office for a pep talk, not unlike a group of coaches about to face their team for the first practice of the year. People who were working on the show elsewhere came as well—the press agents, the music copyists, staff from Hal's office, the hair and wig designer, the makeup designer, the advertising agent, and others. There was much joviality, greetings, laughter, all tinged with nervous expectation. It's an exciting moment—a gathering of people, many of whom have never worked together before, who are about to embark on a creative journey together. When you see everyone in one place at one time, it means one thing: the clock has started ticking. Everyone in that room, no matter what his or her area of focus, had a lot to do to prepare for the first preview in Boston, which was now just six weeks away. Alexis quipped quietly to Ruthie, "This feels like a lousy cocktail party." Not missing a beat, Ruthie shot back, "Without the booze."

Surprisingly, Alexis and her costars were a little nervous, despite having had a head start. Their comfortable routine was now being invaded by what seemed like an enormous group of strangers. There was amusement as the actors portraying the four leads in their youthful

past introduced themselves to, well, themselves. The young versions may not have had striking physical similarities to their elder counterparts, but the personalities matched. Playing Young Buddy was Harvey Evans, an ageless Broadway chorister with a cheerful outlook on life, full of smiles and goodwill. He greeted everyone like a long lost friend. Virginia Sandifur, the Young Phyllis, was tall, dark-haired, and slightly removed from the fray. Phyllis to the core. Kurt Peterson, the Young Ben, cast only last week, was personable and relaxed. He had piercing eyes, but a nice demeanor. He was living with Victoria Mallory, the actress hired to play Young Heidi Schiller. They had been in school together, had fallen in love, and played opposite each other in a production of *West Side Story* at Lincoln Center. It was nice to have a couple already in place among the company. Marti Rolph, Young Sally, was fresh and bubbly, just in from Los Angeles. She had a wide-eyed Sally-like enthusiasm for New York and everyone in it and seemed genuinely thrilled to be here.

The designers arrived. George Martin helped Boris Aronson and his wife, Lisa, carry in a large box containing the scale model of the set. Tharon Musser, the lighting designer, and Florence Klotz chatted quietly. There was also a large contingent of friends and family, including Hal's wife, Judy, who was a particular friend of Steve Sondheim's and had been a champion of *The Girls Upstairs* for years, and John Guare, resident friend and *Follies* fan. All told, there were about eighty people milling about.

At ten, the cast was called into the large room and everyone else was asked to stand by outside in the hallway while the Equity rules were read through. Once all union business was taken care of, the doors were open to the rest of us, as Terry Marone packed up her papers in one large briefcase and left.

The cast sat themselves around the table, positioned roughly by billing and size of role. Fifi D'Orsay, looking for the proper place to sit, said to anyone who would listen, "Zere is no place for me to sit . . ." to which Ethel Shutta, pointing to the seat next to her, responded, "Hey, squattez-vous."

Sondheim was at the piano, surrounded by his music department: Hal Hastings, orchestrator Jonathan Tunick, head copyist Mathilde Pincus, and dance arranger John Berkman. Everyone else filled in around the periphery. Fritz Holt began the proceedings by welcoming everyone, introducing himself and the rest of the stage management

staff, and offering a few pointers—"We're here to help with whatever you need, to solve any problems . . ." etc. Then he introduced Hal Prince.

"Gee, the last time I did this there were fourteen people in the cast, so it's a little different this time." The *Follies* cast numbered forty-nine. "I won't introduce you all; there are too many of you for that. Anyway, you can all introduce yourselves to each other over the next six weeks and in Boston." He did introduce Jim Goldman, Michael Bennett, and Steve Sondheim. Boris and Lisa were fussing with the set model on top of the rolling table. He asked if they were ready to show it. "Still too early," said Boris. So Hal continued: "What we intend to do with this show is to take somewhat of a trip, sort of a group nervous breakdown. Part of its style is in being big and brazen." He explained that to help facilitate the necessarily complex staging, in three weeks' time rehearsals would be taking place on the actual set, which was already under construction in a scenic studio in the Bronx. In order to give the studio time to complete the building of the set, however, we would be rehearsing from four in the afternoon until midnight. Boris announced that he was ready. He turned the model around; the actors got up from the table and crowded around, oohing and ahhing appropriately. Hal explained how the basic set would work. Then the set was turned back to the wall while Lisa and Boris fussed some more. When it was turned around again, the colorful Follies drops were all in place. Everyone was impressed. Realizing an oversight, Hal then introduced "the genius who thought this whole thing up, Boris Aronson. And that lady standing beside him is the only person who can deal with that genius, his wife, Lisa."

Hal went on to say: "There are many decisions which may not be made for a long time, but to help us get an idea of where we're going, I want to get the show up on its feet fast. Seeing it all put together will help us see what it looks like. Now, when we start the read-through, please speak out. Read out, take chances, make mistakes, because that's what we're here for. Ruthie will read stage directions and push you along should anyone lag, and Steve will play the songs when we get to them. For those of you who know your songs, Steve will play them today for the last time. From now on they are yours. Steve also has a new song for Solange LaFitte which no one has heard, so that will be a first!"

And off they went. Ruthie began at the very beginning: "The cur-

35

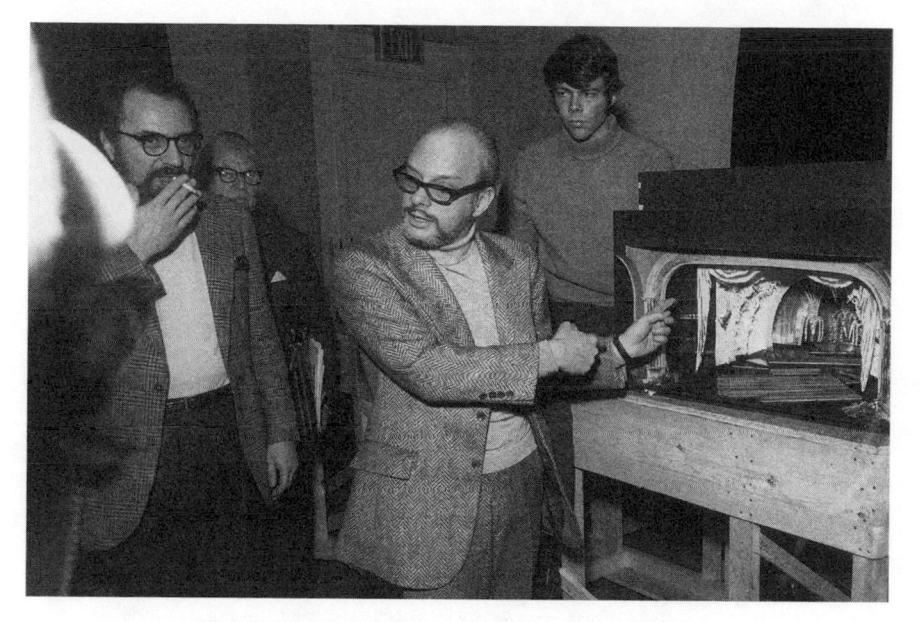

Hal Prince shows off the set model. Jim Goldman,
Michael Bartlett, Fritz Holt watch.

tain rises to the sound of pastiche music, as if recorded years ago, tinny, scratchy, full of ghosts."

The cast read their lines, some timidly, some with gusto. Steve sang all the songs, in a somewhat hurried fashion but to affectionate applause each time. The new song for Solange was part of a three-song montage early in the show. "Rain on the Roof" was first, a throwaway for the husband-and-wife team the Whitmans—originally "the whistling Whitmans"—a short, sweet couple whose song was punctuated with kisses: "Listen to the rain on the roof go pit-pitty-pat . . ." etc. Then came "Broadway Baby," the paean to showbiz, to be sung by old Hattie—"I'm just a Broadway baby, Walking off my tired feet. . . ." Then as he got to the new number, Steve said, "Don't look—I'm going to miss a lot of notes," and he began a vamp in 2/4 time. He sang:

> I have traveled over this earth,
> From Quebec to Venice to Perth,
> I've sailed down to Sydney
> And up to Nome,
> I've been to Rome
> And I've done Stockholm.

> I have seen the gardens of Kew,
> I have been to Timbuktu, too.
> But when I've returned,
> The thing I've learned
> Is what I always knew:
> New York has neon, Berlin has bars,
> But ah! Paree! . . .

He clearly didn't have the song completely in his fingers, so he stopped and started. But the idea, as well as its cleverness, came through. Although several lyrics sung that day were soon changed, I thought these originals exemplified just how fertile Steve's imagination is:

> I've been North and South, East and West,
> I have been to Buda- and -Pest
>
> . . . .
>
> I have seen Calcutta's black hole,
> I have even toured the South Pole,
> But when there's a moon,
> I leave Rangoon,
> And through Montmartre I stroll.

The atmosphere was relaxed. Quips were thrown around from time to time; when Steve got to "Who's That Woman?" he yelled to Michael across the room to make the tap sounds, which Michael accomplished by pounding the table with his hands. Fifi D'Orsay stumbled over the word "nonpareil."

Once they got to the beginning of the yet-to-be-finished Follies sequence, Hal interrupted: "All right, that's all we can do for now."

It was scary to have an entire sequence not yet completed on the first day of rehearsal. Those who had worked with Sondheim before knew that he was, by his own admission, a procrastinator, but that he thrived under pressure. Michael Bennett, who would have to stage each of the unwritten songs, was the most concerned. He knew that he already had his hands full with the older women, for whom he had big plans, and that he had a lot of movement to deal with in addition to the choreography. But, to be fair to Steve, there were also a handful of songs from *The Girls Upstairs* that had been cut over the past few

Ooh, la, la. Miss Fifi D'Orsay.

months: "Pleasant Little Kingdom" and "All Things Bright and Beautiful" for Sally; "That Old Piano Roll" for Buddy; and "Bring On the Girls," an opening number that Michael wanted replaced. He wanted a fresh start and Steve obliged, coming up with "Beautiful Girls." All the cut songs ended up in the show as part of various incarnations of the Prologue, the final version of which was based almost entirely on "All Things Bright and Beautiful."

A break was called. Everyone got up, milled around, Martha Swope packed up her cameras, the room got put back into shape for rehearsals to begin, and I was corralled into helping the Aronsons get back home with the set model.

So began the first week of rehearsal. In two weeks' time there would be a stagger-through, although that was not on anyone's mind at the moment. For the remainder of the day and for the next weeks, the

show would be rehearsed in bits and pieces, over and over again, with as many sequences linked together as possible, and as early as possible.

Although Michael and Hal were codirectors, each had another hat to wear as well. Michael's choreographic hand was needed throughout, since the line between direction and choreography was less clear than in a traditional musical. As the choreographer, he had a lot to accomplish in what now was starting to feel like not a lot of time. Hal had his producer responsibilities, although he infinitely preferred directing. He was bored by producing, and no longer enjoyed the challenge. But he was still brilliant at the job.

As soon as the break was over, Michael wanted to show "Who's That Woman?" to the women who would be dancing it—Mary McCarty in the solo spot, with her backup dancers Alexis Smith, Dorothy Collins, Yvonne De Carlo, Ethel Barrymore Colt, Helon Blount, and Sheila Smith. He knew that in order for it to work, he needed the "old gals" to do some pretty substantial hoofing. He took over the large rehearsal room, gathered the young dancers on whom he had been setting the number, and showed the whole thing, jumping in and dancing the leading role himself from time to time, at one point placing himself in the middle of a blossom of dancers surrounded by dancing petals. He pointed to Mary McCarty and then to himself as if to say, "And this will be you." She guffawed. When the number finished, Michael and Bob positioned the women out on the floor, spaced apart, and began going through the tap steps, slowly and patiently. "Looks like we'll be seeing a lot of each other over the next six weeks," Michael commented cheerfully, as he left them in the capable hands of Bob Avian and Mary Jane Houdina. The ten o'clock call the next morning, and for many mornings to follow, was devoted to learning and drilling the steps for this number. This would prove to be traumatic for some, but once the show got onstage, every minute of difficulty paid off—at least for the audience.

Michael had reconceived the number from what Steve had originally intended. It was designed as a challenge tap number from the old Follies that five of the ex–Follies girls at the reunion decide to perform once again. As they line up, they realize that one of the girls has died. That, however, won't stop them, and they proceed with the

dance, while maintaining a gaping hole in the middle of the lineup. As the show evolved, with a general shift away from a linear story and into a mood piece that moved between the past and the present, Michael's idea was to make it a dance between the present and the past in musical-comedy terms. With the advent of the ghost figures as characters, and with a song whose lyrics turn on the motif of looking into a mirror, Michael created a number with a clear sequence of memory-play: it starts in the present, then conjures up the past in a distant mirror image, then the two come together and coexist side by side, finally merging into one. After the verse and first chorus, during which the backup girls are mainly just posing, they start into a charmingly simple shuffle tap routine, lining up across the stage for a light series of variations, some with individual poses, working down the line. Then they dance around the center, ending up back in a line downstage, but now we see the mirror image of them way upstage: it's their ghosts, young and as they were in the Follies, all dressed alike, in tap costumes flecked with mirror chips catching the light. The two groups continue dancing as mirror images of each other—the reunion gals in their miscellaneous party dresses and the ghosts in identical Follies tap tutus. Then the two groups come together in one big circle, alternating present-day character and ghost figure. They dance together, but, of course, don't relate to each other at all. They are in separate times, though they're actually touching. At the very end, each present-day woman ends up standing in the same position as she did at the beginning of the number, only now she is posing opposite her own ghost figure, mirroring her youth.

It was ambitious. It was also clear from the get-go that it was going to be a lot of work for everyone, since for it to work properly the older gals would have to get their steps down. Michael wasn't interested in having them forget their old routine.

Word had gotten around before rehearsals began that the principal ladies would do well to take some tap lessons. Some did, others did not. Yvonne didn't, and she was having a hard time. "Once I learn them I'm okay, since I am a dancer, but I just can't get the steps." So Dorothy Collins went to Fritz Holt to see if Bob Avian couldn't do some extra work with Yvonne on the side, quietly, so she wouldn't feel bad. "Why don't you say something about the other girls having had some tap lessons—but don't make it sound like that is what you're saying." Bob, who had worked with Michael on every one of his shows,

was a model of tact and diplomacy. He invited Yvonne to come with him off in a corner, where he took her through the steps patiently and slowly. Monday night she appeared on the *Tonight Show* and told Johnny Carson that things were going well with the show, "but I'm having a lot of trouble with tap." In truth, all the women were having trouble learning the number, but most of them suffered silently.

Hal was responsible for the book scenes. The show was episodic, so what he had to rehearse was either scenes among the principals or short bits and pieces involving party scenes with one or two people drifting through clumps of other partygoers. He wanted to stage the show in chronological order, so he began with the opening mono-logues. Only Phyllis, Ben, Sally, and Buddy had monologues, but other characters had specific entrances that would be coordinated with music. "Make your entrances as if you've been having a conversation with the person you're arriving with. Your speech should be sort of a continuation," he told the room. He had a distinctive way of working: he took small sections of scenes, went over them repeatedly, blocked out some staging, and often gave the actors line readings if they didn't get one instinctively right off. "I'm not good at talking or verbalizing the printed page. I am not the kind of director who can talk, talk, talk about a scene. I have to see it." Since the party scenes continued throughout the whole show, he spoke about the need to "orchestrate the party." He kept a careful eye out for focus, so the emphasis would always be on the right place and on the right characters. "You take a drink from this waiter here, and come down this way, wave hello to those people over there, and come dancing over here and stop." He kept on rehearsing party vignettes all week, devising almost cinematic cross-fades as a waiter, a guest, or one of the black-and-white showgirl ghosts wandered in front of a scene as it ended. Some of this looked stagey and clumsy, but without everything else going on around, it was clearly too early to make a judgment. Sometimes Hal would jump up, grab an actor by the arms and pull him through to where he wanted him. Sometimes he seemed oddly preoccupied, and would talk to Ruthie or whoever was sitting next to him while scenes were being run. Perhaps he was discussing new ideas, but it didn't look as if he was pay-ing attention to the actors. Since everyone in the scenes he was staging was also needed by Michael and the music department, he would grab anyone available to stand in. On a couple of occasions, I stood in for a waiter. It felt odd—sort of fun, but I felt as if I really didn't belong. I

was much more comfortable at any of my other tasks, which were beginning to become more numerous and varied.

Hal Hastings started to teach the opening number, "Beautiful Girls," to everyone in the company. He also worked with individual actors on their solos. Often this was done so quietly that no one was aware of songs' being rehearsed until they were ready to be presented in the big rehearsal room. He chose to start with the older actors, since they had already expressed concerns about learning everything they had to learn in the time available and he knew they would need a lot of hand-holding.

A full-page ad for the show ran on Sunday, the second day of rehearsal. This is a tradition that Hal Prince had adhered to for years; he felt that seeing a full-page advance advertisement in the Arts & Leisure Section of the Sunday *New York Times*, with everyone's name in place, always gave the company a boost. It was also another subtle reminder that soon there would have to be a complete show to put in front of an audience.

Hal and Boris had a blowup early in the week. Although Hal liked

Where they were headed: "Beautiful Girls" onstage in Boston.

the rehearsal platforms that approximated the side units of the set, he also wanted to have the set model in the rehearsal room with him so he could make reference to the real thing while he was roughing out his staging. Boris said it was needed at the shop as reference during the construction. Since it was painted in fine detail, it was also vital to the shop's painting staff. Hal had a heated phone conversation with Boris, but because he was needed back in the rehearsal room, he turned the phone over to Ruthie. She shut the door while Hal walked back to rehearsal, muttering, "I don't want to be in there." Ruthie's piercing voice, now rising in volume, could be heard through the door. Then the receiver slammed down and she emerged, heading for Hal, fuming: "Why do you do that to me?" Later on, Hal conceded that Boris was absolutely right, that as producer he understood completely the need for the model at the shop. But as director he wanted it in the rehearsal room.

If Hal had a conflict at this point in the process, it was that he was both sole producer and codirector. He had started his life as a producer, in partnership with a fellow stage manager, Robert E. Griffith. Together they had produced shows that were directed by the A-team of musical theater artists of the 1950s: George Abbott, Jerome Robbins, and Bob Fosse. Hal was the eager-beaver youngster of the lot, and was even parodied in a book called *Say, Darling*, written by Richard Bissell, the author of the novel *7¹/₂ Cents*, on which *The Pajama Game* was based. *Say, Darling* told the story of how a book was turned into a musical. Then it, in turn, was made into a musical, with Robert Morse portraying the Hal Prince character in a not altogether flattering portrait. Nothing fazed Hal, though, and he kept right on producing. By the early 1960s, after the death of his partner, he had struck out on his own as one of the very few producers on Broadway to earn a solo credit ("Harold Prince presents . . ."). He still knew how to produce better than almost anyone else, and had assembled a solid staff. Included was Carl Fisher, an elegant elderly gentleman, nephew of George Abbott, who had declined to be a partner with Griffith and Prince in the early days, but who stayed on as their general manager. Fisher also headed a syndicate that invested in shows in his name and in the case of *Follies* was one of the largest investors. Hal was leaning more and more on Carl and the staff, and Ruthie in the rehearsal room, to take care of business, even to the point of arguing with them over expenditures that

he as director thought were needed. The overall producing scheme and policy was clearly Hal's, but the more he could remove himself from the daily nuts and bolts, the happier he was. One day I brought down a sheet of expenses from Carl for him to okay. It totaled over $200,000. He glanced at it, handed it back to me, and said, "Give this to Ruthie. I don't have the strength to look at it and get mad."

Hal was still the sole producer of *Follies*, although he gave Ruthie "in association with" billing, as he had since *Cabaret*. He had his usual large group of investors: for *Follies* there were somewhere between 170 and 207, each of whom put up between $875 and $52,500 for a total of $700,000. A limited partnership, imaginatively named the Follies Company, was formed as the business entity through which the show was produced; the investors were the "limited" partners who provide the capitalization, and the producer was the "general" partner who finds the property, hires the talent, and does the actual producing. The Securities and Exchange Commission regulates the limited partnerships formed to produce shows in New York, and because of the high rate of failure, the offering papers must indicate the track record of the producer raising money to present the show. The legal partnership documents include a lot of detail about the show, the personnel involved, how much they will be paid, and so on. Each investor and the amount of investment has to be listed and filed. The documents often allowed a producer the right to an overcall of a set percentage from each investor should the show go over budget. If there is no such provision (and there was none in the case of *Follies*), the producer is allowed to arrange for a loan to the partnership that would then occupy a first-payback position. Since the final reported budget for *Follies* was close to $800,000, a loan did have to be made. (Rumor had it that Hal put up the money himself, and in an article in *Forbes* it was reported that one of the obligations when the show made a first distribution to investors was "paying off $78,000 it had borrowed.")

It was easy to sense Hal's producer-versus-director conflict on a daily basis. One day when Ingram Ash, the head of the show's advertising agency, brought down a series of photographs and layouts for Hal's approval, he tried to talk Hal into leasing the large half-block billboard above the marquee of the Winter Garden Theater, where the show would play in New York. Ash had a rendering of how it might look, but Hal rejected it as an extravagant expense. Everyone on the support team thought he should take the plunge, but he saw it through the

prudent producer's eyes and didn't want to take it on. (He was eventually talked into it.)

On the second day, Michael began work on staging the Prologue. Hal would sit in whenever he could, since what they were creating was a kind of mosaic—people arriving at this ghost-filled theater for the party, greeting each other, sensing the ghosts, hearing bits and pieces of shows from the past. The Prologue was to change three times before the New York opening, each version fascinating in its own right. It had been decided that there would be no overture. The house curtain would be down as the audience filed in. Once the house lights dimmed, the curtain was to rise on the half-lit set of the crumbling Weismann Theater after some flashes of lightning. The Prologue set the ambiance of the scene before anyone arrived for the party. We would discover—in some way yet to be determined—the ghosts of showgirls haunting the theater, lurking in the shadows, ready to do the show, only the show wasn't happening anymore. It was to include specific memories from the days of the Follies, although what memories those were or how they would be manifested had yet to be decided. Slowly, the reality of the present would become apparent and the ghost figures would recede into the background, only to appear again when conjured up by the events of the play. The characters would begin to arrive, and each would react differently to the surroundings, as usually happens at reunions, only this time, the feelings would be verbalized and, in some instances, physicalized. When Solange LaFitte (Fifi D'Orsay) arrives, for example, she hears her old applause echoing in the past, and she brightens to its sound. Hattie Walker (Ethel Shutta), ever the pragmatist, enters directly with her black-and-white ghost figure shadowing her every move. The wheelchair-bound Heidi Schiller (Justine Johnston) is greeted by the swirling movement of her "waltz." We could get glimpses into the people they were today before we learned about who they had been in the days of the Follies. When Stella Deems (Mary McCarty) is announced by the Major-Domo of the party by her maiden name, she has no reaction; her husband reaches out to remind her of her previous life. John Berkman, the arranger of the dance music, sat at the piano and created the arrangement as Michael worked, basing everything on elements and variations of the songs in the show. It was moody, atmospheric, and eerie. Each day more characters were introduced, the staging got more specific, and the music related more to the characters. Sometimes the ghost fig-

ures would take over and influence the music with specific references to the past. On the day when Michael finally got to the end of the Prologue, Hal said, "Oh, well, good. It's an opening." And Michael replied, "And what do you know? I don't have a clutch in my stomach."

Another focus early in the week was "Waiting for the Girls Upstairs." In some ways this song was the key to the whole show. Not only had it been one of the first songs written, but its evolution paralleled the evolution of *The Girls Upstairs* into *Follies*. Steve felt it; of all the songs, this was the one he seemed most anxious about. By Monday afternoon it was in presentable enough shape to be run for Hal, Steve, and Jim Goldman. Halfway through, Hal leaned over to Michael and said: "Terrific—it's going to be terrific." Steve was pleased. "It's going to be great, really, you all keep the emotion very well, and it's the emotion that carries the song through." It is the first moment when the lead characters deal specifically with themselves as a foursome—then, and now. The emotions are, necessarily, complex, and since the song comes early in the show, it opens the Pandora's box of emotional turmoil to come. The song begins on stage level with the men singing their verse. Without being quite conscious of what they're doing, Phyllis and Sally climb a staircase on one of the side units, as if going back up to their dressing rooms. When they begin their verse, they are "upstairs," singing about the "boys downstairs." It was a nice moment, and it cleared the lower level for the young counterparts, who take over for the first time in the show. They enter filled with youthful anticipation of an evening on the town, discuss their plans, and then run off, leaving behind the four principals, who are somewhat dazed by the memory. Once the song was run, Michael went into the stage managers' office, took a swig of Hal's Fernet-Branca, and said, "I really like 'The Girls Upstairs' from when the young kids start until the end. I just don't like the beginning. But . . . I've got too much to do to worry about it now." Then there was a brief summit meeting.

In fact, there was a summit meeting almost every day in which Hal, Michael, Jim, and Steve would sequester themselves behind a closed door and discuss the status of the show. This often took place over lunch, but sometimes happened on the spur of the moment.

Of all the creators, the one who was least in evidence the first week was Jim Goldman. He was probably feeling more gun-shy than anyone, simply because as exciting as *Follies* was, it was a far cry from the show that he and Steve had begun. Changing gears to accommodate a

new producer and a new directing team must have made him cautious, and this was the third try, although this time was for real. There had been six complete drafts of the script before Hal got involved, each of which had rough and final versions. (The first one he gave Steve had on its cover: Untitled musical, unpolished book by James Goldman, unfinished music by Stephen Sondheim.) When Hal wanted him in rehearsal, he was always there. And every time he came in, he brought new revisions, sometimes just a line or two, sometimes a new lead-in to a song, sometimes a shift of sequence, sometimes an entirely new scene. He was game, certainly, and appeared to be very laid-back, and very un-showbiz. I found this letter stuck in an earlier draft of the script in the stage managers' office:

Dear Hal,

What you've got here is a first attempt at 1) clarifying and improving Ben and 2) tightening the first sag in the show, the area between "The Girls Upstairs" and "Who's That Woman?"

It wasn't that what Ben did was so wrong. The problem was that he didn't do anything. Being unsure of him, I had taken the sure course of leaving him out, with the result that between his opening monologue and his scene with Sally after "The Girls Upstairs," he had something like two lines of dialogue.

I've come across a way of formulating what the past means to our four people. I've found it enormously helpful and before you read this stuff, particularly with Ben in mind, I wanted to offer it to you.

It's just that when the past stays alive in our lives in harmful or damaging ways, it means we have unfinished business with it. For Ben, Sally represents unfinished business. It's not the lady herself who attracts him and evokes old feelings. It's the past within himself that he has never faced or come to terms with.

This may be a highly personal way of putting it and of no help at all. But I've begun to feel so much clearer and more certain what this piece is all about by thinking that our people have unfinished business with the past and when the show is over, they have finished with it.

Anyway,
Jim

At one of the summit meetings during lunch (I brought in the food—gofer, remember?), Jim announced that he had found some answers the night before but had had no one to tell them to. This seemed like a slow-track comment delivered to a bunch of people on a fast track and brought the conversation to a bit of a standstill. But soon the conversation was focused on the Follies sequence. Steve was lying on his back on one of the stage units, Jim was puffing away on a pipe, Ruthie was seated, looking up at Hal, Michael and Bob were sitting quietly, and Hal was pacing. The discussion turned to how metaphorical the entire Follies sequence should be. Steve wasn't sure exactly where he stood; he had mentioned to me a few days earlier that Hal was injecting a lot more obvious "meaning" into the show than had originally been intended. Ruthie said: "This is the first chance all evening for the audience to enjoy something without having to think every moment of the time, and I think it should be kept that way."

A digression. On Tuesday night, Mary Rodgers and her husband, Hank Guettel, came to our house for dinner with my parents. They were friends, and we had gone as a family to Hank and Mary's on Christmas night for dinner. Steve Sondheim had been one of the other guests, and since I knew I would be working on *Follies*, I asked about it. He said his greatest fear was there would be no one boss; Hal was the logical boss, but because he knew Michael Bennett was going to be a real force this time, he was concerned there might be a tug of war between the two. So on this Tuesday night, four days into rehearsals, Hank and Mary brought gossip from Steve, whom they had spoken to earlier that day. Steve had helped Mary out of a crunch with *The Mad Show* a few years earlier, when, under the pseudonym Estaban Rio Nido, he wrote a funny set of lyrics to Mary's music in "The Boy from . . . ," a parody of the then-popular song "The Girl from Ipanema." Their song told the story of a young woman's frustration with her man who lives in places with unpronounceable names, and somehow seems unresponsive to any woman's affection, which she just can't understand. "Why are his trousers vermillion? . . . Why do his friends call him Lillian?" It was the hit of the show. Steve paid homage to them both with a line in *Company*: "Hank and Mary get into town tomorrow." Listen—it's still in the score.

Mary said Steve had reported that the show was "terrible—if people thought *Company* was depressing, wait until this show opens. It really is very depressing." She didn't give much credence to his comment, explaining that songs are never sung the way you, the composer, imagine they would and should be, and it's always a shock when you first hear them coming from the mouths of actors. Hank said that *Follies* was a labor of love: "If someone is able to come up with something as brilliant as *Company* when he said his heart wasn't really in it, imagine what this score, which has indeed been a labor of love, is going to be like?" He also said to keep an eye open—in *Company* the whole score didn't come together until Steve wrote "Being Alive" in Boston. He suspected something similar might happen on this show. They also both stressed that they had the utmost respect for Hal as a producer. "He is high above other New York producers in the way he handles his backers. He treats them well without pandering to them and prefers to have many people invest small amounts rather than a few big investors."

Back at Nineteenth Street rehearsals were forging ahead. Hal Hastings took any actor who wasn't otherwise occupied to teach and drill music. He would play the song for the actor first, then give the piano over to a rehearsal pianist so he could concentrate on coaching—phrasing, breathing, enunciation, and rhythm. He wanted to spend the most time with those who needed him the most, and Michael had made it known that he didn't want to work with any of the solos until the actors knew their material cold.

Ethel Shutta was one of the first to learn her song and begin staging rehearsals. She was a delight. Of all the actors in the show, she became the embodiment of what the show was about. She had been a big star in the 1920s, appearing on Broadway in shows like *Whoopee!* and in several editions of the Follies. When married to bandleader George Olsen, she became a well-known vocalist, and even went to Hollywood, where she appeared in several films, including the film of *Whoopee!* Her career had stalled in the 1950s, and drink became something of a demon for her as she tried to return to the stage. Her most recent Broadway credit was an unsuccessful Mary Martin vehicle called *Jennie,* but she had been plugging away, looking for jobs wherever she

could find them. She was grateful for the role in this show, and it would prove to be her last great hurrah. The song given to her character, Hattie Walker, "Broadway Baby," was a pragmatic statement of a Broadway hopeful. She sang the words with such conviction, spirit, and determination that you couldn't help but smile. "At!! My tiny flat!! There's just my cat!!" She was easily a favorite among the company, and every time she rehearsed, people would laugh. In response to my compliments, she replied, "Well, you know, I was in six Ziegfeld shows starting with the Follies in 1925. Don't expect a grand voice from an old girl like me. When you start singing after not having sung for so long—I am so bad about exercising—you have to get worked into it again." She told me she thought I looked like Ryan O'Neal, and ripped an ad out of the newspaper for his movie *Love Story* to prove it. She was worried that she was going to have trouble remembering things, but she was a trouper. When she was passed on to Michael for staging, he began by just letting her do what she wanted. When something pleased him, he would tell her to keep it in. She would stop in her tracks and look at him whenever he spoke, affording him the courtesy traditionally given by a performer to her director. She was fighting to remember things, but that didn't stop her from trying. At the end of each rehearsal she would thank him for taking the time to work with her. She was having trouble with her small part in the Prologue. Michael wanted her to enter, walk five steps in rhythm, stand still for four counts, and then walk downstage for sixteen more counts. When she finally got it right, Graciela ran over and threw her arms around her in a big bear hug. "Hey, I didn't know acting could be so hard!" she exclaimed.

In the middle of the week, two dancers who could pass for an older ballroom couple were chosen from a last-minute audition. For some reason, signing them to a contract took a lot of doing, so they were on again one minute, off again the next. I suspected it was the budget. By the end of the week, Jayne Turner and Don Weismuller joined the company. Another woman was also hired as a swing dancer. She stood four feet ten inches tall in her fraying pink high-heeled dance shoes, cascades of obviously dyed red hair falling down over her character's face, and had a name Michael couldn't resist—Sonja Levkova. The next morning she was hard at work with Mary Jane Houdina, learning the tap steps to "Who's That Woman?"

M y gofer errands multiplied. For script and lyric changes and revisions, I would type pages on a red IBM electric typewriter set up
on an old desk in the front hall of the Lab. I would use carbon sets and
keep copy number four (of ten) for a running and up-to-date copy of
the script, which I would hold on to in case I had to make subsequent
copies. If I was going up to the Rockefeller Center office, I would bring
new pages to Xerox. But I wouldn't always have access to the machine,
since the office's world was more than just *Follies*. The touring production of *Company*, for example, was being cast, which meant that notes
from Joanna Merlin to Hal had to be brought down to rehearsal for his
responses, which I would then communicate uptown. Bills would be
brought down for Ruthie's okay. Petty cash was needed at rehearsal,
and contracts signed downtown needed to be brought to the office for
the files. I would be sent on occasional shopping excursions, like buy-
ing five umbrellas for the Prologue when the decision was made that
the show would take place on a rainy night. And, yes, I made endless
runs for coffee, tea, sandwiches, and oddball food requests—say, for
Hal's lunch, two hard-boiled eggs, a pickle, and soup. The music
department also kept me pretty busy, fetching and delivering.

When Steve Sondheim finished writing a song, he would play it for
Hal, Michael, and Jim. If everyone approved, he would then turn in his
manuscript. This would consist of a vocal line, lyrics under, and two
accompaniment lines playable on piano. While some Broadway com-
posers' manuscripts are sketchy, Steve's are clean, precise, and full,
with musician's shorthand used to save time. The next person to get it
would be Mathilde Pincus, the music copyist, whose task was to write
out a clean copy of the song in a legible and reproducible fashion. She
used a flat pen with black ink and wrote on 11" × 14" sheets of opaque
paper called deschon, which had the musical staff lines printed in
reverse on one side. Writing with ink on the other side allowed for
errors to be erased without affecting the staff lines. This sheet was then
placed on top of a piece of specially treated paper and run through an
elaborate machine that reeked of ammonia. The treated paper could
accommodate four pages of deschon at a time, and out would come a
perfectly clear and readable copy of the song that looked almost like
printed music, with the notes and staff lines equal in value, although

done by hand. The three pages would then be folded, accordion-style, and taped together so the song was ready for the rehearsal room. These were the copies that were distributed to the rehearsal pianists and cast on the first day of rehearsal.

Once the keys were set (depending mostly on the actor's vocal range) and the routining established (dance arrangements, how many times through, etc.), the song was then handed over to Jonathan Tunick, the orchestrator. His task was to apportion the music among the specific instruments chosen for the orchestra to give the musical impression desired by the composer. The size and makeup of the orchestra is a group decision, influenced primarily by the composer and the producer, the composer with artistic concerns and the producer with budgetary ones. (Theaters on Broadway also have union-determined minimum numbers of players that vary with the seating capacity of the theater.) The orchestrator also has to take the dance arrangements and blend them with the songs and any underscoring to create a score that flows together as one piece. He then creates the full orchestral score on a long piece of paper with a musical staff line for each instrument, starting with the woodwinds at the top, going through the brass, percussion, and ending with the strings on the bottom. Each page of full score usually contains only four bars of music, so one song can take up to twenty pages or so, and a long dance routine can fill many more. Once the score is completed, it goes to the copyist, whose next job is to extract parts for each instrument—the flute part, for example, is created by taking the line at the top of each page. When that job is finished, each player in the orchestra will have only his part, although the conductor will have the full score in front of him so he can see what everyone is playing. And this process goes for every piece of music in a show. In the case of *Follies*, there would end up being twenty-three songs and a Prologue. And, of course, every new song had to be taken through the entire process; there is no way to circumvent any of the steps if a musical is to be accompanied by an orchestra of any size. The *Follies* orchestra would have twenty-seven players. Each step takes time, a lot of effort, and money.

My tasks were mainly to ferry different pieces of this score-in-progress around the city. Steve would usually bring the new song down to rehearsal, and he would tend to give his manuscript directly to Mathilde. But sometimes he would be working at home and word would come that a song was finished, so I would be sent over to his house in

Bob Avian, Larry Cohen, Michael Bennett, Hal Hastings—in front of the mirrors at the American Theater Lab, watching the showgirls run through "Loveland."

Turtle Bay to pick it up and take it to Mathilde. When she was finished with the piano/vocal, I would bring copies down to rehearsal, and once everyone had decided on the key, I would take a copy to Jonathan Tunick's apartment on the Upper West Side. When he was finished with a score, I would pick it up and take it to Mathilde for the extraction of instrumental parts. Every day included some element of this circuit.

By Thursday, the end of the first week of full rehearsal, the logistics were changing subtly. More and more of what Michael was doing needed the large rehearsal room, as numbers were being put together with the full company. That put a squeeze on Hal, who was eager to put pieces together and have a run-through to see what they had. Michael, in addition to overseeing the ladies learning "Who's That Woman?" was working his way through the Prologue and starting "Beautiful Girls," both of which depended on the set for much of the movement. In addition, although solos would be worked on in the smaller room, it became more important to bring them into the large room to get a sense of the space. On Thursday, Hal was able to run scenes from the beginning up to and beyond "Waiting for the Girls Upstairs." At the end of the day, Ethel Shutta came into the large room and ran through "Broadway Baby" for the first time "in public." It was great. "That girl is precious," said Hal Hastings.

Friday was the day off.

3

"Girls Looking Frazzled and Girls Looking Great"

REHEARSALS CONTINUE AT THE REHEARSAL STUDIO,
JANUARY 16–29

Hal came bounding in late on Saturday morning and announced: "One hour is all I'm allotted today, so I want to do the scene following 'Waiting for the Girls Upstairs,' and I've got a new idea." The idea was to change two of the waiters to photographers. "I had the idea in bed last night. I began thinking that I hated what I had done, and there was no one from the production to talk to." He began by telling the photographers to shoot indiscriminately. He then found places where some characters could be posed, and he put several of the older women on one side of the stage against one of the units. Ethel Barrymore Colt posed perfectly, her hand held at a discreet position away from her body, middle finger ever so slightly lowered. "I want everyone to examine that hand," Hal noted. Mary McCarty laughed heartily, and he said, "Try not to knock it, Mary. Achieve it." He realized he could use the photographers to help sweep focus from one part of the party to another, like a cinematic cross-fade. So he had both photographers stand in front of the Whitmans, take one shot, then part to the sides, revealing the couple for "Rain on the Roof." It looked like a nice way to get into the song.

He was longing to see sequences put together. He wanted to run the beginning of the show and continue through Ben and Sally's song "Don't Look at Me" and Ben's song "The Road You Didn't Take." On

54

Sunday he was able to muster the opening monologues, and then the book scenes, including "Waiting for the Girls Upstairs." He also integrated Sally's "In Buddy's Eyes" and Ben's "The Road You Didn't Take" for the first time. Dorothy did fine, John muffed several lyrics, but they both got a nice round of applause from everyone in attendance.

Monday brought the first attempt at staging "Beautiful Girls." The music had been learned, sort of, but this was the first go at getting it on its feet. Although Roscoe had the solo part of the song, it involved all the old gals. Hal Hastings assembled everyone in the middle of the room to sing through the song once. Michael Bartlett was very nervous, having to perform in front of everyone, sang in half-voice, missed most of his lyrics, and didn't attempt the high note at the end. But it sounded pretty good. The room was turned over to Michael Bennett, who began with Roscoe. In an early script he was described as "an aged tenor in white tie and tails [who] appears high on a stairway, strikes a magnificent pose, opens his mouth and, in a glorious tenor voice, sings." It didn't look as if Michael Bartlett was going to strike a magnificent pose high up anywhere; just getting him onstage and in a downstage position looked as if it was going to take a lot of hard work. The women could strike their poses just fine, but getting them to where they were supposed to be, *when* they were supposed to be there, was a challenge. Michael began to stage a true Miss America–style entrance for each woman: presentation, walk down the stage left stairs, and promenade. It was slow going, especially since there were more steps on the actual set than there were on the mock-ups in the studio, and that took some explaining. But he was patient. Later in the day, the rest of the party guests and waiters, who had spent the morning learning the song, came in. After one musical pass-through, Hal Hastings stopped and said, "Kids, you've forgotten everything we were doing in the other room. I am trying to get every note. It can't be slop time, it's got to be crisp. If you will attack each note, it will sound full of energy. Please don't get jazzy on me and don't hoax it up. Don't do me any favors. Don't let it get marshmallowy." He asked for a chord at the very end: "You can sing any note you want on the final beat as long it's either a C, an E, or a G, because I want the major triad, and ladies who can hit the high C, please do." The day was getting late, but everyone stumbled through it one last time. "Maybe it was real, what was beginning to happen, but it was also getting to be boring," Michael said. He realized that he had to make certain the transition into the next scene was correct and that all

the actors finished the song in the positions Hal had assigned them for the party scene that followed. His solution was to have a brief encore, with Roscoe turning around like a majordomo, taking charge so everybody could move gracefully to where he needed to be.

Before breaking for the day, Michael brought in all the dancers to go through as much of the Prologue as he had finished. It looked quite marvelous.

Hal Hastings, as administrative head of the music department, was kept busy on all levels. Aside from teaching and coaching the songs, he had to find players for the onstage band. Because the players would be both visible and audible, he needed musicians who would also be believable as a band hired for a party. He was having a harder time than he thought he would, having auditioned and interviewed several candidates, all of whom had been found wanting. He had found a trumpeter in Taft Jordan, whose playing was deemed acceptable. There was a logistical problem with the onstage band since Boris, when he designed the platform, hadn't taken into consideration the proper size of a piano. The space was large enough for a small spinet, which is the size of piano used in *Cabaret*. But this time the piano needed to be full-size upright, so someone made a paper template and the stage managers moved it around the mock-up platform to see if a solution could be found. Since the set was already in the shop, no one wanted any structural changes. As it happens, a slight adjustment could be made relatively easily. Also, in the script Carlotta's escort was supposed to be a piano virtuoso, so they tried to find a position that allowed an actor to take over the piano. Unfortunately, that proved to be unworkable, so before too long, Randy, the escort, became just an escort. The actor didn't know how to play the piano, anyway.

The *Follies* family was starting to find its character. The social ones lingered in the common hall chatting with anyone who wandered by. Dorothy Collins was warm and chatty—at one point so chatty that Ruthie said, "Save your voice!" Gene Nelson was in perpetual motion, always interested in any conversation about Hollywood. Alexis Smith never lingered long, but sometimes paused for a quip. Seeing an article about the show pinned to a bulletin board in which she was referred to

as "tall and striking," she remarked: "I wish I could someday play someone short and fat." Yvonne enjoyed talking and giggling—anything but going over her tap steps or working on her solo song "Can That Boy Fox Trot!" Justine Johnston rarely took her eyes off the clock—either the one on the wall or the one hanging around her neck. She was a one-woman union police force.

A new observer joined the ranks. His name was Larry Cohen, and he seemed to be very chatty with Hal, Steve, and Michael. He was the legitimate theater critic for the *Hollywood Reporter* who was following the rehearsals of *Follies* with the idea of writing a book about the process of putting on a musical. There had been a comparable person following *The Rothschilds*, the last show for which I had gofered, and since I had never spoken with him, I decided to sit tight and ignore this guy, too. (That book did come out: *The Producer*, by Christopher Davis, all about Hillard Elkins.) But Larry was involved in some interesting conversations, and he seemed bright and well informed, so I started talking with him. We had very similar points of view about the state of the theater and the movies, we were both fans of the musical theater, and we had both figured that if anything in the musical theater was going to be exciting this season, it was *Follies*.

Michael took over the large room to continue his painstaking way through the Prologue. Each time he worked on it, he added more people, having begun with the dancers as ghost figures, then added party guests, and, finally, the principals. The aim was to integrate the monologues Hal had been working on and segue neatly into "Beautiful Girls." When he got to Justine Johnston's Heidi Schiller, after spending some time trying to figure out how to maneuver her wheelchair on, he remarked, "Heidi, I think you're going to be on a cane very shortly." On Sunday Michael attempted to put all the elements together for the first time. He gathered the whole company and sat them down. "We must get across to the audience what this evening means to each and every character we see enter. We must realize that as each person enters, he or she has had some business with this place in the past which has really ended. That is partly what this show is about. We must also establish the fact that time as we know it has no relationship to this evening. The show is really about time and what it does to people, so we must establish that we are going to stop it at will, turn it back and twist it around whenever we so desire. I realize that crossing on a count of eight can be tricky, but I want everyone to become so well

drilled that it never looks like anyone is counting. In order to make sense of the whole show, I need everyone to pay close attention to their counts and where they are supposed to be going." Then, slowly, he began to put it all together.

Steve Sondheim came by rehearsals on Sunday in a relaxed mood. He asked me how I thought things were going. It was a tough one to answer, because I didn't know. The atmosphere was so charged—personalities emerging, work at such varying stages of development—that I couldn't figure out how things were in relation to the whole. I told him I really couldn't tell this early, but that some of what I had seen looked pretty good. We talked about the company; he was worried that there might be friction between the generations. From my vantage point, I told him, it looked like the opposite, that there seemed to be friendly and collegial support between the two groups, along with respect. He said he preferred to stay away for another week or so before coming to rehearsals with any regularity.

This was Sunday, a week and a day since we had begun. As far as any of us knew, Sondheim still had at least five songs to write: one song for the Young Four in Loveland ("Love Will See Us Through"), Buddy's character song ("The Right Girl") and Follies song ("The God-Why-Don't-You-Love-Me Blues"), Ben's Follies song ("Live, Laugh, Love"), and a bolero for Vincent and Vanessa. It was unclear what Phyllis and Sally would sing in the Follies sequence, since both "Losing My Mind" and "The World's Full of Boys" were still being discussed. Despite not knowing where he was in the creation of those songs, he did seem to be in an expansive mood.

Sondheim is a complex character. To those in the business, he has always been acknowledged as brilliant—"as close to a genius as anyone working today," some have said. He could be charming, and he could be intimidating. He was thoroughly professional with everyone connected with the show, and quite gracious and giving when he wanted to be. But when he didn't, he could certainly make you feel small. My first encounter was indicative. I had written to him during my freshman year of college asking if he knew where I could buy a copy of the even-then rare hardcover version of the script of *Anyone Can Whistle* for a friend who was desperate to get a copy. He sent me a copy, inscribed to the person for whom I was asking, with a cordial letter.

"Any time you and/or your friend would like to meet with me in the city, I would be delighted." Then, the last paragraph: "One piece of advice: learn how to spell 'inconvenience.' I promise not to tell your father."

His work is complex, too. "He's a lot simpler now than he was," Hal said, "and we really have to keep him simple. Richard Rodgers, who now likes Steve very much, used to say that as soon as you're with him and all is going well, he'll go and get complicated on you." Alexis described what his songs are like to learn: "When you hear him play the songs they sound so easy, then you start to learn them and after two bars you stop, exasperated." Michael described *Anyone Can Whistle* as being "pure complicated, intellectual Sondheim left to his own devices."

It is precisely his intellect at work in a field not known for its intellectuality that makes him unique. It's also what makes him controversial, since the Broadway musical-theater industry relies more on the popular success of the *Hello, Dolly!*'s than on the prestige of shows like *Company*. He had his coterie of fans who felt he was breaking through into new territory, but he was still considered primarily a lyricist; his music was not getting the recognition it deserved. To him, lyric writing was a puzzle, and he loved puzzles. He was good at them, but they took a lot of work. Composing wasn't a puzzle; it was more emotional, and perhaps it was because of his awesome skill with words that people were reluctant to accept him as a composer. But he thought of himself as a composer. *Company* had begun the process of educating the larger world to just how extraordinary he was. *Follies* would be the catalyst that made the skeptics aware of his full talents. Fully appreciating him was still not such an easy thing. When I first encountered *Anyone Can Whistle*, I had no idea what to make of it. On second and repeated hearings, however, I began to realize just how extraordinary a piece of work it was, with melodies that at first seemed to go by without making much of an impression but which became more and more intriguing. A fifteen-minute piece in which a fake doctor separates a stageful of people into two groups—Group A and Group 1—called "Simple"? I had never encountered anything like that. My mind was as engaged as my feelings. That's what he demanded of an audience, and that was new. His work took some getting used to, but it was worth the effort. Yet at this point in the process of *Follies*, I was concerned. There were two distinct styles of songs—the "book" songs, sung in the present, and the songs that echoed the past, which were more accessible. Sondheim

59

Michael Bennett stages "Love Will See Us Through" with Marti Rolph,
stage manager George Martin in the rear.

referred to these songs as "pastiche." I feared audiences would prefer
one style over the other, and I feared that the "book" songs would lose
out. Perhaps the key will be "Waiting for the Girls Upstairs," I thought,
which combines both past and present—and has a catchy tune.

On Wednesday, Steve finished the other Follies songs for the Young
Four, making two sunshiny DeSylva, Henderson & Brown–style songs
about the blissful future: ". . . You're gonna love tomorrow, I'm giving
you my personal guarantee" and ". . . No matter what goes wrong,
Love will see us through till something better comes along." There
was relief from the actors. "Guess what?" Kurt Peterson said to his
agent over the phone. "I have a number!" Michael took the songs and
the four actors into the dance rehearsal room and began to stage them.
He seemed somewhat relieved to be working with young actors who
could learn fast and retain what they were shown. There was starting to
be no time for contemplation, and Michael was starting to get annoyed
at Steve. He wanted the rest of the songs finished.

There was tension when Steve came by on Thursday. He came into the stage managers' office and cornered John Grigas and me. "Which one of you typed the lyric to 'The World's Full of Boys'?" I explained that it had been delivered to us from the Prince office uptown in the form that he was holding. "Well, whoever typed it corrected my lyrics as he went along. I carefully spelled 'galop' g-a-l-o-p, and all the way through it was 'corrected' and spelled with two *l*'s." He marched into a summit meeting with Hal and Michael. I took it upon myself to retype the whole lyric, including the proper spelling of "galop," which, I didn't realize, was an indication of a style of dance. A few moments later, Hal emerged from the meeting to take a phone call, saw me at the typewriter and asked, "Why are you doing that? I think the number is being cut." He sent me to find out from Steve whether the song was in or out, which struck me as odd since he and Michael could surely have asked him directly. But something was up, and I was the fact-finder. Steve was in one of the rooms, talking with one of the actors, and as I waited, Hal and Michael asked, "What did he say?" I told them I hadn't yet had an opportunity to ask him. "Hell!" one of them replied. When I finally did get to Steve, with a bit of a smirk he said that yes, the song had been cut.

Peter Feller stopped in on Monday. He was the owner of the scenery studio bearing his family's name. Feller's was one of the two studios that built sets for Broadway shows, and they were building *Follies*. He had come by with some questions about the Follies drops and some of the rubble. His domain was a natural focus for tension between the desires of the designer, the needs of the director, and the producer's budgetary concerns. But Feller was a diplomat, even though he looked like a character out of a 1940s movie—slick black hair parted in the middle, thin mustache, and black suit. He had four or five henchmen with him, similarly attired. When his questions got to budget, Hal had him speak first with Ruthie. Looking at some plans, Hal commented that "realism is slowly leaving our sets—doors went out last year, and table and chairs are gone now."

Tharon Musser, the lighting designer, came around on Thursday for a meeting with Hal and Michael. She hadn't turned up since the first day of rehearsal, nearly two weeks earlier, but she had been thinking and poring over the blueprints for the set. Obviously she was inter-

ested in knowing how the blocking was coming along so that she could figure out where she would need to hang the lighting instruments. Michael explained some ideas he was having about silhouettes and how they could be achieved. Tharon suggested backlighting. Michael described the Prologue and explained that he would need light coming from "all the diagonals," and that he would need "a lot of light all over." I gave her an up-to-date copy of the script with all the latest revisions, and she left.

Yvonne De Carlo was starting to master the dances for "Who's That Woman?" She was also beginning to spend more time with Hal Hastings on her solo song "Can That Boy Fox Trot!" Rumor had it that Steve was expanding the song for her, and everyone was waiting for the new material to arrive. The song, and the role of Carlotta, was intended as a cameo with a one-joke song tossed off. The character was a faded movie queen who had appeared in the Follies and whose one big number had been cut but has decided to come to the reunion to do her damn song once before the theater goes. She says the song is a college number about picking a guy for her first dance, but the lyric tells a slightly different story:

> I know this grocery clerk,
> Unprepossessing.
> Some think the boy's a jerk—
> They have my blessing.
> But when he starts to move,
> He aims to please:
> Which only goes to prove,
> That sometimes in a clerk you
> Find a Hercules.

Turns out that despite his looking "reptilian" and "as for being saintly, even faintly, no," what he can do well is "fox-trot," with an emphasis on the first letter. One joke.

Yvonne had flown to New York to audition for the role of Phyllis. She was certainly in keeping with the kind of Hollywood personality being considered for the show, but she didn't seem to have the right style for Phyllis. However, when she sang the song she had prepared for the audition ("Ten Cents a Dance") someone said: "Carlotta." She embodied Carlotta, but if she was to be cast, everyone knew that the

role would have to be made more than a cameo. Hal wasn't all that fond of "Can That Boy Fox Trot!" but he liked the marquee value of Yvonne's name. He felt that she would need more than a one-joke number. Why not expand the song? Steve knew what it was and was reticent about adding to it, saying he would favor writing an entirely different number. But there were too many other concerns, and once she was cast, the decision was made to expand the song.

Alexis Smith was quietly working away. No one was aware of it, but she was working harder and pushing herself further than anyone else. To all appearances, she remained cool and relaxed. And the more she relaxed, the funnier she became. She chanced to walk by a dancer, one of whose roles was a waiter with whom she is caught necking late in the proceedings. He was crocheting. She looked slightly bemused, and asked what he was crocheting. "A pair of pants." Her hairline rose slightly and her eyes slanted ever so slightly. "Oh." As she walked down the hall she muttered under her breath, "That was not exactly the kind of young lover I had in mind." Yvonne overheard her and chimed in with a complaint about the actor playing her escort. "I expected some-one tall and dark. And I got a guy as tall as I am. He's strong, but I'm just as strong. Here, feel my muscles."

Fifi D'Orsay felt faint, tried to break a capsule of smelling salts, and was comforted by one of the stage managers, who sent her home for the rest of the day. When she appeared the next day, once again made-up and fluttery, she told anyone who would listen how marvelous her number was and how she needed to have more rehearsal to get it down pat. Michael began to stage it over the weekend, assisted by Graciela. Fifi was in her usual flustered state, muffed most of the lyrics, replacing them with "Ooh, la la!" Michael calmly stopped her, came over, put his arm around her. "Well, you know, I have my tricks, which I will put into the number when I am onstage, but I cannot show them to you now because I am not on the stage." "Well," Michael said, patiently, "you can tell me what you are going to do because I don't want to be surprised every night." "Don't worry about it, chickie-poo, believe me, I am not a fool and I will give a real performance when I have my audi-ence." Michael took her by the hand, stood alongside her, and with Graciela close by, showed her some simple steps that he wanted her to try. She moved with him without looking to see what he was doing. He tried again, and then demonstrated a move that necessitated a turn-around. Fifi muttered that she didn't want her back to the audience.

That was enough. Patiently, Michael asked that everyone else clear out of the room so he and Graciela could work with her in private.

Ethel Shutta was getting more and more confident each day, although still fighting to learn her lines and lyrics. But she was having none of Fifi, who was trying to use her as a security blanket. She was actually older than Fifi, and was happy to be friendly, but, "Jesus, I can only take it to a point. And the only thing I don't like about her is that goddamn hamminess." She also pointed out that for all Fifi's nervousness, she was like an eagle when any new line was given to someone else. "Shut up," she told Fifi, "you ought to feel damned lucky to be working." When Mary McCarty was on the *Tonight Show*, Fifi complained that *she* wasn't asked. "There is no end to what I will do when it comes to publicity," she told Mary Bryant, the show's press agent.

Charles Welch and Dortha Duckworth were always sitting together, so much so that it seemed as if they *were* the Whitmans instead of *playing* the Whitmans. They were both short and slightly homey-looking. Their characters' minds were going slightly, such that they didn't really remember what in their past really happened and what was part of their old Follies act. Their number, "Rain on the Roof," was, according to Dortha, "the most ingenuous example of love in the entire show." When they were brought into staging rehearsals, the rehearsal pianist played the introduction and Hal Prince said, "God, that is so dreary. It should be a real introduction and come down the scale with pizzazz and not be so draggy." Hal Hastings went over to the piano, played something frilly that fit the bill, and from then on that's how the song began.

Since Michael had now worked with Fifi D'Orsay, Ethel Shutta, and Charles Welch and Dortha Duckworth, he could begin to assemble the Montage. The Whitmans would begin with "Rain on the Roof," to be followed by "Broadway Baby" and then "Ah, Paris!" At the end, all three songs would be combined into a finale. Steve had composed all three songs with the idea of putting them together, but they didn't quite fit. Hal Hastings was endeavoring to figure out how to adjust them so they would at least give the appearance of blending together. This was going to take up a lot of rehearsal time, and in Boston, once the audience's response to Ethel's "Broadway Baby" became apparent, the order would be changed so that her song would be last. And before the show even got to Boston, Dortha Duckworth would be fired.

"Who's That Woman?" was rehearsed and rehearsed. It was hard

for everyone. Ethel Barrymore Colt recounted the trials and tribulations involved in learning all the tap steps for the number and revealed that all the older women were afraid to admit when they got tired, but that every rehearsal winded them all. Privately, she said, they'd agreed that "tap" was a dirty word. They kept hoping and waiting for the young dancers to admit they were tired, too, and ask for a break, since Michael and Bob would be more likely to listen to them. And when Michael wanted to add a series of pirouettes to the number, she confessed that she just burst into tears. Sheila Smith said that the dance was indeed difficult and that she was amazed Michael had just plunged in with untrained dancers and given them such hard steps right off the bat.

On Thursday, Steve brought in a theme to use as the basis for the ballroom specialty dance, "Bolero d'Amour," for Vincent and Vanessa. He had composed it in the taxicab on the way down to rehearsal, the only time, he said later, he would ever do that. He played it for Hal and Jim, both of whom approved. Then he gave it to John Berkman, the dance arranger, to play for Michael; it would be Berkman's responsibility to fashion an arrangement to reflect the dance that Michael would create. A few moments later it was heard coming from the dance rehearsal room. There was some muttering that the theme sounded a little like the theme from *Auntie Mame*. "Bolero d'Amour" was to occupy a lot of time over the next several days. The other numbers had been mapped out, so Michael could turn rehearsals over to Bob and the assistants, but he would do "Bolero d'Amour" alone. It was in a different style from anything else in the show and was probably different from anything Michael had ever choreographed before. This was a big flowing ballroom dance, sexy in its undercurrents and gorgeous in its scope, with lots of long skirts, deep back bends, high kicks, and swirling around. Vincent and Vanessa would be shadowed by younger counterparts, played by Graciela Daniele and six-foot-tall Michael Misita. There were two other couples upstage. Michael had to work on his feet, and fast. Originally in four sections, it ended up in two. I think Michael wanted to show people he was capable of a sweeping romantic dance. He seemed fixated on it. It was the one number that Hal Prince, in retrospect, said he should have cut.

Saturday morning brought the first attempt at a run-through. The actors were, for the most part, off book with lines learned. Of course until this stage of rehearsal, most of the acting feels like word reciting

and being in the right place at the right time; performances begin to emerge from this point onward, so whenever an actor showed a glimmer of a final performance, it was thrilling to everyone. The Prologue was included in this partial run-through, as were "Beautiful Girls" and "Waiting for the Girls Upstairs." Then four book songs between Sally and Ben, which had been rehearsed sporadically, were included: "Don't Look at Me," the first time Sally runs into Ben, the man for whom she has been secretly pining all these years; his response, "The Road You Didn't Take," in which he thinks he's justifying the decisions he has made in his life ("The Ben I'll never be, Who remembers him?"); then Sally's heartfelt lie about how wonderful her life is "In Buddy's Eyes" ("I'm young, I'm beautiful . . . I'm still the princess, Still the prize"); and, finally, Ben's admission to Sally of his mistake in marrying Phyllis: "Too Many Mornings" (". . . Wishing that the room might be filled with you"). There were fumbles, but not from Dorothy, who got everything letter perfect. She and John McMartin were clearly working hard. Justine Johnston's number, "One More Kiss," the very first song ever written for *The Girls Upstairs*, was included for the first time. Left out was the Montage, "Who's That Woman?" and all the songs that while being rehearsed were not yet ready to show, like the Young Four's Follies numbers and "Can That Boy Fox Trot!"

A few people turned up to watch the run-through: Tharon Musser, Joanna Merlin, and Hal's dynamic secretary, Annette Myers. It ended up looking pretty lame, and from the expressions on the faces of these few "outsiders," it didn't look as if they were having a great time. The book scenes were boring, and there was a sameness to the tone of the show: bickering among the principals, song, bickering among the principals, song. Yvonne's line "What this party needs is a good kick in the ass!" got a weird laugh. Even taking into consideration the numbers that weren't included, it was hard to discern any shape to the evening. Once it was over, Hal wasted no time. "Tomorrow morning I'll need the first hour and a half to clear up a thousand things. We're going to change the order of parts of the script, and it will cost some people some lines, but it's all in the interests of improving the show, and that's what we're all really interested in." He turned to Ruthie and said, "There is one thing that is different on this show from any other I've ever done: on this one I never have to take my script home and do my homework, since I always have enough time during the day when there's nothing for me to do."

Steve handed Yvonne the middle section of "Can That Boy Fox Trot!" "Well, I've finished it now. From here on, it's up to you." He had created a routine in which Carlotta looks for the guy and runs into two possibilities, a football hero and a poet, the former with a low-pitched voice, the latter with a high one, both of whom vie for her affection. Of course, Carlotta sang all the parts. (A new line, cut within a few days: "You never know—the poet was the better lay.") By the end, all three were singing together. "Now this gets tricky." She was to explain, "They start singing counterpoint . . . any music lovers here, take five." Yvonne was thrilled and couldn't wait to get started, but it was clear that Steve had handed her a challenge. And Michael made it known that he didn't even want to talk with her about staging until she knew the words and music.

Once Hal heard the extended version, he decided to switch the order of "Fox Trot" and "One More Kiss." Originally, "Can That Boy Fox Trot!" was to be tossed off just before the emotional dénouement that prompts Phyllis's song "Could I Leave You?" and the group nervous breakdown. Now that it was a real piece, he felt that putting it in the middle of the action and having a wistful, haunting waltz at the end would feel tighter and prepare the audience better for the emotional bloodbath to come. "One more kiss before we part, One more kiss and—farewell . . . Dreams are a sweet mistake. All dreamers must awake . . ." He kept making other small revisions—arranging for a curtain call for the Montage, moving party people into different positions, etc. He began to get hard-edged with some of the actors: "Don't worry, it'll work. And if it doesn't, we'll change it later." When an actor made a suggestion he didn't care for he said, "Don't do me any favors. Just do what I ask you to when I ask you to do it."

The second and final week in the rehearsal studio was to culminate in a run-through on Thursday afternoon before the day off, and before the move to Feller's Scenic Studio on Saturday. Suddenly there seemed to be a real push to integrate all those pieces that had not yet been put in sequence nor finished being staged and choreographed.

Hal Hastings was spending a lot of time with Yvonne and with Gene, whose character song, "The Right Girl," had quietly made its way down to the rehearsal room earlier in the week without many people noticing. This was to be a solo dance number for Buddy in which he expresses anger and frustration at his personal situation, ultimately deciding that he doesn't love the right girl. It was being worked on by

Steve Boockvor, Yvonne De Carlo, and Dorothy Collins in a cheerful moment.

Michael and Gene alone, at odd times of the day, usually late in the evening or early in the morning. Gene, who hadn't danced onstage in eleven years, was obviously nervous, and Michael wanted this to be a tour de force. Neither man wanted to let on what they were up to, or to show any of it to anyone.

Alexis was rehearsing her solos behind closed doors. In addition to "Could I Leave You?" Phyllis's angry commentary to Ben ("Could I leave you? Yes. Will I leave you? . . . Guess!"), she presumably was rehearsing "Losing My Mind." There was no way for those of us not in the summit meetings to know where things stood with "Losing My Mind" and any other songs in the Follies sequence for both Alexis and Dorothy. If they were concerned, they were keeping it very quiet. Dorothy just kept radiating good cheer. In fact, on Sunday she and Yvonne were sitting around chatting amiably, and when, at one point, Dorothy threw her arms around me, Yvonne shouted, "Oh no, you don't. He's mine!" Dorothy was happily married, and everyone knew that. Yvonne, on the other hand, appeared to be away from home and very much on her own. I wasn't sure what to make of her, and the night before she had asked me to dinner. I couldn't go, so I declined.

More production people came by and more meetings took place behind closed doors. Pete Feller sat with Michael and Hal for a long time, going over problems with the set construction. Press agent Mary Bryant arrived with a photographer from the *Daily News* for a spread that ended up appearing only in the early edition of the paper— bumped for some man throwing himself into the East River and drowning. (Hal, on seeing that the spread was captioned "Nostalgia for '71," said, "All this nostalgia shit gives me a pain in the ass.") She also had to gather biographies from the actors for the Playbill in Boston. Hal Hastings was interviewing new rehearsal pianists since David Baker had, somewhat mysteriously, left the production. "It's a long story that I will tell you sometime if you're really interested," he said. I never got the story. Florence Klotz appeared with some new costume sketches. Joe Tubens, the hair designer, came by with the makeup designer, Charles La France. Harold Friedlander, the man in charge of the printing for the advertising agency, came down with mock-ups of the poster. This was an expensive poster, not only because it used a lot of color, but because it had gradations of color, most prominent in the neck of the figure. Hal didn't care; he loved it. There were some suggested adjustments to the billing, which didn't work. There was also a "herald" for the theater in Boston, a 6" × 8" one-sheet flyer used traditionally as a handout at the box office with all perfor- mance and ticket price information. This was being done simply and economically and was based on a costume sketch so it could be printed in only two colors. Mary Bryant asked that I not pass it around as it had been printed before John McMartin joined the company and listed only three stars.

Michael relied more and more on his assistants to run those num- bers that needed constant drilling so he could concentrate on finishing up "Bolero d'Amour." He took as much time in the large rehearsal room as he could, often taking over the mornings and not calling in the rest of the company until the afternoon.

On Tuesday, Hal spent the afternoon staging the one part of the show that hadn't yet been touched: the scene following "Could I Leave You?" when the generations start turning on each other, resulting in the breakdown that leads into "Loveland" and the Follies sequence. He had the full company present, and before beginning he asked to run the prior scene, including "Could I Leave You?" This was the first time Alexis had performed it in the big room for people, and she gave

a real performance, quite stunning in its strength. When she finished, there was a brief moment of silence, and then the entire group burst into applause. She just giggled and smiled.

Staging the new scene was a little like planning the strategy for an invasion. There was a script, and it had everything that was needed: present-day characters turning on their spouses, starting with Ben and Phyllis. Then ghost figures would enter, yelling at their partners. Slowly, the characters would begin crossing over the time line and turning on themselves in the other reality. Those multiple confrontations would lead into the "group nervous breakdown." There were lots of ideas tossed about, all of them having to do with planned confusions and who was actually hearing whom, as if the whole sequence were unfolding one step at a time. Hal would push people around, look at what he'd done, like it or keep moving bodies around. "Every once in a while I think, 'Ooh, is that pretentious.'" Gene Nelson had an idea, but hesitated to throw it in. "You have an idea? Let's hear it!" Since his character came on to confront Ben, he thought it would be interesting if when he stormed in he went first to Young Ben, stared into his eyes for a moment, then broke off and went over to the older Ben. Hal liked the split second of confusion, then decided that it wasn't right. He thought he should keep the generations separated in groups, the old ones on stage left and the young ones on stage right. Then he realized that that worked directly against the point of the scene. He tried to get the Bens and the Buddys all to huddle in the middle, then have both Young and Old Sally enter; because she is the reason for the tension among the characters, we could see each man react differently to the two Sallys. When he was done he felt the action looked right. "Everybody take it down and then let it build up from there. When we get to performance, the emotions will be growing as the scene goes on." Knowing that there would be music underscoring, he said, "You know, I'm glad this is a musical, because if it were a straight play, I wouldn't have any idea what to do with this scene."

Tensions were mounting between Steve and Michael. Steve watched, stone-faced, as "Who's That Woman?" was performed without the old girls. When it was over he smiled, said a quick word to Michael, and went over and conferred with Hal Hastings and the pianists. A few weeks before rehearsals began, Steve had warned Michael that he might not have all the songs until the third week of rehearsal, largely due to the indecision about the specifics of the Fol-

lies sequence. Michael and the dancers were now finishing up their fourth week. It became clear to everyone associated with the production that it was past time for the score to be finished. Every time I went to the Prince office I was asked about it. Mathilde who, like Michael, knew that Steve needed to finish before she could start her work, said she wouldn't badger him about finishing because she had done it once and gotten her head handed to her. She was quick to point out that Steve had called back to apologize, and Steve knew that she had thin skin and would cry at the drop of a hat. David Wolf, assistant to Joanna Merlin, made a joke that maybe the solution would be to have a drop made with the words "STILL TO BE WRITTEN" that could be flown in to end the show. The feeling was that the summit meetings behind closed doors were at least partly about doing whatever needed to be done to get Steve to finish.

Hal's need for a bona fide run-through on Thursday won the day. The show was written to be performed without an intermission, but there was much discussion about whether it would have one. It was felt that it might be just too long to run as one act, but it was decided to run it straight through. The company sat around the periphery of the room and cheered everyone on when they weren't performing. Still skipped were "Can That Boy Fox Trot!," "The Right Girl," and "Bolero d'Amour." The run-through began at eleven A.M. and finished a little after one P.M. When they got to the end, Michael asked that they run "Loveland," even though it hadn't been run in days, and "You're Gonna Love Tomorrow" and "Love Will See Us Through," which had been staged fairly quickly and weren't finished. Many of the company members were seeing numbers they had never seen before. It was especially gratifying to see those pieces of the show that were integrated into the whole for the first time. Ethel Shutta was a favorite, as she continued to be. "Who's That Woman?" was cheered as well, although everyone was beginning to get sick of it. Mary McCarty had been downplaying the fact that she was the lead singer and that the other women were all, in fact, her backups. Whether she was being clever or just unaware, it was working well. It wasn't for several more weeks that it would become apparent that the stars were actually being used as a chorus—a brilliant stroke. Now it was just that the damned number was taking up so much rehearsal time.

For the first time, with the inclusion of "Loveland," the company began to get the sense of how the Follies sequence was going to work.

"Loveland" would take us into Loveland, a place where "Time stops, hearts are young," and where our principals would crack up.

All in all, the run-through was a fair sight better than the one earlier in the week, and it was encouraging enough to have everyone finish up in the rehearsal room on a high note. I got excited. For the first time I realized that the Follies in *Follies* could be even better than the cabaret in *Cabaret*—so many of the songs in the body of the show are Follies songs, but because they're ostensibly sung by old people at a party, they bring up the question of whether they're really at the party or back in the Follies, at least in their own minds. The fact that each of these numbers is slightly different from the others in feel and staging only adds layers to the show. In *Cabaret*, even the book scenes took place within the frame of the cabaret. Here, we're both in the Follies and not at the same time, depending on who's singing what. And then, of course, we do go "in" Loveland at the end, but even then the show continues to operate on many different levels at once. If this thing works, it's going to be truly remarkable. And for the first time, it felt as if there really was a show.

Once the run-through was over, Hal, sensing Michael's increasing annoyance, took him off to a room alone. They were sequestered for a long time. Afterward, they went back to work, cleaning up sections they wanted to keep working on—"Bolero d'Amour" and the Montage—and sent the rest of the company home early. The next step was to decide upon how the Follies sequence—Loveland—would end, for Steve to finish the score with enough time to choreograph and stage the new numbers, and see how everything fit on the actual set.

No one had any idea what was in store once we got to the scene shop, but because we were starting on a weekend, at least the first two days could be at normal working hours. There was both excitement and trepidation. It was quite unusual for a show to rehearse on the actual set, so that would be an adventure. Nor was it normal to rehearse from four P.M. until midnight. And it certainly wasn't normal to take a motley group of people to a corner of the South Bronx several blocks away from Yankee Stadium to rehearse on a multileveled structure still being constructed in the middle of a workshop. But there was a lot about *Follies* that wasn't exactly normal, if there is such a thing as normal in the theater.

4

"But Every Height Has a Drop"

ON THE SET AT FELLER'S SCENIC STUDIO,
JANUARY 30–FEBRUARY 5

Feller's Scenic Studio occupies a nondescript, two-story brick factory building in the Bronx, a couple of blocks off the Grand Concourse and a few blocks from Yankee Stadium. Nothing about its exterior is inviting or interesting, let alone theatrical. The doors are of unfriendly steel, the windows, framed in standard-issue factory metal. Whatever its original use, it hardly looked like a place that was about to house the eclectic family of *Follies*, few of whom, one would have to guess, had ever been anywhere quite like it.

Everyone converged at 10:45 A.M. Most of the company came in a very full chartered bus, having departed, in a wonderful reversal of usual matinee theatrical practice, *from* a Broadway theater, the Alvin, home to *Company*. There was lots of gossip about what everyone had done on the day off—Fifi regaled everyone with accounts of all the fascinating and expensive things she'd bought; Mathilde Pincus mentioned that she had copied out a new song for Buddy in record time and that Steve had called to thank her. As the bus drove up avenues, over bridges, and under highways, it was clear that getting to wherever we were going wasn't an easy feat. No one ventured to guess what kind of public transportation might be an alternative. As the bus arrived, so did the limousines carrying the honchos. Everyone had the same response: "Where the hell are we?" As Alexis emerged from her car she looked around and commented, to no one in particular, "Well, this is certainly a curious place to be."

73

Inside, the building seemed to consist of one large, vast space punctuated by columns, with workbenches all around the perimeter. Areas were dedicated to different aspects of making scenery and large props—carpentry, metalwork, plastic and fiberglass fabrication, painting, even an enormous vacuum form in which 4' × 8' sheets of plastic can become fake brick or stone walls, bookshelves filled with books, and even armor. Every nook and cranny seemed to hold some magical machine designed to do something specific. Situated at various places around the studio—laid out on the floor, standing up against columns, leaning across sawhorses—were bits of scenery for two other musicals scheduled to open on Broadway in the spring: *Lolita, My Love*, and *70, Girls, 70*. The sets for *Lolita, My Love* were decidedly weird, with walls cut on the diagonal every couple of feet revealing different wallpapers. The small solid standing units for *70, Girls, 70* were much more conventional, with rooms, a bar, seating areas, all of which seemed full scale yet remarkably small. Never far from each project was its appropriate shop drawing, drafted and painted by the designer or an assistant on cardboard, with notes about dimensions, colors, and other details. Often a quarter-inch or half-inch scale set model would be used as reference as well—the one for *70, Girls, 70* was in one of the offices, along with the model for another musical, *Ari*, based on *Exodus*, which had left the shop shortly before we arrived. Odd props and old pieces of scenery were leaning up against back walls, out of the way. There was a stairway leading up to a second floor that had enough empty rooms to serve as impromptu rehearsal spaces, actors' hangout, and a stage managers' office.

Feller's was known as the best studio for three-dimensional, constructed scenery. The main competition, Nolan's, was known for its painting, so they tended to get the shows that relied on drops and scrims. *Follies* was clearly a show that had to be built, so Feller's was the logical choice. There was also a long-standing relation between Hal and the Feller family, since Pete had been investing in Hal's shows for years, including *Follies*. It must have been because of this connection that the company was allowed to rehearse on the set, which had to be an inconvenience to the shop. For the Feller family it was challenge enough to find and hold on to good craftsmen for a job that was cyclical by nature; to have their space invaded by a bunch of actors who would be using the very set they were trying to finish couldn't have been their idea of fun. But they were as accommodating as they could

At Feller's: Michael Bennett, Fritz Holt,
Ruth Mitchell, Hal Prince, and Steve Sondheim.

be; an integral part of the Broadway community, they always came through. During the pre-Broadway run of *The Rothschilds*, I remember Pete Feller himself struggling to fix a renegade wall panel on a central piece of that set—on the stage of the Fisher Theater in Detroit, and during a performance!

Dominating the entire central area of the studio stood the basic multitiered set for *Follies*. All the levels—the basic raked stage and the three platforms resting on top—were in place. All the side units stood roughly in their offstage positions, and were constructed as high as the

ceiling of the studio would allow; most didn't have their uppermost platforms in place. Nothing was finished or painted, but it was an amazing sight. No matter how many drawings or models you might have seen, there is nothing like the excitement when you first see a set. It's also always a little shocking, because it's never exactly as you imagined it. And seeing this particularly vast set fill a place that seemed large to begin with made it seem gargantuan. The set was very big, very tall, very unfinished, and without a single level playing area. I walked around to the rear, and stood dead center. The basic raked floor came up to my chin. In the theater, I figured, no one will realize it's five and a half feet off the floor, but here, where the set is isolated, it felt as if the actors would be performing in the trees. With the exception of two escape stairs at the very rear of the set going off on each side and a couple of isolated locations, everything on the stage would be in full view of the audience. There would be no place to hide. Nothing quite seemed to relate to anything else. For a depiction of something in a decrepit state, it looked awfully complicated. An upright piano had been placed up on the platform, where it would remain as part of the onstage band, to be used for all the rehearsals on the set. Upstairs, an old spinet from *Cabaret* would serve to accompany rehearsals in the largest of the rooms.

Even though it was Saturday, the distinctive sound of power tools being turned on, ripping their way through their designated task, and then being turned off could be heard everywhere. Workmen were wandering all over the set, banging and sawing; clearly, every bit of time was being used. Meanwhile, in one quiet corner of the studio, observing everything, stood Lisa and Boris Aronson.

Hal and Michael had arrived earlier than everyone else. They knew what to expect. Standing directly in front of the set, in the spot that would be the orchestra pit in the theater, they gathered the company together. "Okay, when the workmen are finished, we'll give you five minutes to look around, walk all over the set. You can use the time for all the bitching you want. Bitch, complain, and get mad. But after five minutes, I don't want to hear another word, because we have to realize this is our set and we'll have to make it work for us."

The actors wandered around, cautiously. They walked up stairs that somehow seemed twice as tall as they had ever imagined. They peered around steel pipes welded together in odd configurations. The older actors expressed concern for others rather than admit their own fears;

Ethel Shutta remarked that it was too bad Fifi would have to "climb around all those stairs with her bad eyesight and bad ankles." Entrances and exits were marked, and stairs and units were not where anyone thought they would be. Alexis climbed up one of the two permanent downstage towers and peered down over the main stage area onto what looked like a vast cavern of empty space, a slightly seasick expression on her face. Comments: "My God, it's huge." "Oh, Lord." Ethel announced: "I don't know about the set, but the noise here is killing me." Steve Boockvor, the actor playing Yvonne's escort, Randy, looked around and said, "I think they've got a fuck of a lot of work left to do."

Indeed they did. That is why, starting on Monday, the shop would have the normal working hours of the day, and we would work from four P.M. until midnight. Hal and Michael were anxious to use more and more of the mechanics, so they would exert gentle pressure on the Fellers to finish up. The side units were a particular concern since many entrances and exits were timed in conjunction with their movements; until they were up and running, the transitions could only be approximated. But every day, a little more of the set would be finished and painted. Of course, once the set was finished, mechanized, painted, and tested, it would have to be taken entirely apart, fit into trucks, driven to Boston, and reassembled on the stage of the Colonial Theatre. That would all happen in two weeks' time. One added bonus: the stage of the Colonial Theatre is smaller than the one at the Winter Garden, so backstage would be cramped and the downstage towers virtually obscured by the proscenium arch.

"Okay, the five minutes is up as far as Hal Prince is concerned," came the authoritative voice. "Let's work our way through the show, starting at the top, and let's stop, please, whenever there is a problem. We'll adjust all the entrances and exits as quickly as possible. But, please, let's not waste time." Michael added that all dances would only be marked, warning everyone that the raked stage would definitely take some getting used to. He didn't want anyone to get hurt. Hal then asked for quiet from the workers in the shop and in that moment told the cast there would be "no talking or we'll leave you in the Bronx!"

The work-through went amazingly well. Starting with the Prologue, the staging transformed itself from the flat floor of the rehearsal studio to the levels of the set with remarkable beauty. The ghosts seemed interestingly placed, giving the impression of being in their

own world, not quite part of the scenery, not quite part of the action, inhabiting the farthest corners and highest platforms. The actors' entrances and exits were tricky to execute, and time had to be taken to figure out exactly where they were meant to be. The side units affected every entrance, since they filled the entire space on each side of the stage. Entrances were either through, over, or under one of them, and sometimes more than one. It had been a lot easier in the rehearsal studio simply to walk across tape on the floor or over a plywood platform. Breaks were called when Pete Feller and his crew needed to finish something that was deemed of vital importance to allow the staging to progress—like cutting a groove in the floor so the unit containing the staircase for the "Ziegfeld" entrances of "Beautiful Girls" could be pulled manually into its proper downstage position.

The Montage proved to be the first stumbling block. The entire weight of it fell on the shoulders of four older actors out on a raked stage—alone. It was scary. Dortha Duckworth had trouble adjusting to where she was supposed to be and remembering her lines, and Charlie Welch was quietly supportive. Fifi D'Orsay was terrified. Ethel Shutta didn't like all those weird angles, but once she planted her feet on the stage and belted out "Broadway Baby," it was clear she was well on her way to delivering a showstopper. The three-way ending was beginning to work. Steve Sondheim, too curious to stay away, seemed happy throughout, but especially overjoyed at "Broadway Baby." Jim Goldman sat next to him, beaming.

The idea of rehearsing on the actual set was Michael's, and it was clearly a good one. He knew how difficult it was going to be for the older actors to adjust to the various levels, but he also knew how treacherous it was to dance on any raked stage, let alone on one with multiple levels. (Several members of the company remarked years later that they never really recovered from injuries suffered dancing in *Follies*. Actors' Equity even created a rule determining how much of a rake their members would be required to dance on.) The more familiar everyone in the cast was with the set, he reckoned, the easier time they would all have in Boston. Michael had loved the different levels in the initial sketch, and he wanted to use them as much as possible, even though he knew they would be a challenge. He thought they gave "the feeling of Ziegfeld stairs without having the stairs there." Hal was fine with Michael's input, as was Boris, who liked the way Hal worked, talking mood and feel and what he wanted to accomplish, and then letting Boris come up

with a concept and a design. "If you can do a show with no scenery, then scenery is a waste of time and energy," Boris had said, and since every inch of this set was clearly being used, he was a happy man. "If his set isn't used, Boris is unhappy," Lisa said. I noticed that the farthest unit upstage right included a solid piece of brick wall, and that none of the others did. I said that I liked how it set off the structural nature of all the others. Lisa smiled. She said Boris had insisted on one solid unit, and although Hal had initially balked, he had come around.

Lisa also said she was amazed at how quickly the set was coming together. She lamented the changes that had been made for economic reasons—first and foremost, changing the floor from wood planking to a flat floor painted to look like planking. There had been a compromise step contemplated—cutting grooves into a solid floor to make it look like planking—but painting the floor won out in the end. I would be surprised if Michael hadn't chimed in on that decision, since anything that would have made the dancing surfaces potentially uneven could have proved devastating.

Several members of the Feller family stood around, taking it all in. They were used to visits by designers, directors, and producers, but an invasion of this many actors was a first. "This is the last of the biggies," Pete said. And then, in a very straightforward manner, without any particular emotion, he observed: "It will be very good, be a hit, and not make money, although it will run." He said he didn't expect to see any profits from his $14,000 investment.

There had been progress in the music department on the day off. The song Steve had delivered to Mathilde was for Buddy in Loveland. I was handed a copy from which I was to extract the lyrics for the script. By this time I had learned how particular Steve was about how he wanted lyrics typed. In the script, they were to be in capitals with all punctuation in place—lines ending in commas, semicolons, periods, question marks if the line is a question, quotation marks if the line is a quote, and no punctuation only if the next line is a continuation. All slang was to be kept as written but vowels would be restored to words if they were removed in the piano/vocal sheet to indicate how specific syllables were to be sung. (For example, "EVERY" would go in the script, while "Ev-'ry" would go with the two corresponding notes in the score.) Spoken lines were to be written with normal usage of lower-

Not for long: John J. Martin and Dick Latessa as the costumed objects of Gene Nelson's affection. They were replaced by bona fide women in Boston.

and uppercase letters. The new song was entitled "The God-Why-Don't-You-Love-Me Blues." It included internal dialogue, quotes, hyphens, and slang—the whole bit. As always, the stage managers were anxious that I get the lyrics typed out as quickly as possible. On the typewriter, the hyphen was a lowercase key, the capital letters, of course, uppercase, which meant constant shifting. The following was typical: "I'VE GOT THOSE 'GO-AWAY-I-NEED-YOU,' 'COME-TO-ME-I'LL-KILL-YOU,' 'DARLING-I'LL-DO-ANYTHING-TO-KEEP-YOU-WITH-ME-TILL-YOU-TELL-ME-THAT-YOU-LOVE-ME-OH-YOU-DO-NOW-BEAT-IT-WILL-YOU?' BLUES." The song was written for two men in drag to represent Sally (Buddy's wife) and Margie (his mistress). From this moment on, it was alternatively titled "Buddy's Blues."

The work-through took until 4:30. Hal said he was very happy with how good everything looked and how the set seemed to enhance the show at every turn. Michael was most eager to work through the big dances on the set, so he took it for the rest of the day. Hal took the

80

party scenes upstairs to "change some color and some style." Steve found another room upstairs to work out some lyrics for a new song. He was in an expansive mood, praising the work done on the show so far and saying that he felt that every single movement on the stage was fascinating.

Hal cheerfully adjusted to working in a decidedly smaller space, a plain factory room with dirty white walls. He began by giving John McMartin a new line for Ben as he pours two brandies and drinks them both himself. After hearing it a couple of times, Hal said, "Well, John, I don't think they're going to fall out of their seats screaming with laughter and call for the author over that line, but I do think there's more of a laugh to be found." John listened, said nothing, then did the line completely differently and got a chuckle from everyone in the room. There was a new line for Dimitri Weismann, the Ziegfeld-like character, about how the party was tax deductible. Without a moment's hesitation, Hal said to Edwin Steffe, the actor playing Weismann, "That is a new line and I haven't given you a line reading yet."

The day ended at 6:15, and everyone piled back into the bus. I sat with Fritz Holt, with whom I rarely had much opportunity to talk—no one is busier during rehearsals than the production stage manager. He mentioned that Hal had been concerned about working on the set this early, but that he understood Michael's strong feeling about getting on those levels as early in the rehearsal process as possible. Fritz also knew that Hal wasn't thrilled to realize that from here on, the only times the stage would be his was during run-throughs and cleanups. Run-throughs were going to start happening with increased regularity, to be sure, but scene work was going to be relegated to any place other than the set itself, which Michael would need for musical staging.

By the time everyone arrived for rehearsal on Sunday, the novelty of coming to the Bronx had worn off. Hal decided that he was going to be difficult. There were too many clamoring workmen around the set, and despite all pleas, there was still noise throughout the rest of the studio. He picked up the microphone that had been rigged up so he and Michael could be heard by everyone and announced that he wanted quiet, that he was not in a good mood, and that he intended to get a lot done today. Leaving the set to Michael, he took the actors in the book scenes upstairs.

Michael began with "Loveland." For the first time, the pie-shaped steps were put in place. The workmen pushed the upstage side units to

their extreme offstage positions, removed wedges underneath the two three-step units, and pivoted them down. The center of the stage then seemed like a big circle, although the steps weren't actually on the same axis. Once they were in place, the dancers walked up and down, getting a feel for them. Michael blocked out the staging he had created in the studio, positioning the principals, young and old, downstage center, where they will be "having at" each other. The chorus then sweeps on from all sides and takes over the stage, enveloping the principals, who are cleverly removed without the audiences realizing what's happening. They will be gone by the time the chorus pairs off to sing: "Time stops, hearts are young, only serenades are sung in Loveland, where everybody lives to love." After a verse and a short dance, a V-shape will be formed along the sides, with everyone pointing to centermost upstage position. There, each showgirl makes an entrance, one at a time, accompanied by a recitation of a couplet about love assigned to the male dancers. Each costume is to be inspired by its corresponding couplet, and each showgirl will pose, then parade around the stage, displaying her outlandish and fantastical garment for all to see. Even with the dancers in motley rehearsal clothes, you could sense how the levels would all work together to give the audience the feeling that they were viewing everything slightly from above—halfway between a Ziegfeld staircase and the June Taylor dancers from the *Jackie Gleason Show.*

Hal remained upstairs, going over transitions and party scenes. He worked on Heidi Schiller's speech about her beloved composer who wrote the waltz "One More Kiss" for her. "Oscar Straus . . . or was it Johann?" She was now out of the wheelchair and on a cane. As her line was being shortened, Justine Johnston elongated whatever words she had left, as if filling her allocated time, no matter what. Yvonne rehearsed her speech about how wonderful it is to be in the movies because it keeps her young, although acknowledging that her type isn't used as much as it once was: "Used to be I played the bitch who lost the boy; now I'm somebody's hot-pantsed mother, stinko by my swimming pool and all my kids are acid heads. I love it!" Hal's direction: "Make the 'I love it' really big." Yvonne was feeling frisky. She had a lot of ideas. What if she said her speech to one person only, to Heidi, who happened to be standing right next to her? Hal said no, that Carlotta would never have a conversation with any one person; she would address a group. "I may be the son of a bitch who did this to you, but it

will only bring out more vitality," he said. He had her pose for several photographs during the scene, but she didn't want to keep having to stop and start. She wanted to change a line from having "lost the boy" to having "stole the boy." Hal reassured her that Jim had intended the line the way he wrote it. Ed Steffe couldn't get enough lechery into his line with a young waitress: "So you want to be a star, my dear?" Hal thought maybe smoking long black cigars would help, and said that he didn't mind if Ed smoked them all night long. Yvonne chimed in, "Not before my song!" "You know the trouble with that girl?" Hal said to the assembled group. "She's a gun collector, and she'll take out a Luger and shoot you." Everyone laughed. Her mind was on "Can That Boy Fox Trot!" which was ready for Michael. They began working on it during the lunch break, and although she was excited, she said later that she didn't care for some of the "suggestive gestures" Michael was contemplating.

Putting "Beautiful Girls" on the set proved to be a challenge. The plywood platforms back in the rehearsal room had been mastered, but the reality of the set was another story. The side unit that contained the stairs was designed to look like a collection of rubble. As a result, even though the rise was the same, each step was a different size and shape. The women were unnerved. Descending without falling down was one challenge, but to gain access to the top of the stairs for the entrance itself, everyone would have to climb up an offstage ladder attached to the furthermost downstage unit, cross over a plank behind the stage band, and then emerge, one at a time and on the proper beat of music, at the top of the next upstage platform. All the actresses were in some version of panic at the very thought, and the really smart ones realized that some of them were going to have to do this in long dresses. Michael and Bob, along with George Martin and John Grigas, lined the girls up and slowly walked them through and down the stairs. This took a lot of cajoling and hand-holding. And as if the actresses needed one more thing to be concerned about, they began to realize that once they stepped off the staircase onto the stage area to promenade around Miss America–style, they would cross the very front of the stage, which in the theater would drop off into the orchestra pit. There was a uniform look of panic on all faces.

Jonathan Tunick came with Steve and Jim in the afternoon. Although he had already been at work orchestrating much of the score, he was eager to see any newly staged numbers in context. Like any

good orchestrator, he always liked to see the staging before beginning his work. Details, subtext, and punctuation can be influenced by performances and staging. He pulled out his tape recorder as "Loveland" was run, followed by "You're Gonna Love Tomorrow" and "Love Will See Us Through." Steve and Jim watched as well, looking increasingly like proud parents.

It was approaching the end of the second day in the Bronx, and Monday was going to begin the four-to-midnight schedule. It had been two difficult but exhilarating days. It had also been tiring for everyone. Hal wanted to close the rehearsal by starting at the top of the show, after the Prologue, and working through until time ran out. He stopped after "The Road You Didn't Take." Lots of mistakes were made in "Beautiful Girls," in the blocking and in entrances. Hal addressed the company: "I am sick and tired of hearing errors in the lyrics on the opening number. From now on, I will not tolerate any more goofs. It's ridiculous. We've been at this for three weeks. We'll never get this show together if we can't remember things." Michael, who, unlike Hal, had started the day off in a good mood, added: "Listen, this is a very difficult show, and there is a lot of work involved in putting it all together. If you find it necessary, carry a pencil and write down the movements, because I am tired of seeing, as I saw time and time today, the same mistakes being made over and over. If you have one song, there's no reason why you shouldn't know the lyrics. It's nonsense. That's all I have to say. I'll see you tomorrow."

The cast shuffled out to the waiting bus, tired, exasperated, and chagrined.

Costume fittings were beginning to be scheduled during the daytime hours. The nighttime rehearsal schedule freed up the day, but any actor called to a costume fitting would be available for that much less rehearsal time, since actors were allowed to work only a set number of hours per day, and the clock started at their first call. One more thing to be coordinated by the stage management.

Hal asked me to take some dictation. He had the scene at the very end of the show on his mind. It didn't yet exist, and he wanted to try to create a version that he could put into rehearsal. The challenge was to figure out how to get the principal characters out of the Follies sequence and back to reality. Steve wanted to try for a Pirandello

moment in Ben's song, in which somehow the character and the actor get confused and the audience wouldn't be sure what was going on. (He succeeded skillfully in the song ultimately titled "Live, Laugh, Love.") Steve also suggested they try an idea that was originally contemplated for *Gypsy*, in which the lead character becomes caught up in a kaleidoscopic nightmare of her life, with characters and bits and pieces of songs mashed together. (This became "Rose's Turn.") Hal's concern at the moment was the scene that would follow the end of the Follies sequence. The assumption was that the four principals would be left alone on the stage. They would recover somehow from the group nervous breakdown and go back to their lives. But what would Ben, Phyllis, Sally, and Buddy be feeling? Hal was at somewhat of a loss to figure that out, since Ben's number was only in discussion. "Loveland," the songs for the Young Four, and "Buddy's Blues" were finished, but there still was no determination about Phyllis's and Sally's numbers, so the problem of what they would actually say after going through their specific experiences hadn't been solved. Hal had two different drafts from Jim Goldman, along with some pages of his own notes. Quietly reading from all the pages, flipping back and forth among them, he dictated his own version of the ending, very pensively, hardly raising his voice over a whisper. I wrote down whatever he said. When he was done, he asked that I type it up and bring a couple of copies to him so he could go over it with Michael. Two days later I was summoned to his office at Rockefeller Center, where he was going over the scene—his version, and a slightly different one he had received from Jim the night before. Jim sat silently as Hal discussed a couple of details, and then handed me a draft that he wanted typed out and distributed to the actors.

It was time for Michael to mount "Who's That Woman?"—which was soon to get the nickname "the mirror number"—on the set. As with the Prologue, what started to become apparent was the brilliance of the staging as it was placed on the angular set. When the young characters appeared upstage in mirror image, with their backs to us, they were higher than the older women and fanned out on two levels. You almost got the feeling that there was a tilted mirror allowing us to see the dance from above at the same time we were seeing it from the front. When the older and younger characters melded into one at center stage, it looked cinematic. And when everyone danced around in the circle, they were actually dancing up and down several levels, so it

looked like pure Busby Berkeley. Michael knew he had to keep running the number, so that the older women could feel comfortable with the rake, and also get their not-yet-mastered tap dance steps down cold. He didn't want a day to go by without working through it on the set. And if the gentle walk and promenade of "Beautiful Girls" was panic-inducing, imagine what the first pass through the tap steps of "Who's That Woman?" was like. But, as always, Bob Avian, George Martin, and Graciela and Mary Jane were there at Michael's side, ready to encourage, cajole, assist, and lead the cheers when things went well.

"Bolero d'Amour" was also taking up as much rehearsal time as Michael could find. I wasn't sure why; one new number had come in and was being staged pretty quickly, but this one was taking forever. Fred Kelly, one member of the company who had pretty much kept to himself, was watching from the sidelines. I asked him if he had any thoughts. "Are you in college?" he asked. "Then do you mind if I answer you on a psychological level? When you have a fey director and fey dancers trying to create a dance between a man and a woman, you find that it takes a long time to get anything good. They add the same things to the dance and don't know how to get it to the level they want. Of course when I worked with my brother, Gene, we both knew how to get the same result. One time we were choreographing a dance together, and my brother was late. So I worked alone—and when he finally arrived and saw what I was doing, *he* had come up with exactly the same steps."

When the rehearsal was over, Michael called all the dancers together to tell them that he had decided to fire Don Weismuller, who was playing Vincent. He asked if any of them knew any dancers who were tall, of a certain age, and could dance well; any names, he said, would be appreciated. Graciela, who was one of Michael's assistants as well as playing Young Vanessa, had been involved in every rehearsal of the number. She wasn't thrilled at the thought of having to teach it to someone new. "Why not just get rid of Vincent and have Vanessa do the number by herself?" she asked. She was one of the few people in the company who could make Michael laugh.

Tuesday brought a small contingent from the press. Rehearsals went on as if they weren't there. Sam Norkin, the *Daily News*'s answer to the great Al Hirschfeld, was in attendance, sitting quietly in the background, sketching faces and poses on sheets of paper. He would

Using the set: Several of the women—Sonja Levkova,
Mary Jane Houdina, Sheila Smith, Ethel Barrymore Colt, and
Jayne Turner—pose for a photograph at the party.

simply draw on one sheet and then place it on the bottom of the pile. Norkin was happy to show his preliminary drawings to anyone, and only Ethel Barrymore Colt and John McMartin seemed recognizable. There were two photographers as well, one of whom came with Louis Botto, who had been given the go-ahead to proceed with his article on Hal for *Look* magazine—"The Prince of Broadway." He and his photographer, Bill Yoscary, would follow the show along its developmental path from now to Boston. Hal, although encouraging, did caution them by saying, "I hate to do this to you, but I must have approval over

all the photos to cut out any of the old ladies that are really awful. If anyone comes across like Elaine Stritch in the film of the *Company* recording session, that's one thing. But I don't want any of these ladies to come off badly in any article." He reminded them that Actors' Equity has strict rules about using photographs, and that it can involve "a lot of dough." "I think there would be a story here as long as it's not indulgent," he told them all. The other photographer, Robert Galbraith, was taking photographs of the set for Boris. And for the first time, one of the doily Follies drops was laid out on the floor—large string netting over which some liquid plastic substance was poured to make the filigree.

Both Steve and Jim began to be around more and more, even though the writing wasn't finished. The show was starting to look and feel like a show, and it was their baby. They were often pulled aside into one of the rooms upstairs for discussion. They were also giving notes—for example, Steve wanted a clean musical end to "Too Many Mornings" before the next line of dialogue.

After one of the runs of "Who's That Woman?" Hal decided to keep moving, linking it to the scenes that follow. The next song in sequence was "Can That Boy Fox Trot!" Yvonne, who had been working with Michael, had been telling everyone how great it was, but she had also been saying that the number "wasn't ready for public display." Still, she allowed herself to be coaxed into doing as much of it as she could. The stage managers had to prompt her a lot, but she charged ahead and, with a twinkle, even used the "suggestive" gesture that Michael had devised for her and about which she had expressed concern—hands clasped together in front, bending at the elbows and bringing them up to her chest while making a slight grind with her midriff on the word "fox-trot." Everyone applauded, and Steve complimented her. She was pleased. Hal kept moving on, staging her exit from the number. "Do you know it must be a week since we last did this scene—I don't remember any of it!" he said.

I sat with Dorothy Collins, John McMartin, and Ruthie Mitchell during the dinner break. Dorothy was saying how thrilled she was to be part of *Follies* and what a brilliant director she felt Hal was. "I go out of here exhilarated every night." Ruthie said that he actually hadn't been such a great stage manager but that he sure was impressive as a producer and director. "Boy, oh, boy, I'll say," Dorothy agreed, going on to recount how her first husband had made her feel that she had no

acting talent whatever, so she took it upon herself to attend some acting classes. Sanford Meisner at the Neighborhood Playhouse was useless for her, but Uta Hagen was brilliant, giving her great confidence. She also thanked Ruthie for being so patient when she had auditioned years earlier for *She Loves Me.* Hal came by, sat down, and she gave him her compliments directly. He then explained how the ending of the show was shaping up. Jim had an idea that after the group breakdown, the four principals pick themselves up and leave as if they were just leaving a cocktail party—niceties exchanged, nothing dramatic, just platitudes. Hal wasn't convinced it was a good idea and wondered whether an audience would be able to make the shift so quickly after having been through the whole Follies sequence. "It may sound like I'm putting Jim down, but I'm not. I'm only expressing my fears. We all have to be big enough to let our honest thoughts affect how we deal with each other."

That evening Hal walked through, and restaged, the tricky moment after "Could I Leave You?" when the present-day characters turn on their former selves. Now that Hal had the actual levels to use, he played around with entrances and blocking. First he tried moving all the action onto one level, and rejected it right away. Then he tried different levels, and when he saw something he liked, he said, "I'm almost there, but it's still static." One moment had Ben all alone on one side of the stage, looking lost. Hal turned to Jim Goldman and said, "See what I mean by needing more for him here?" He brought Buddy on upstage right and then had Young Buddy enter downstage right—he liked the idea of the two characters confronting each other across the whole stage as if no one else were present. "It just looks terrific." When something didn't work, he'd say, "That's just awful." But he was cooking tonight, and having a grand time almost conducting the action.

I had become something of a chauffeur, as I had made myself available to drive people to the Bronx in my red convertible Volkswagen Bug, a hand-me-down from my grandmother. I was asked to fetch and carry some of the principal actors and, on occasion, some of the staff. Larry Cohen was a frequent passenger as well, and he always had interesting gossip coming from the Michael camp, since he had become friendly with Michael and Bob Avian.

The next day Hal made his first attempt at rehearsing the very end of the show with the actors. He gathered all four principals and their young counterparts upstairs, handed the pages out to them all, and had them read through it once. Silence. He made some encouraging remarks, and they read it again, with Hal making more observations, giving direction, answering questions. Then he got them up on their feet. The initial idea was to have each character hug his or her younger counterpart, but it was awkward, and it clearly wasn't making the actors happy. Hal moved his actors around; then he would run through what he had done. The actors would look to him for reassurance. He tried changing one of Sally's lines to a gentle singing of a section of "In Buddy's Eyes." Then, as they are left alone, he had the four young characters break away from their present-day selves and drift up to the corners of the set, back into the shadows. As this was happening, the present-day characters expressed their cocktail-party niceties and exited, leaving the ghosts in the theater. The actors remained glum. Only Alexis seemed to find a way to make her lines work. Since the Young Four had no lines, the whole thing felt awkward to everyone. Hal asked me to find out when Michael would be on a break so he could try to stage it on the set. A few minutes later, down everyone went, and after making a few slight adjustments to the placement onstage, he ran it a couple of times. You could have heard a pin drop. "Well, we'll show it to Jim later when we run the whole thing. We'll run it with and then without what we've just done, and we'll see what it looks like."

Wednesday night's run-through was the most complete so far. Beforehand, Hal said to me, "In a week we'll really have something to look at." He then gave the company a pep talk: "Let's not stop and fix things tonight. Let's go through everything, absolutely everything we've done so far, and see what we have. Energy—that's the word. Lots of energy. That's something that will help us through the next few weeks." Hal wanted to do it without a break, to run the whole show as one entity. They did; it began at 9:15 and ended at 11:15, even without "The Right Girl," which was still not ready, and much of Loveland, including the songs for Phyllis, Sally, and Ben. Most of the winching mechanics for the side units were finished enough for the moves to be attempted; despite some skepticism, they ran smoothly, with only a single stop all evening to get one unit back in its track. Lyrics were still

Jim Goldman confers with Hal Prince.

flubbed by Michael Bartlett, Ethel Shutta, and Fifi D'Orsay. One change that had been made, which struck many of us as a surprise, was that Alexis performed "Could I Leave You?" drunk, reeling around the stage, even clutching Ben's leg at one point. None of us knew where the idea came from, but it was clearly a big mistake. Still, Alexis was roundly credited for throwing herself into it full force. It turned out she had thought the song would be her one musical moment in the show and therefore asked that it be staged by Michael. For whatever reason, he decided to stage it as a drunken rampage. She was supposed to sing "Losing My Mind" in the Follies sequence, but she must have known instinctively that it was the sort of number she couldn't really deliver.

As the polite applause died down, Michael, knowing how incomplete the Follies sequence was, yelled: "*This* is a work in progress!"

Following "Loveland," the only other finished songs run were "You're Gonna Love Tomorrow" and "Love Will See Us Through." Once they were done, Hal skipped to the new ending scene that he had rehearsed earlier in the day. Both Steve and Jim sat forward. When it was over, there was general silence, just a little too long for comfort. Hal called for a break, and then turned to Steve and Jim and asked to speak with them about several things—"not just that shitty ending which I did to show you but which I don't think is right."

There was quite a production meeting following the run-through. The clearest evidence of something that had been brewing came out right at the beginning of rehearsal the next day. Michael gathered the full company on the set and announced: "I am now going to begin version number three of the Prologue." It hadn't occurred to me, but Michael hadn't worked on the Prologue in days; it had simply been part of the run-throughs. I also didn't notice that there had been more than one version so far. "You will all please be patient. I am going to have people moving in different tempos, so everyone must be with me. Pay attention and be patient." He then addressed the dancers and showgirls: "For those of you who have seen your costumes at fittings and know how big they are, please let me know if I am asking you to do something that you won't be able to do—that will save us all a lot of time." Although it was hard to see what had been considered wrong with the Prologue, one of the goals of the new version was to tie music more into each character. The first version had begun with eerie, atmospheric music composed by John Berkman that emphasized the ghostlike world of the Weismann Theater. Michael added some of the ghost figures to his second version, without necessarily driving the point home that they were actually the same characters who were inhabiting the theater.

Nothing seemed to faze Michael. There was no visible limit to his energy, his drive, or his choreographic imagination. He was of a different generation from the rest of the creative team, the youngest by far, and his career was on the rise. Hal, Steve, and Jim were all successful and in their forties. Michael was twenty-eight. He simply thought and behaved differently—he was obviously from the drug generation, while the others were from a drinking generation. To many of us, he was the discovery, and watching him work was eye-opening. I mentioned to a college friend at the time that I thought he would end up being the Jerome Robbins of our generation. Some of us sensed that

Michael Bennett with his ever-present floppy leather hat.

this was the last time he would share the leadership position with anyone, and yet we all knew that the collaboration on this piece would result in something very special. In a weak moment he had confessed that he hated the idea of getting older, and here he was, working on a piece dealing with the confrontation of youth and age. He was pushing the cast to do things they might not be able to do, and he hated seeing

his dances not at peak form. He saw Gene going through hell, longing to be able to do the kind of acrobatic and lengthy dances he used to perform in the movies with ease. Even though Michael had already made the change from dancer to choreographer and director, something about watching Gene work through the number in rehearsal piqued him to say in a quiet moment that no one should be surprised if on his forty-fifth birthday he were found with his wrists slashed, so real was his terror of getting old. Musical theater, he believed, was a place for the young. It's haunting to reflect that Michael Bennett died when he was forty-four, of AIDS.

Finally, a decision was made about "Losing My Mind": it would be sung by Dorothy. She had been a trouper, never asking about what was being considered for her. She was thrilled to hear the news, and when Hal took her aside to tell her, he remarked, "enough of the little flowery dress. You'll get a long silken evening dress and sing the song in a big spotlight." One had to wonder why it had taken three and a half weeks of rehearsal for everyone to realize that "Losing My Mind" made much more sense for Sally than for Phyllis. Hal Hastings took Dorothy upstairs to teach her the song. She then came back down, lyric sheet in one hand, the other hand behind her back, and wandered around the shop, memorizing. Petite and vulnerable, she walked among the half-finished Follies drops, carefully sculpted piles of Styrofoam rubble, and the few remaining bits and pieces of other shows, learning the song that would define her character. Soon Steve was working on a leggy dance number for Alexis. Turns out that following the rehearsal during which the drunken version of "Could I Leave You?" was performed, Alexis had gone over to Steve's house to talk. She was worried about "Losing My Mind," admitting that Dorothy had a superior singing voice, and could probably deliver it better than she. Why not give it to her? And since Alexis had good legs and could move well, she said, why didn't Steve write her a dance number? Steve was intrigued, so that's what was decided: "Losing My Mind" went to Dorothy, Hal got to stage "Could I Leave You?" and Steve would write Alexis a new number.

Run-throughs were becoming almost a daily occurrence. *Follies* seemed to be kicking into a higher gear. Everyone felt it—as if the show were entering the home stretch. There was an increased level of energy and excitement.

One night when I drove Alexis and Yvonne home from rehearsal, Yvonne asked me to go with her for a sandwich at the Copacabana. I said sure, and ended up feeling like a young hustler hanging on to a movie star. It was an interesting night. I had never been to the Copa. The maître d' recognized Yvonne instantly and led us to a ringside table. A couple of the other guys who ran the place came over and kissed her hand. A chorine came by and sat down next to me, complaining about some of the other girls in the show. Drink and food were plentiful; many hours passed and no check was ever presented. At one point, late on, I began to feel responsible for this cast member who was needed at rehearsal the next day and suggested that we go. Yvonne agreed and said a cheery goodbye to everyone seated around her. As I was getting her coat, one of the guys who had been particularly friendly asked if I would like my pin. I didn't know what he was talking about, but he seemed to mean business. He asked me to sign a paper. Fortunately, Yvonne hadn't gotten my name right all evening, so I signed some mangled form of whatever she had called me. He handed me the pin, which I put in my pocket. Evidently Yvonne had observed this transaction, because as soon as we got into my car, she turned to me, laughing, and said, "So what does it feel like to join the Mafia?" I laughed, but nervously. The atmosphere of the place certainly felt underworld, but I had no idea what a pin meant. I didn't look at it, or put it on. But I knew I didn't want it, so after dropping her off at the apartment where she was staying on West End Avenue, I drove back to the Copa, parked the car up the street from the club, and walked in. The same guy was standing inside, near the entrance, and I handed him back the pin, saying that I just didn't feel right about accepting it. He took it back without comment; I turned around, walked back into the street and got back into my Volkswagen. By this time snow was falling, so I drove home slowly. And it was very late. I found a parking place on the street. I got home, got into bed, and sat up for a few minutes playing over in my mind exactly what had happened that night. Is this show business?

5

"Clicking Heels on Steel and Cement"

riday was the company's day off. To the craftsmen at Feller's, that meant a day without us, for which they were grateful. But a lot was going on back at the American Theater Lab. As I entered, I heard "Rain on the Roof." Dortha Duckworth had been fired, and her replacement, Marcie Stringer, was being taught the song and choreography. Her stage husband, Charlie Welch, was there with her, day off though it was. It seems Hal and Michael had changed their minds about how they wanted Emily Whitman to be played. Instead of someone sweet, modest, and warm, they had decided they wanted a Nancy Walker kind of belter. To tell the truth, Dortha wasn't ever really on top of what little she had to do in the show, and Michael complained that he had to cut back on the staging because she couldn't handle very much. Even so, it seemed an unnecessary change to me, and I liked the gentle quality Dortha and Charlie Welch brought to the proceedings. They seemed like a sweet suburban couple who, in addition to performing their little number at local Rotary Club talent shows, had also actually once been in the theater. That struck me as the point of the Whitmans, to show that some just plain folk ended up in the Follies as well as the tortured characters around whom the show was based. Replacing Dortha seemed an odd use of what little time there was remaining. Marcie Stringer did have sharper edges, but at

96

this rehearsal, she seemed to be having as much trouble learning her dance steps as Dortha had had.

On this day off, Hal was wearing his producing hat. There were problems with *Company*: the box office gross had dropped precipitously and was hovering around break-even for the first time in its nine-month run. It had grossed even less than *Fiddler on the Roof*, which was still hanging on, six years into its run. Hal was not happy. He had a commitment to play *Company* in the summer for Edwin Lester's Civic Light Opera series on the West Coast—eight weeks in Los Angeles and seven weeks in San Francisco—and he had planned to mount a new company to play those dates and then go out on tour. Now he realized that if business in New York dropped off too much, he might be forced to close the show here and move that production west. He was on the phone: "I don't care what I have to do, I want that fucking show playing at the Alvin all next year!" He was reminded that January and February are notoriously bad times for Broadway and that perhaps he should give the show a few weeks to see if business improved. Auditions would continue as if there would still be a second company. The leading role, originally played by Dean Jones, needed a star. From one of Joanna Merlin's memos to Hal: "Richard Chamberlain adores *Company* but doesn't want to follow anyone in it in any company." Robert Morse—"any interest on your part?" George Hamilton—"wants to audition. Do you want to read him as well as sing?" George Chakiris— "Billy Cohen thinks he has no box office value." There was a list of women for Hal to consider for Joanne, Elaine Stritch's role in New York. They ranged from Kaye Ballard to Janet Blair to Eve Arden to Gisele MacKenzie. Next to some Hal wrote "NO!" while others got a "to read" or "can't sing" or "too fat" or, in the case of Angie Dickinson, "won't." (Business did improve, and the tour did go out, headlined by George Chakiris. Elaine Stritch went out on the tour as well, replaced in New York by Jane Russell, who had come up to Boston during the run of *Follies* to audition for the role.)

Don Weismuller, who had been fired early in the week, appeared at the rehearsal studio. He refused to be bought out of his contract. When an actor is let go, he is usually either paid for the balance of his contract or paid a negotiated settlement amount. It's generally considered bad form for an actor to stand up to a producer and say that he has the right to play the role for which he was hired, but Don had decided to do just that. Hal chose not to fight it, so a character named Vincent

would have to remain in the show. The solution? Change the name of the dance specialist to Vernon and his partner to Laverne; Vincent would become a partygoer and an understudy. (In the end, they went back to Vincent and Vanessa and changed the name of Don's character to Vernon, and everyone seemed happy.) A replacement had been hired, Victor Griffin, who was, according to the stage managers, "just like Don only thinner." So once again the dancers in "Bolero d'Amour" were in the big rehearsal room, this time working Victor into the dance. Graciela had been looking forward to spending her day off working with a Spanish-language production of Federico García Lorca's *Yerma*, grateful for the opportunity to get her mind off *Follies* for a few hours. No such luck.

Back in the Bronx on Saturday, Marcie Stringer was introduced to a slightly disbelieving company. Nothing makes a company more nervous than to have one of their fellow actors fired, especially when it takes everyone by surprise, as this replacement did. It becomes a game of "Who'll be next?" The two people feeling this most directly were Peter Walker, who had just had his role as Major-Domo in the Prologue taken away, and Ethel Barrymore Colt, who was keenly aware that she was barely keeping her head above water, especially in the mirror number. These two shared another problem: they had been hired to understudy Ben and Sally and must have been afraid that they couldn't pull off those roles. Hal had become aware of Peter's inability to remember lines and blocking during the work on the Prologue, and had quietly asked Dick Latessa, who was already understudying Buddy, to take an unofficial look at Ben. He also confided that if Dorothy were ever out, he would be tempted to cancel the performance rather than have Ethel play the role. Some of these uncertainties must have made their way to the two actors. They often sat together, off in a corner. Added to the anxiety about the firings was the appearance of Dortha, who showed up at the studio in the Bronx, hoping to remain a part of the company. It had worked for Don Weismuller, but it wasn't going to work again. Hal took Dortha aside and spoke with her quietly, thanking her for her talent and saying that he would be happy to work with her again if the opportunity arose. That got translated back to the company as Hal's having promised her a role in his next show.

The entire Feller studio was now taken over by *Follies*. The set

had been painted black, and the floors on the two smaller platforms looked like the gray planking in the model. In one large corner of the shop a black-and-white photograph of a city street scene was being transferred to a large drop laid out on the floor. A scene painter was standing, holding a paintbrush attached to a four-foot handle in one hand, the actual photograph in the other. He would look at the photograph, dip the brush into one of the several paint cans on the floor containing blacks, whites, and grays and re-create the image on the much larger canvas, guided by a faint chalk-line grid on the drop that corresponded to a grid drawn on the photograph itself. This drop would be used in the final image of the show, the morning after, as daylight peeks through a portion of the rear wall of the theater, revealing the street. The vacuum-form machines were commandeered to create silver fountains that would end up behind Alexis and the dancers in their bright-red costumes in her Follies song—whatever that would be, since it was still not written. Piles of debris and crumbling proscenium pieces were at various stages of construction and painting in any available vacant spot. On the downstage floor of the set itself, the cross-sectional outline of the proscenium arches of the Colonial and the Winter Garden theaters had been painted. Everyone could see how the set would fit in the two theaters and appreciate what the eight-feet difference in proscenium opening would mean. Anything taking place on the extreme downstage towers wasn't going to be seen by a lot of the audience in Boston, and no one was happy about this.

Hal took the set first because he wanted to try reversing the order of "The Road You Didn't Take" and "In Buddy's Eyes." The section of the show following the Montage, which included these two songs and "Bolero d'Amour," had been tinkered with since the beginning of rehearsals. It is the first time we see the four principals paired with their "other" partners—Ben with Sally, Phyllis with Buddy—in the present, while simultaneously we see scenes of them in the past with their eventual spouses. It was a tricky mosaic to get right, and instinct more than anything guided the shaping of the sequence. Originally, "In Buddy's Eyes" came first, but Hal felt it might tip the hand too soon. The song is, in essence, a lie: try though she may, Sally can't convince herself that she really is "young and beautiful in Buddy's eyes." She is, after all, standing with Ben, the true love of her life, the man she didn't end up with. Ben's song, "The Road You Didn't Take," is an honest statement of regret and is at least truthful—"The Ben I'll never be,

Who remembers him?" "Bolero d'Amour," a sumptuous dance of passion, would come between the two songs, but Hal was sensing that it would be stronger if Ben's song came first. The switch would also allow him to cut a few extraneous lines, and that would help get the show moving a little faster. After he made the shift, he wanted to run it with "Bolero d'Amour," but Michael had the dancers rehearsing upstairs, so Ruthie and George Martin danced the lead roles—or attempted to, much to everyone's amusement. George knew the moves; Ruthie had only a vague notion of where to go. Hal ordered the party people populating the sides not to look and act bored, explaining that the party hubbub would be important to the feel of the show and asking that they all try to maintain a level of animated interest, even if they were, for all intents and purposes, the background. Of course some were ready to act up a storm, like Sonja Levkova, who performed every scene as if it were the last she would ever be in, and somehow always found her way into a position of focus, dead center. When he was finished, Hal confessed to all that he wasn't used to rehearsing directly on a set and that he found it unnerving.

Michael took the set back and worked through the new Prologue. He was clear, animated, and uncompromising, demanding attention from everyone. His directions were precise: "Don't enter in rhythm. Just come in as if you were arriving and getting out of the rain, but get to your designated spot on the right count of the music." Sometimes he would sit on his stool, deep in thought, tuning out whatever else was going on around him and tapping his finger in the air in rhythm. He would mutter, "Please start doing something, because my finger is getting tired." He worked the beginning through to Ethel Shutta's entrance over and over until he was satisfied. "I like it, which means there probably won't be another version of this." (There would be, but it wouldn't happen until Boston.) Having shown a great deal of patience with the older women, he now had to find a new source of patience for the showgirls. "Do not walk in the same tempo as the party guests. You are in a different reality. You must walk to your own rhythm, slower." Their method of working wasn't really the same as that of the Broadway dancers. One of them remarked, "In Vegas all we do is walk. We really should just come out in those gorgeous costumes and parade around for everyone to look at." Getting them to move to different rhythms was proving tricky. But Michael kept plowing ahead, ever focused.

Some members of the company were starting to get sick. Mary McCarty felt rotten and Ethel Shutta had stayed home. Others started to complain about various ailments. Hal had little sympathy: "Even if people don't realize it, this is the most important thing going on in the world!"

On Sunday, I picked up Steve and Jonathan Tunick, who were coming to see "The Right Girl" performed for the first time. In the car Steve talked about how Jim Goldman was struggling with the character of Sally and the problem of how to have her go crazy at the end of the show without making it seem like a soap opera. Jim had come up with an idea that he hadn't yet told Steve and which he said was probably the most pretentious idea he had ever had. Steve said that *Follies* was now fulfilling two of his dreams: to have a character crack up onstage and to begin a show with an orchestra tuning up, which was being contemplated for the Prologue.

Fritz Holt took the whole company up to the second-floor studio to run through sections of the show so Gene could go through "The Right Girl" for the higher-ups only—Hal, Michael, Steve, Jim, and Jonathan. Screens were pulled around to discourage anyone else from watching, since Gene was still nervous and uncomfortable about performing it publicly. I remained discreetly in the background and watched. It was amazing. The song was built around an agitated nervous vamp, with each verse punctuated by tough, rhythmic, edgy dance sections. This is Buddy expressing his frustrations at the mess he has made of his life, realizing, as the song ends, that he'd chosen the wrong girl. Michael's staging utilized the entire set, which would be completely empty for one of the very few times all evening. He had Buddy dancing from platform to platform, jumping about, swinging around pipes, and even, at one point, leaping from one raised platform to another, landing solidly on both feet, ten feet above the stage floor. He even tried having Gene in tap shoes to increase the percussive quality of the dance, but thought better of the idea. At the end he did a twist with his whole body, ending up in a crouch downstage, facing out. "I don't love the right girl," he sang, then concluded with a simply spoken "Oh, shit." It was angry, strong, tough, and arresting. A tour de force, obviously hard to execute, and dramatically compelling. In fact, it proved to be too hard to execute and was softened considerably as

the weeks went by, yet it still held on to the dynamism of one of those tough Gene Kelly concept dances from 1950s musical movies. It also clearly added another layer to the score; up until this point it was only the pastiche memory songs that were choreographed, not the book songs. Here was a book song, a soliloquy, sung by a stage-door Johnny, not even an old Follies performer, heavily choreographed but entirely in a fantasy moment within the present. It was another example of how the creative forces behind this show were twisting and manipulating the levels on which their songs and dances operated.

I drove Hal, Steve, and Jim back to town. They had noticed, they said, that Yvonne seemed to be taking quite a shine to me. I told them about the night at the Copa and added that I had escorted her to a preview of John Guare's *The House of Blue Leaves* the night before, and that she had taken me to Asti's restaurant, a hangout of the Italian opera singing crowd where the waiters are apt to burst into song at any moment. They were aghast. I thought it was fun to pal around with Yvonne—she was a movie star, after all, and someone who liked attention paid to her. I didn't mind having a glamorous lady in a white fur hanging on my arm, but I didn't take it seriously and wondered why they seemed almost parentally concerned. I wasn't interested in pursuing her, and I couldn't tell if she was pursuing me. But months later I found out that once when Yvonne had mentioned to Dorothy that she thought I was cute, Dorothy had warned her to "Keep your hands off that nice young man." I did escort her to many a dinner in Boston, drove her back to New York, and visited with her from time to time after the show opened. And there the story ends. Probably a good idea: as Steve reminded me later, she did have a gun collection, and a husband.

On Monday Steve was hard at work on Ben's Follies number, "Live, Laugh, Love." He had figured out a way to construct a debonair Fred Astaire–like song that would include a moment for Ben to catch himself off-guard, leading to the Pirandello moment when he would forget the lyrics and stumble. I was sent to Mathilde's to pick it up, but she had been given only the music and some of the lyrics; Steve was still phoning them in, line by line. Everyone at rehearsal was anxious to get the song, so after running some other errands, I arrived back at Mathilde's as her newly inked piano/vocal copy, in an unfinished state, was literally emerging from the ozalid machine. Each new lyric phoned in would be

Gene Nelson attacks "The Right Girl," jumping from platform to platform.

written down on her reference copy in red ink. Steve promised every-one he would have the song finished by that evening.

When I got to rehearsal Ruthie was standing at the desk in front of the set, on the phone with Steve, taking down more lyrics for the song. With the rehearsal proceeding noisily, inches away from her ear, she dictated them to me as she was getting them. I went upstairs to type them out, then decided I had better check them with Steve directly, since they had arrived in piecemeal fashion. He made a couple of changes to what I thought I had heard, then asked if I could put Hal Hastings on the phone. He sang the song to him, explaining that it should be done "in a nice, easy, Fred Astaire tempo." Now that this song was done, he was about to begin Alexis's Follies number. "Remind me of her range, which I know is about three notes." Hal Hastings obliged.

At nine there was a run-through incorporating a large chunk of the new Prologue. Everyone was in residence for this one, including light-ing designer Tharon Musser, press agent Mary Bryant, Hal's secretary Annette Meyers, the guys from *Look*, and two photographers. Hal asked me to sit next to him and take his notes. Ethel Shutta was still sick, so Mary Jane Houdina, who played Young Hattie, played present-day Hattie as well. Her performance of "Broadway Baby" was simple and precise. Here was a young woman singing the song as it might well have been performed back then, in the place in the show where it was to be performed by an older person now. Hearing Mary Jane sing about "making rounds all afternoon," and wanting to be "on some marquee, all twinkling lights," seemed perfectly appropriate, innocent and youthfully hopeful. Mary McCarty was also sick, but her memory figure couldn't jump into her role in the mirror number because the two of them danced together, so Michael jumped in and danced her role, poker-faced, performing it to the hilt and clearly relishing the moment. Everyone loved it—maybe it was an insider's delight, but it certainly made for an accurate run of the number. Stage managers filled in during the dialogue scenes.

"The Right Girl" was performed for the first time in sequence. It had picked up the nickname "The Mystery Number" around the com-pany, so everyone was eager to see what it looked like. Gene was extremely nervous and muffed several of the lyrics, but he was greeted with sustained cheers from his fellow performers. He looked relieved, but totally wiped out. Yvonne now had "Can That Boy Fox Trot!"

*Michael Bennett steps in for Mary McCarty in "Who's That Woman?"—
backed up, on the right, by Dorothy Collins, Helon Blount, and Yvonne De Carlo.*

pretty much under her belt, including the elongated middle section, so
it was performed in full. She missed a fair number of lyrics but got
through it in high style. (Truth: Gene and Yvonne rarely sang all their
lyrics correctly throughout the entire life of the show.) "Beautiful
Girls" looked good, and each pass strengthened the women's confidence, although Michael Bartlett still had trouble mastering the
words, often singing lines like "Nothing detectable half so inspectable"
instead of "Nothing respectable half so delectable." "Rain on the
Roof" was tentative, as Marcie had been rehearsing only for one day.
The book songs went well, as did what was ready of the new Prologue;
indeed, it did look cleaner and more focused than the previous version,
incorporating more pieces of memory music linked directly to the
present-day characters. The five lead performers were given clear
entrances, all linked to music they would be associated with later on in
the evening. "Loveland" was fine, but the Follies sequence following
still only consisted of the two songs sung by the Young Four. Dorothy
was learning "Losing My Mind"; Gene Nelson had been focusing on
"The Right Girl" and hadn't gotten to rehearse "Buddy's Blues" much;

John McMartin was waiting for Michael to stage "Live, Laugh, Love"; and Alexis simply said, "Just think, if I get my number on Wednesday, I'll have ten days to learn it before the first preview."

What didn't feel up to the musical numbers were the book scenes.

The book of a musical is its most vulnerable component. It must provide the framework for the score, and is often "cannibalized" in order to create new songs. It's said that a good score can make a successful musical, but a good book can't do it alone. The truth is that it takes both a good score and a good book to make a first-rate musical. Part of the job of a book is to get from musical moment to musical moment without anyone's really realizing that's what's going on. It's a tricky task, especially on a conceptual show like *Follies* that doesn't provide opportunities for standard storytelling devices. And so the pressure on the book of *Follies* was enormous.

It's dangerous to assess how well dialogue is working during rehearsals of a musical; listening to actors repeating lines over and over is a lot less interesting than listening to them singing songs over and over. Both Jim Goldman and Steve Sondheim understood that this particular play had a decidedly dark side, and both were interested in writing about characters in various states of crisis. But in choosing a party as the framework for their show, they established the need for small talk. How clever, pointed, and witty that small talk was could well be the key to the success of the book. There were areas of the book that were still being discussed, like the very ending of the show, about which everyone involved seemed to have a strong opinion. But what this run-through made clear was that the dialogue had too little in the way of wit and humor—or if it had them, they weren't coming through. The characters came across as humorless, and that was worrisome; if they didn't express themselves somewhere with humor, their individual plights were going to be awfully hard to sit through. But the numbers were coming together, and there were enough good and witty moments to justify confidence.

There was discussion among the company about whether the two

different styles of song—the "book" songs like "Waiting for the Girls Upstairs," "The Road You Didn't Take," "Don't Look at Me," "In Buddy's Eyes," and "Could I Leave You?" and the "pastiche" songs like "Broadway Baby," "Who's That Woman?" and "Beautiful Girls"— would work together and feel like a unified score. Of course Steve was composing very consciously and was very aware of mixing up the styles. But the more the show began to come together, the more the differences among the songs became apparent, and the more I began to wonder whether pastiche might not win out over the book songs. After all, the pastiche songs were simply more fun.

A production meeting followed the run-through. The lines among the creative staff were starting to be drawn, and as time was ticking away, opinions were starting to get heated. Jim started off by saying how happy he was with the progress of the show. Michael was angry, wound up, and frustrated; that was the last thing he wanted to hear. He said he felt the audience would have a hard time getting to know the people in the play and as a result he was worried that they wouldn't be interested in staying with them for an entire evening. He complained about a lot of the book, starting with the monologues used in the Prologue; he pointed out that the ones written for Ben and Phyllis were originally conceived for the characters driving in a car on the way to the party and that now they made no sense. "I want two new monologues." "Is that an order?" Jim replied. "Yes," Michael answered. Jim fired back that while he had been listening over the past weeks to a lot of talk about polishing the gem that is "Can That Boy Fox Trot!" he felt the song was no gem at all. There was agreement that the length of the song was a problem, now that the middle section had been added, and concern over whether Yvonne would be able to sustain interest in it. Steve said he hated "Ah, Paris!" Hal was worried that "Bolero d'Amour" wasn't working and might have to be cut, but acknowledged that so much work had been put into it that he didn't want to consider actually cutting it until he could see it in front of an audience. He also brought up the question of an intermission, saying that they might have to try one in Boston, and his vote would be to place it after "Who's That Woman?" Concerns were voiced about the character of Ben, and whether he was the least complete of all the principals. Michael had no patience for Ben, and wondered whether Jim and Hal identified in some ways with the character, which would be a hindrance

in their ability to zero in on the problems. He also felt there were important moments missing from the dialogue, although he insisted he wasn't criticizing the book. "Yes, you are," Hal said.

By the end of the meeting it seemed clear that if there were to be opposing views from here on, the antagonists would be Michael and Jim. Steve understood the give and take of the collaborative process, and didn't take offense when his work was criticized; at least he never showed it in front of his collaborators. He and Hal had known each other for so long that they spoke in a kind of shorthand. Steve was supportive of Jim, and confessed quietly that he thought Michael, although terrifically talented, was getting a bit too arrogant for his own good. That was making it hard for him to deal with Michael in production meetings, even though he acknowledged that he agreed with some of Michael's concerns. Hal was trying to play the mediator, but his own tension with Michael was apparent.

After the meeting, Michael confessed to Larry Cohen that he hated the book of the show and hoped never again to find himself in this kind of collaboration. In his opinion what the show needed was George Furth or Neil Simon to come in and write twenty good jokes.

Tuesday was a workday, devoted mostly to cleanups and slight modifications in staging. Michael, having stated his concerns about the book—and gotten nowhere—decided to solve the problems himself. One of his ideas was to turn the show over to the ghosts whenever possible, since many had no lines at all and he found them far more interesting than the characters. He began at the top of the Prologue and changed the order of the entrances of the principals, making Phyllis and Ben enter first, and together. Since, as he noted, their monologues were carryovers from an earlier draft and had been written to take place in a car, and since Jim Goldman seemed unwilling to change them, Michael thought that they'd make better sense as the first dialogue we hear. He also thought it would be "cleaner" to have them enter, say what they had to say, and then leave, so Sally could come in next, alone. (In the earlier version Ben froze when Sally entered.) Buddy would be last, since he has come separately and doesn't quite know what mood he's going to find Sally in. Michael had the ghost figures physically shadow the corresponding characters as soon as they arrived; that would help the audience make the connection between the memory figures and the present-day characters. He gave Yvonne a

long movie-star entrance, crossing the whole stage, while the ghost of the choreographer complaining that she's on the wrong foot is heard, and six of the dancing-girl ghosts come running on behind, almost as if they were backing her up. It will work, I thought, if the audience recognizes Yvonne. He also took Fifi D'Orsay's behavior in rehearsal as inspiration for her entrance by underscoring it with riotous echoing applause—from way back when, when her character had been a big star. Of all the actors, Fifi had the toughest time dealing with the reality of the present. Let her live in the past.

Hal gathered the whole company together to give his notes from Monday night's run-through. Many were about cleaning up entrances and exits. He cut Carlotta's escort, Randy, out of her number entirely, though he was to remain her escort. She would now do the number entirely on her own.

Ethel Shutta was back on Tuesday, ready to work but clearly not fully recovered. She made a perch for herself off in a corner to rest when she wasn't needed. She brought me a little present, as she did from time to time. I decided that I could do a lot worse than having Boris Aronson and Ethel as grandparents. I gave her a ride home, and she started talking about the show and about how she didn't like certain people. She hesitated a bit, then said, "I don't care, I'm going to tell you the truth. I don't care if they let me go. If I'm fired, I'll look at them and say, 'Goodbye,' because I did this show to prove to myself that I still had it, that I could still make people laugh and keep them entertained." Two things were bothering her. First, she suspected that several cast members whom she felt weren't as good as she was—Fifi in particular—were being paid more than she was. The other thing on her mind was Hal Hastings, who in her opinion was rude and cruel to people, especially to Michael Bartlett, "who has such a lovely voice and has done so much with his life—to be treated with such little respect is just mean." The company continued to adore Ethel, and every time she did "Broadway Baby," people would watch and laugh.

With more songs completed and staged, there was an increasing amount of shuttling music elements around the city. Jonathan was finished orchestrating "One More Kiss," so it had to get to Mathilde's for the orchestral parts to be extracted. As Jonathan wearily opened his apartment door to hand me the score, I remarked that this one was probably simple because it was short. "To an orchestrator, a bar is

Run-through position: Fritz Holt, Steve Sondheim, Jim Goldman, Michael Bennett, me (notepad in hand), Hal Prince, Tharon Musser, Ruthie Mitchell.

a bar," he said, "and all the songs in this show are long. This one is a hundred bars, which makes it probably the shortest." He still had a long way to go, and many more bars to orchestrate.

Wednesday brought the second full run-through of the week. It felt better and more confident than the one on Monday; there were fewer lost lyrics, and fewer missed entrances. Two more Follies songs were being incorporated. First was "Buddy's Blues." As soon as the Young Four finished their double love songs, Gene came out to the center of the stage, wearing a derby and driving a little prop car, Donald Duck–style. He started the song as if peering through a parted curtain. "Hello, folks, we're into the Follies," he sang and at a certain point, drove his little car around the stage, evoking the life of a traveling sales-man. On one side of the stage his mistress, "Margie," deadpanned non-passionate love for Buddy, while on the other side "Sally" exclaimed how much she loved another man. Both "Margie" and "Sally" were played by men—the robust John J. Martin and the average-built Dick Latessa—replete with feather boas. Gene dropped two full choruses of

lyrics, but it didn't matter. It was a tongue-twisting lyric, with lengthy and slightly variable descriptions of blues: "I've got those 'tell-me-that-you-love-me-oh-you-do-I'll-see-you-later' blues" etc., but everyone got the point nonetheless. The ending was raucous, Gene forgot all his lines, but the company applauded loudly. You could see that Gene was relieved. I didn't get the drag idea, but surmised it was a reference to some old Follies convention with which I was unfamiliar. One more number moving toward completion.

As soon as the applause died down, Hal Hastings moved to the piano bench, replacing the rehearsal pianist, and began to play a slow four-bar introduction. Dorothy walked to center stage, turned slightly, looked up and out, let her arms fall straight down at her sides, and sang:

> The sun comes up,
> I think about you.
> The coffee cup,
> I think about you.
> I want you so,
> It's like I'm losing my mind.
>
> The morning ends,
> I think about you.
> I talk to friends,
> I think about you.
> And do they know?
> It's like I'm losing my mind.
>
> All afternoon,
> Doing every little chore,
> The thought of you stays bright.
> Sometimes I stand
> In the middle of the floor,
> Not going left,
> Not going right.
>
> I dim the lights
> And think about you,
> Spend sleepless nights
> To think about you.

You said you loved me,
Or were you just being kind?
Or am I losing my mind? . . .

She turned and moved very slightly as the music went on. Then she repeated the last chorus, finishing quietly. Hal Hastings played the final two bars and ended on one slow arpeggiated chord. He let the notes die out slowly. There was a moment of absolute silence. Then the entire place burst out in prolonged cheers, applause, and cat whistles. Dorothy shyly broke character and smiled, then turned on her heels and began to blush. She laughed her nervous laugh, looking embarrassed, and wandered over to where Hal and Michael were sitting. They got up and hugged her. So did Bob Avian, who, it turned out, had done the staging for the number. Everyone was smiling. It had to do with a combination of circumstances—the mounting pressures, the realization that Boston was upon us, the growing recognition within the company of tensions among the creative staff, and just plain exhaustion after four hard weeks of rehearsal—but the release was overwhelming.

As soon as the applause died down, every member of the company went over to Dorothy individually to give her a hug, pat her on the back, and tell her how moved they were. Several told her that her singing "Losing My Mind" would be the glorious culmination of a glorious evening. This happy moment meant the world to Dorothy, because earlier in the day Mrs. Pete Feller had, with impeccably bad timing, sidled up to her to confess how dull and boring she thought the whole show was. Dorothy hadn't told anybody about that conversation, but with this triumph she got a new burst of energy. She knew that *Follies* was a great opportunity for her, the best she had had in a long time and probably the best she would ever have again, and she had been very patient over the past several weeks, waiting for a decision to be made about her song. If what Lynn Feller said had shaken her confidence—in the show, or in her own abilities—delivering the song so successfully restored it. She was as happy at this moment as she was ever going to be on the show. She had conquered.

I drove Steve home from rehearsal and took the opportunity to ask him how he thought the show was progressing. He was concerned

Pleased and smiling, Steve Sondheim.

that there hadn't been enough run-throughs but admitted that that was partly because so much of the score was late. And he acknowledged that part of the reason was his procrastination, but he also complained that it had taken so long for the creative staff to come to agreement about the Follies sequence. He said Hal may appear to hate rehearsals, but he told me to wait until Boston, when he would kick into action as soon as the show was put in front of an audience. He expressed concern about the tone of the show, which he said was still somewhat up for grabs. I asked if the show was still a labor of love for him, and he said his guts weren't in it anymore, that it was definitely more theatrical but he wasn't sure he liked it as much as *The Girls Upstairs*. He liked most of the staging, but wasn't happy with "the way Ben runs around in 'The Girls Upstairs.' " But he said he would stand behind the show wholeheartedly, and even in the state it was in six months ago, it was better than much of what's out there on Broadway. He asked me what

I thought, and I didn't really know what to say. Okay, I was intimidated.

The next day I volunteered to play chauffeur for Steve and Judy Prince, who were off to *The House of Blue Leaves*. The two of them had been friends for years, and their banter was comfortable and witty. As Judy climbed into the backseat, she asked Steve how things were going. He said that he was in the middle of writing Alexis's number for the Follies sequence and had found himself in "a fit of rhyming fun" of which he was proud. He then proceeded to recite the following lines. The song, designed for a woman unable to reconcile the bohemian life she once led as a Follies girl with the conservative, sophisticated life she has ended up living, was called "Uptown, Downtown."

> She sits at the Ritz
> With her splits
> Of Mumm's
> And starts to pine
> For a stein
> With her Village chums,
> But with the Schlitz
> In her mitts
> Down in Fitzroy's Bar,
> She thinks of the Ritz—oh,
> It's so
> Schizo.

(This lyric did end up in "Uptown, Downtown," but the song was replaced in Boston.)

When I got home, I decided to write down my feelings, directly, for the first time. Here is an excerpt:

I am now sitting here thinking about today, what it was like, what the show was like, where my head is at, and what I really think about both the show and my life. Monday's run-through brought out all the bad things in the show. I was convinced the book was a total bore, that there was no human warmth on stage, and that if any critics in Boston say anything positive about the show they would be crazy. Well, tonight that run-through took on a perspective, since today made me realize

there is a hell of a lot about the show that is really great. The staging is brilliant—no arguments. There is some humor in the book, but as Steve said, Jim's brand of humor is very subtle and not joke-oriented at all. But it's hard for me to differentiate what I am really feeling from what is merely a conglomeration of what I've heard expressed by others, what I have been told, and what I've been influenced by. How do you keep perspective when you're so close to something?

So what is my opinion of *Follies* at this point, one week before going to Boston? I really don't know. I guess I think I fear the show will be brilliant, funny, witty, full of adroit observant things, and yet cold. Will it appeal to those who adore Steve's work? Is that too small a group? Is the show, and the theater in general, a place for a small group of elitists to go to be amused or entertained? Can you try to teach things, even unpleasant things, to audiences who only want to be entertained? Will they accept it? The few isolated examples of successful "serious" musicals have been able to reach audiences by playing directly on their emotions. What of Steve Sondheim's and Jim Goldman's genuine emotions come through in this work? I don't know. I firmly believe that the best way for theater to teach is through humor. An audience will cry a lot more if it comes out of laughter than if it comes out of being told to cry. The whole idea of people's relationships with their past is intriguing, but is it as insane-making as the creators of *Follies* seem sometimes to believe? As written, *Follies* says that 1) man's inability to deal with his past eventually leads him into some form of breakdown, and 2) his past is terrifying when he looks back on it, sees how he behaved, and realizes how little he knew. I would like to see the show deal with the feeling that 1) coming to terms with the past will eventually leave you better equipped to deal with the present, 2) there is an innate loveliness in the innocence of youth, and 3) delving into the past makes one understand that we never stop growing. My beliefs tend to side with a basic hope in people, in the mind and heart to pull us through life, if you will. *Follies* is an important show, and I frankly hope it will run longer than any of Steve's other shows, but for that to happen I think the four main characters must be better off for having lived through the experience of the show. I am not talking about

cheapening it for New York audiences. I am talking about being careful not to be indulgent. What got me to feel as I do this evening, and to write this all down, inarticulate though it feels, is because "Losing My Mind" moved me more than anything else has over these past several weeks.

Thursday was the company's final day on the set at Feller's. The last few rehearsal days in New York would be back in Manhattan, at the American Theater Lab. Before driving up, I was sent to buy a slew of Styrofoam boaters for the chorus in both "Live, Laugh, Love" and the nearly finished number for Alexis, which we now knew was called "Uptown, Downtown." Michael spread the chorus out across the stage and tried out a lot of different old hat-and-cane steps. He was playing around with every clichéd step he could think of. Michael knew that both numbers would have top hats and canes, and therefore would be somewhat related choreographically. He knew the shape of "Uptown, Downtown." Alexis had been given most of the lyrics. Fritz was anxious for me to get them typed out so he could insert them in his stage managers' script, and since Alexis seemed to have the only copy, I had to peer over her shoulder to get them. She gave me a quizzical glance. Fritz also wanted me to make sure all the new script pages generated over the past few weeks were organized and in one place so they could travel with the stage managers' desk to Boston. I had kept one clean copy of every page that was changed during the rehearsal period, each one dated. I was prepared for the request.

The final New York run-through on the set took place Thursday at seven P.M. Judy Prince and John Guare were on hand, as well as Steve's respected agent, Flora Roberts. Martha Swope came with a small crew and many cameras. The creative staff was in place. I asked Jim Goldman how he was doing. "I'm going to be fine, no matter what." Guare, who had not been to any previous run-throughs, sat with a permanent half-smile on his face, and when it was over he could only shake his head and repeat "Fantastic . . ." over and over. Ethel Shutta was out; her return on Tuesday had proven to be too hasty. (She missed Wednesday's run-through as well.) Buddy's car had been painted blue. One truckload of scenery was already gone, so the studio was beginning to thin out. And as soon as the rehearsal finished, the crew would begin to take the side units and the stage itself apart. Because very lit-

Working out preliminary staging for "Live, Laugh, Love"
upstairs at Feller's. Paul Gemignani at the percussion, John Berkman
at the piano, Graciela Daniele, Michael Bennett, Bob Avian.

tle could fold up, it would take a total of seven trucks to get the entire physical production to Boston.

By Friday morning, Steve had finished "Uptown, Downtown." Mathilde sent her sister to Steve's to fetch the manuscript at nine A.M. At 11:30 I was sent to pick up the hastily copied piano/vocal copy, which I was to take immediately down to Nineteenth Street. Hal Hastings grabbed it and went into the small room by himself to play it through. Mary Jane Houdina and Bob Avian were taking the dancers through some movements, including experimenting with hand clapping for the dance section. Michael and Bob had done some quick research on 1940s dance steps and were teaching them to the fourteen

members of the dancing ensemble; and once Michael heard the song played through a couple of times, he grabbed a Styrofoam boater from one of the dancers and jumped right in. Alexis went into the music room with Hal Hastings to learn the song. When she felt confident enough to join in with the dancers, they went into the large room. With John Berkman at the piano and Paul Gemignani at the trap set, Michael worked through some ideas. It was a group effort as ideas were tossed back and forth among Bob Avian, Mary Jane, and Graciela. After a little while, Michael announced loudly to the room that he was ready to begin on the staging, which he acknowledged he was making up as he went along. He had the chorus keep their backs to the audience all the way through, allowing Alexis to be framed in the center, facing front. He was also experimenting with having them each remain in one place for the entire number. Soon he asked the stage managers to postpone John McMartin's call, as he'd decided to spend the whole day working with Alexis and the dancers. The more they all worked on the number, the more the steps involved removing and tipping the stiff-brimmed hats, and the more little pieces of Styrofoam brim began breaking off and flying around the room. By the end of the day, the shape of the number was blocked out completely, and the hats were all but destroyed.

Hal Hastings had a rare moment of respite and we had a chance to talk. At this point in the process, the "musicality" of his job seemed to include a lot more hand-holding and cajoling than actual music-making. He felt slightly overwhelmed by the enormity of the show, which was long on songs, long on dance music, and included an onstage band that was playing almost all the time the pit orchestra wasn't. Every cast has its own personality, he said, and this group was certainly growing into its own. He admired Gene Nelson, who was still having trouble remembering his lyrics and staging but who worked continuously and tirelessly, even on his days off. "He has a good voice, but it's not inside a great actor." Yvonne was having some of the same problems, although she wasn't inclined to work outside of rehearsal; she preferred to take her chances and just do as well as she could. Victoria Mallory had had her wisdom teeth removed, and he was concerned that that might have an adverse effect on her singing. Of Dorothy Collins he said that underneath that bouncy, cheerful exterior lurks a rather sad and somewhat neurotic woman. He

explained that her first husband, Raymond Scott, hadn't treated her well, but that she was now happily married to Ron Holgate.

On Friday evening at seven P.M. there was a session to record the background for the new Prologue. All the fragments of specific characters' songs had been orchestrated; some were to be only flashes of memory, others were to be longer and more prominent. All the announcements were to be recorded as well, so they were "in memory"—a change from the last version of the Prologue, in which the Major-Domo at the party announced each guest. To be used were "Bring On the Girls," the original opening song, in a Rudy Vallee–like crooning voice provided by Kurt Peterson; "Broadway Baby," sung by Mary Jane Houdina; and fragments of several others, sometimes with speaking over them. I got all the orchestral parts from Mathilde, picked up Jonathan Tunick, and went down to a small recording studio in the West Fifties.

This was the first time any of the *Follies* songs would be heard with an orchestra of any size. For this purpose, the orchestra was only fifteen strong, with Paul Gemignani front and center at the drums and dance arranger John Berkman at the keyboard. Hal Hastings conducted, with Steve, Michael, and Bob Avian in the booth. The first song "played down" was "Bring On the Girls." The orchestration was pure 1930s dance band—saxophones, clarinets, and one syrupy violin, giving a kind of Tommy Dorsey sound. The orchestra, made up of first-rate New York musicians, many of whom would be in the pit when the show got to the Winter Garden, got the style on the first take. "Who needs rock-and-roll?" quipped Jonathan, after winning praise from everyone in the booth. Steve complained that one note was wrong, but quickly conceded that he was more concerned for the copy of the tape that would go into his personal archives. (Interestingly, the orchestration to "Bring On the Girls" was very similar to the one Jonathan did several years later for the film *Stavisky*, in which this tune was used in a dance-hall scene.) Once the orchestral portions were done, the musicians were sent home and the voices were laid down. Michael, perhaps seeking revenge for the amount of time Yvonne was taking in rehearsal, stepped up to the mike first to play the choreographer: "and . . . a *one* two *three* four—Carlotta, you're on the wrong foot, get on the other foot. Now you're *behind* the beat. Come on, Carlotta, catch up! Carlotta!" Dick Latessa did several of the announce-

ments, including "the whistling Whitmans," complete with two tracks of whistling. Everyone thought it would be fun to get into the act, so Hal Hastings announced "the girl of your dreams, Miss Stella Deems," and Jonathan Tunick and Bob Avian each did one. Michael and Steve discussed the importance of determining what each recording was: an actual performance from before ("Bring On the Girls"); an old shellac 78 recording ("Broadway Baby"). They also wanted to make certain the audience didn't think the recorded orchestra actually was the orchestra in the theater. The engineer played around with some echo, differentiating between the various segments, paralleling the mood and state of mind of the characters whose memories they were. Hal Hastings, John Berkman, Bob Avian, and Michael stayed until five A.M., editing the finished tape.

There were only three days left before the company moved to Boston. Alexis arrived early at the studio on Saturday morning, in her red knickers, ready to work through "Uptown, Downtown." In one week she would be performing it before the first preview audience. She worked on Friday, so by rights she had Saturday off, but she wasn't about to rest; she needed to master her number. This was her chance to shine. Michael spent most of the day working with her.

Hal began Sunday's rehearsal with notes from Thursday night's run-through. He was going to make a few changes before leaving for Boston, he said, including new monologues for Ben and Phyllis in the opening scene that Jim had just completed (in response to Michael's particular beef), a new version of the final scene, and a restaging of Ben's "The Road You Didn't Take." In addition, Hal knew that he needed to see how "Live, Laugh, Love" was going to look before staging the hallucinatory scene that followed.

Michael and Bob had started the day doing more research on dance styles for "Uptown, Downtown." Michael liked the song, but wasn't sure how much he could get Alexis to dance. She was tall and had great legs, which he wanted to utilize as much as possible; but figuring out how to point up the difference between the two sides of the character in a decidedly low-down dance was a challenge. The chorus would go on doing the whole dance with their backs to the audience, but he was making certain that their steps remained active

and interesting, and, whenever possible, that they commented on the lyrics. He also wanted a showstopper and knew that one way to get one was to build up to a section where one step could be repeated over and over. (Donna McKechnie told me years later that Michael would design dance numbers in such a way that he could determine the exact bar of music at which the audience would start to clap, and that repetition was one of the keys.)

Jonathan Tunick had completed several full scores, and for a change he brought them to the studio himself. He watched "Uptown, Downtown," took notes, and wondered whether this job would ever come to an end. He was having fun with the onstage band, however, and was proud of a moment he had finished in "Beautiful Girls" when the onstage band is overtaken by the entire orchestra, in the style of an old MGM musical. It came at the end of Roscoe's verse, just before the first woman appears at the top of the stairs. He had orchestrated it to feel like a movie opening up to Cinemascope, with the full orchestra booming out for the first time all evening, and he couldn't wait to hear it played by the full orchestra in Boston.

Ethel Shutta was back and feeling fine. Some of the other older members of the company still had trouble remembering their words and staging, but she had retained hers. She now tended to be a bit mischievous, which the rest of the company adored. After singing "At my tiny flat, there's just my cat," for example, she ad-libbed, "Here, pussy, pussy." She also illustrated the phrase "a spark to pierce the dark" with an imagined bow and arrow shot offstage left while raising her leg to help aim the bow. The line "From Battery Park to Washington Heights" often became ". . . way up to Washington Heights," whispered in Jimmy Durante–style while she swung her arm way up. Today's addition was a yelled "I can play the part!" after "making rounds all afternoon." On days when she was annoyed, she would arch her finger right at Hal while she sang "Say, Mr. Producer, I'm talking to you, sir." She didn't enjoy participating in the group numbers; once while crossing the stage in "Beautiful Girls" she caught my eye and mouthed: "I hate this shit!" But her spirit was indomitable.

Hal wanted John McMartin to perform "The Road You Didn't Take" as if it were a Henry Higgins monologue, in speech-song style. He realized this song was Ben's credo, in which he tries to convince himself that he has made the right choices, and he felt that Ben should

be unsuccessful at doing so. "The Ben I'll never be, who remembers him?"—this was the line Hal recognized as the most important character insight in the song. There isn't going to be another Ben, the Ben who would be willing to go off with Sally. Hal wanted Dorothy to realize during the song that she isn't going to get Ben for her own, that she is part of "The Road You Didn't Take."

When the new dialogue for Ben and Phyllis in the Prologue was read through, Alexis got a laugh on "Who's in love with you, Ben, your editor at Random House?" "My God," she quipped, "a laugh!" Hal couldn't resist, either: "What's that funny noise? Laughter? Whatever it is, we don't want it!" The general feeling was that the new dialogue was an improvement over the monologues.

M onday was the last working day before Boston. Since "Live, Laugh, Love" was now blocked out, Hal could work the company step by step through the end of the Follies sequence, what was being referred to as the "chaos." The idea was this: Ben comes out to perform his number in a completely debonair fashion—white tie, tails, top hat, and cane. He sings about pulling yourself out of your personal doldrums: "When the winds are blowing, That's the time to smile. Learn how to laugh, Learn how to love, Learn how to live, that's my style." This is the successful Ben, who's found his successful way through life. The beat is gentle—Fred Astaire comfortable. The dancers back him up with a gentle tap chorus, lined up on either side of him, also in top hat and cane, listening to his every word and responding. (John, it turned out, had to be cued through the number by Graciela and Mary Jane, who pointed their canes or threw a beat.) After a circular dance, the second chorus begins and, as cleverly constructed by Steve, Ben catches himself when he sings, "Me, I like to live, Me, I like to love, Me . . ." What he hears, of course, is: "I like to love me." He stumbles and goes up on the words. The chorus continues dancing in line, but he's forgotten his lyrics. He asks the conductor for his line, and briefly gets back on a solid footing, only to lose it once again, this time for good. Then he breaks down. He stops and yells, "I don't love me!"

What was to follow was the theatricalization of a total breakdown. Scraps of everything we've been seeing and hearing all night coming back at us. Hal began to stage it by assembling the entire company—minus the four principals, who don't partake—and assigning each per-

son a place onstage. Carlotta would stand up with the onstage band, singing "Can That Boy Fox Trot!" Hattie Walker would stand on one of the staircases, belting out "Broadway Baby." Stella Deems would be on top of a platform, belting out "Who's That Woman?" Hal positioned people, told them approximately what they would be doing, and tried to make sense out of it all. It was a bold, experimental thing to do, and even though the company had known that something like this was in the works, they all found it a little weird. Hal called for Michael, admitting cheerily that he should have had Michael stage it in the first place. Michael looked at what Hal had done, then said to the company: "To begin with, the only way this cacophony will work is if everyone will pick up his or her cue and do the scene as if you were down center and alone. Don't try and play to the audience when you're standing high on top of one of the platforms." He asked that the dancers just keep dancing Ben's number as if nothing odd were happening, even though Ben would exit discreetly in order to make a costume change for the last scene. He had the two men in drag from "Buddy's Blues" come down and join the line of dancers backing up Ben. Bit by bit, he and Hal began to shape something that was either going to be quite startling and extraordinary or a big mess. At this early stage, it was hard to tell, but everyone was game to try to make it work. ⸺

Dorothy had a costume fitting, and since I had some rehearsal skirts to be returned, I went down with her to the costume shop. Flossie had stopped by rehearsals from time to time and had attended a couple of the run-throughs, but since this was the first time I had been to the costume shop, she gave me a guided tour. The showgirl costumes were in their final stages of construction. Several women and a few men were sitting around large worktables, sewing, ironing, putting finishing touches on these big, beaded dresses (I had never seen so many beads in my life). Some dresses were hanging on model forms, with people sewing hems and sleeves. Birdcage hats, a large dress with three cherubs hanging on for dear life, different-colored skirts and dresses— the place looked like a fantasyland. With great pride, Flossie showed me the cape Alexis would wear for the opening, large and purple with appliqué patches of beaded strips in different colors. I found it hard to imagine anyone actually wearing it. It looked very regal, as if Phyllis were some sort of queen to Ben's king, if you were willing to give the

show royalist overtones. In fact, Jim Goldman's most recent success had been *The Lion in Winter*, and I wondered whether he liked to think of his characters as kings and queens.

After a generous lunch break, Michael and Hal ran the end of the Follies sequence from Sally's "Losing My Mind" through Phyllis's "Uptown, Downtown," which was coming together, on to Ben's "Live, Laugh, Love," into the cacophony and through to the final scene with the four principals. Then Michael gave a pep talk: "I want everyone to really *give*. If you don't have the poles on the actual set to hang on to, find something or someone to hang on to so you can really sing out. I need to see if this thing is going to work or if I am going to have to go home tonight and figure out something else." It seemed to work.

The day ended early so everyone could get home and pack for Boston. New York rehearsals had officially come to an end. Next would be a new town, a real theater, dressing rooms, costumes, lighting, sound, the orchestra, the "ten out of twelves" when the show can rehearse for ten hours straight, and then, finally, on Saturday, an audience. In five days everyone would have a sense of how good *Follies* really was.

6

"Why Am I Here? This Is Crazy!"

ON TO BOSTON, FEBRUARY 16

There is no place more theatrically prestigious in the United States than New York. "If I can make it there, I'll make it anywhere," as Kander and Ebb once wrote. And because new plays and musicals aren't hatched in a state of perfection, taking a show to some other city (or cities) before opening on Broadway is an age-old tradition. Traditionally, everyone on the creative team stays with the show during its pre-Broadway tryout, and work continues at whatever pace seems necessary. There are as many stories of shows being turned around because of what was learned from audiences and critics in Philadelphia, Washington, Baltimore, or Boston as there are stories of shows that closed ignominiously in one of those towns when everyone realized just how dire the situation was. No one tries to produce a failure, *The Producers* notwithstanding, but the surprises that come when first confronted by a paying audience can be enormous. Better to face those surprises in a place where the stakes aren't so high, and there is time for changes to be made.

To many within the Broadway establishment, Boston was a favorite stop. Its audiences were thought to be intelligent and fair-minded; somehow, they understood and enjoyed their role. They understood they weren't getting a completely finished Broadway product, but that was part of the challenge. They felt part of the development process. One very New England cousin of mine, whom I saw only in the sum-

mers, took pleasure in describing moments of discovery. She relished telling her story of *Mame*, when the audience applauded the title song during the overture, not because anyone had heard it before, but because it just felt like a hit song. She remembered the moment when she realized that both halves of "You're Just in Love" in *Call Me Madam* were going to fit together. She couldn't wait for the next new show to open. But Boston audiences could also be tough and uncompromising.

There were critics in Boston who were helpful. Elliot Norton, the chief critic for the *Boston Record American* and unofficial dean of American theater critics, was well-respected. He was always willing to meet face-to-face with the creative team of a new show and give his critique, including suggestions for how the show might be fixed. In his later years, he had a television program on Boston's WGBH in which he would invite members of the creative staff for a very public, but gentlemanly, discussion. Kevin Kelly, a younger and often more acerbic critic who was coming into his own, had been one of the first to sing the praises of *Company* in the season before *Follies*. And as we will see, a then unknown young man—still an undergraduate at Harvard—not only surprised everyone connected with *Follies* with his astute and brilliantly written review, but he also became the first person to predict the legendary status the show would eventually achieve. He was Frank Rich.

Boston has its own small theater district, downtown, just off the slightly seedy corner of the Boston Common. In 1971 there were three theaters that welcomed pre-Broadway shows and touring productions—the Shubert and the Wilbur, both on Tremont Street, and the Colonial, on Boylston Street. Hal Prince preferred the Colonial. Though built as part of an 1899 office building facing the Common, it had a bona fide marquee and a proper theater lobby, so once you were inside, it didn't feel at all like an office building. It was also the most beautiful and ornate of the Boston theaters. There was plenty of marble and gold leaf in the lobbies, lounges, and auditorium; cherubs adorned the front of the boxes and balconies; and the ceiling was decorated with frescoes. The back of the stage opened onto a small alleyway named in honor of "Allen's Alley," the final segment of the popular radio program hosted by Fred Allen. Loading and unloading trucks full of scenery was tricky and decidedly a one-at-a-time proposition.

Once a truck had backed into the alleyway, getting to the stage door meant sliding alongside with inches to spare.

When *Follies* arrived, two pre-Broadway tryouts were already playing in Boston. *And Miss Reardon Drinks a Little*, the Broadway debut of Pulitzer Prize–winning playwright Paul Zindel, was in the last week of a sold-out run at the Wilbur prior to moving to the Morosco Theater in New York. The Shubert was housing a new and interesting-sounding musical titled *Prettybelle*, by Bob Merrill and Jule Styne, who together had written the score to *Funny Girl* and individually had had great success in a number of other musicals through the years. Gower Champion, who had twice won double Tony Awards as both director and choreographer (for *Hello, Dolly!* and *The Happy Time*), was in charge—the credit above the title read "A Gower Champion Production." Oliver Smith was the designer and Alexander H. Cohen the producer. The star, with her name as large as the title, was Angela Lansbury, by this time a two-time Tony winner for Best Actress in a Musical. All these award winners made the *Follies* creative staff a little nervous. Since the Tonys were presented in April for a season that ran from mid-March to mid-March, *Company*, which had opened in April of 1970, would be competing with every musical that opened before March 16, 1971. Alexander H. Cohen, in a stroke of producorial and promotional cunning, had scheduled *Prettybelle* to open on March 15th, the last possible day for eligibility. It would therefore be directly up against *Company*, which was, so far, the perceived front-runner in the musical categories. Cohen, who also produced the Tony Awards telecast, was delighted at the prospect of a last-minute publicity-stoking challenge.

Word was starting to drift back to the New York theater community, however, that *Prettybelle* was in trouble. Angela Lansbury played a proper Southern woman, unfortunately also an alcoholic schizophrenic, who seeks revenge on her late husband when she discovers he had been a brutal racist. At first she supports liberal causes (which gets her into enough trouble), but then decides to allow herself to be raped by a series of men of various non-white minorities. Not exactly the stuff of musical comedy, and not how the audiences who had been charmed by Angela Lansbury in *Mame*, or even *Dear World*, wanted to see her. It appeared that despite all the best of innovative intentions, the show was doomed. None of the collaborators did work of great dis-

tinction, and the production looked cheap. Halfway through the Boston run of *Follies*, *Prettybelle* put up a closing notice and canceled its New York opening.

While the *Follies* cast was finishing up rehearsals in New York, a caravan of trucks loaded with equipment, costumes, props, scenery, and music had begun the journey north. Costumes constructed at Barbara Matera's shop on Broadway and at Eaves Costumes on Forty-sixth Street, music copied at Chelsea Music on Sixtieth Street, lighting and sound equipment from Ninth Avenue, scenery from the Bronx—all were converging on a theater in Boston where everything was about to come together under one roof for the first time. Once in the theater, each department was going to need space in which to function: the lighting department had to have a large enough area to spread out and check all the lighting instruments and cables before they were hung. Barbara Matera needed enough curtain rods to hang all the costumes, now numbering close to two hundred, in addition to needing enough workspace to make alterations or even construct new costumes that might be needed during the run. The carpenters needed room to swing a hammer and adjust things in the set that didn't quite fit. The sound department, pretty much a one-man operation, commandeered space in the auditorium for laying out its cables, speakers, and microphones prior to having them installed around everything else. Mathilde Pincus and the music department needed to set up all her equipment, which included a traveling ozalid copying machine and desks for the copyists, several of whom would be on the scene the whole time. At least she didn't have to be in the theater; a suite at the Bradford Hotel became her domain.

Along with the tradition of Boston theaters is the tradition of Boston hotels. Because the idea was to stay as close to the theater as possible, it was a fairly small pool of hotels that served the visiting theater community; within that pool there was a clear pecking order: the top of the line was the Ritz-Carlton, an elegant hotel on the far side of and overlooking the Public Garden. Next came the Statler Hilton, a vast triangular affair closer to the theaters but also near the bus station. Lower down were the Bradford and the Avery, both short walks from the theater. The Bradford had decidedly seen better days but was large enough to have useful amenities, such as a large ballroom on a lower

floor and a smaller one on the top floor. The Avery was on the edge of Boston's "combat zone," an area that seemed not to have found priority placement on any list of urban renewal projects. Its carpets were stained and its curtains frayed. Everyone was on per diems and could therefore decide how much to spend on a hotel. The thrifty ones suffered at the bottom of the heap; those whose comfort was more important to them went slightly higher. Of course those familiar with the road were quick with advice for the neophytes, like the showgirls from Las Vegas, for whom the whole experience was overwhelming. Since the management was paying for my hotel, having decided it would be useful to have me remain throughout the Boston run, they chose to put me in the Avery.

No one stayed at the Ritz-Carlton. Most of the principal performers and the creative staff opted for the Statler Hilton, while the great majority of the company stayed at the Bradford. Only the most intrepid and the extremely ill paid ventured to the Avery. Yvonne De Carlo decided she needed to cook for herself, so she stayed at the Lenox Hotel, where she could have a kitchen, although it was a long cab ride away from everything. There wasn't going to be a lot of time for luxuriating in the hotel anyway. If any spot other than the theater served as a central gathering place, it was the Statler Hilton, with its several restaurants and bars. And although there would be contractual days off, they were rarely for sightseeing and adventuring. The work was going to be hard, with rehearsals continuing during the day while performances took place at night. Since the theater was ours, all rehearsals would take place there, on the stage, in the lobby, even in the men's and women's lounges. There was a certain amount of jockeying for position, but the by now traditional roles usually applied: Michael took the stage and Hal took the ladies' lounge for notes and book work. Music rehearsals tended to be in the men's lounge on the lower level. Most every change would be run before the half-hour call to make sure all departments knew what to expect. And once the orchestra ventured into the pit, any rehearsal involving them took place before the audience was allowed into the auditorium. Even new songs or new orchestrations would be read by the orchestra while in their places in the pit. Notes would generally be given after the performance at night. So any free time people were actually going to have was going to be needed for rest.

Two buses were needed to ferry the company up from New York.

The honchos flew up during the day at their leisure, but some of their luggage went along with the company. A few of the more experienced dancers found their own way and avoided the school-trip nature of the bus ride. I was assigned to pick up Alexis's luggage. When I arrived at her hotel, she was standing in the lobby in a floor-length brown coat surrounded by a large set of slightly faded matching floral bags, looking quite properly like someone from Hollywood ready to spend a few months off adventuring somewhere. I'm still grateful that the cabdriver turned out to be an aficionado of 1950s Hollywood movies, because our trip was not what he was expecting. Loading a set of bags into a New York City taxi is normally the precursor to a high-paying trip to the airport. We were taking them six blocks, from the Manger Windsor Hotel on Sixth Avenue and Fifty-eighth Street to the Alvin on Fifty-second Street. But he knew exactly who Alexis was and was thrilled to see her in person.

Many of the actors paired off on the bus as they paired off onstage: Harvey Evans sat with Marti Rolph, Peter Walker with Ethel Barrymore Colt, and so on. Jokes were tossed around—Dick Latessa, seeing Justine Johnston's mother waving her goodbye, asked if she had packed her boots. After the requisite stop at a highway Howard Johnson's, the buses arrived on schedule, shortly after three P.M., and dropped everyone off at their hotels with most of their correct luggage. Opinions were voiced and some changes made. Ethel Shutta complained that the Statler Hilton was too far from the theater and that she wouldn't be able to get there without crossing treacherous intersections. Ursula Maschmeyer, one of the showgirls, hated her room because it was too small. Dick Latessa took one look at his room at the Avery, turned in his key, and hightailed it to the Bradford.

As soon as I checked in and dropped off my bags, I walked over to the theater. Rounding the corner of the Common, the first thing I noticed was the marquee. It was an ornate version of the kind you typically see at movie theaters, with permanent white sides, lit from behind, on which rows of red plastic letters can be hooked. *Follies* clearly had too many names for those letters, so the solution was to print the necessary information—the four names above the title, the title of the show, and Yvonne—on a sheet of clear plastic that was then attached to the marquee. It looked very neat and classy. (Several years later, a truck smashed into the marquee, and rather than have it

repaired, the owners removed it entirely.) In front of the theater, two "three sheet" *Follies* posters had been pasted onto two large rounded columns framing the entrance. (I'm not sure where these posters got the name "three sheet," since they appear to be made in two sheets; they were the standard-size posters commonly seen in subways and train stations and in front of theaters.) Framing the entrance to the theater, these two leering and colorful Byrd posters were quite a sight. All the credits were there, naming the people I had been watching at their individual jobs. Seeing all the names up there in an organized fashion was one more indication that performances were really soon to begin. The outer lobby was spacious, full of veined marble and gold metalwork, with a vaulted ceiling. Along one wall was a pair of box office windows, and opposite were two shallow exhibit cases, both of which had a "window card" (18" × 24") poster in the center—the sort traditionally used for ticket brokers, hotel displays, and framed in the hallways of producers' offices—surrounded by black-and-white photos taken by Martha Swope on the first day of rehearsal. They were a bit of a shock. Everyone had arrived that first day looking tidy and pulled together, but ever since, rehearsal togs and minimal makeup had been the order of the day. Mustaches had been grown or shaved off, hair had been restyled and cut. These looked like people with only a vague connection to the *Follies* cast, and yet the photographs had been taken just five weeks earlier.

Someone in the box office buzzed me into the lobby of the theater itself. Although now only in worklight, the gilded mirrors, rococo fretwork and lighting fixtures, as well as the grand staircase, were plainly visible. This was what the Roxy must have been like before Gloria Swanson stood in its rubble. It was said to have been inspired by the hall of mirrors at Versailles. No wonder Hal Prince liked this theater—it was a glorious place to be.

It was exciting, yet unsettling, to walk into the darkened auditorium and see the set on the stage. We had been told that the Colonial would have a narrower proscenium opening than the Winter Garden, but I hadn't anticipated how high it would feel. What had looked wide and low in the studio, here looked cut off at the sides. The proscenium was almost square; it was as if you were looking at a wide-screen movie through a square opening. The hanging pieces, now off the floor and placed where they belonged, looked properly ragtag and ominous, and

*Lighting designer Tharon Musser and costume designer
Florence Klotz in the Colonial Theatre, Boston.*

they did give a definition to the top. The two downstage towers were hardly visible from the center of the auditorium, and the side units simply disappeared when in their extreme positions.

Tharon Musser, until now someone who appeared at rehearsals for meetings and run-throughs only, was stationed in the middle of the auditorium, seated with Spencer Mosse, her assistant, at a makeshift table—a sheet of plywood laid over several seats. She was clearly at "mission control." Her impromptu desk was lit by an old-fashioned gooseneck desk lamp with a rounded metal hood. There was a microphone with wires leading up, out, over, and back, giving her communication with everyone involved with the lights—hanging, cabling, focusing, gelling, and connecting each instrument to the dimmer boards. They included the stage managers backstage, electricians on the fly floor high above the stage, and the members of the lighting crew stationed backstage, at the front of the balconies, in the follow-spot perches, and on the sides of the proscenium. Her papers were spread out, including large blueprint plans indicating where each and every spotlight would hang, where it would be focused, and what color

the gel should be. The auditorium was in darkness; the stage was lit only by whatever single lighting instrument was being focused. It was a one-at-a-time procedure, and Tharon was in total charge—the theater was hers. Carpenters were wandering around the stage, trying to do their work while keeping out of the way of the lighting crew and occasionally begging for more light, but her needs came first. Because of the structural and constructionist feel of the *Follies* design, she and Boris had decided that there would be no masking for any of the lighting instruments. Trusses were constructed to hold lights, both vertical, behind the proscenium on the sides, and horizontal, above the stage.

Despite the best intentions of the most talented of artists, there is no such thing as everything working on the first try when a new musical is being put together. Adjustments and alterations are the norm; all anyone can hope for is efficient use of time. The larger the show, the higher the number of things that can go wrong. Over the next few days, time would often prove more valuable than money, since come hell or high water there had to be a performance on Saturday.

The orchestra assembled for the first time on Tuesday afternoon in the rooftop ballroom of the Bradford Hotel. This was a preliminary rehearsal, without singers, and it provided an opportunity to play through everything first before presenting it to the company. The music staff was there in force: Hal Hastings, facing the orchestra at a makeshift podium; Jonathan Tunick, John Berkman, and Mathilde sitting at a table behind him with piles of full orchestral scores and instrumental parts. And, of course, Steve Sondheim. For him, it was the most thrilling moment, to hear the score as Jonathan had orchestrated it. Arranged fanlike over the floor of the ballroom were music stands and chairs for the twenty-seven players who made up the *Follies* orchestra: five reed players who, among them, played flutes, piccolo, clarinets, bass clarinet, alto saxophone, tenor sax, soprano sax, baritone sax, oboe, English horn, and bassoon; one French horn; three trumpets; three trombones; two percussionists (Paul Gemignani was one; the other doubled as the drummer for the stage band); one harp; one piano (which would also be used in the stage band); six violins; two violas; two cellos; and one bass. The only player in the orchestra to have been part of the rehearsal team was Paul Gemignani, and now he sat among the local players. Each city hires its own orchestra, coordinated

by a contractor who is familiar with the local talent. To first-rate musicians, it's a gig. Usually there's a general lack of interest in the music they've been hired to play, although there is a certain amount of fun to be had with a new show. Since Boston boasts several conservatories of music, a good orchestra can usually be assembled without too much trouble. The contractor's task is to find players who are knowledgeable about the musical style of the show, who are able to read quickly and accurately, and who are willing to show up eight times a week and sit in a pit. Rarely do players feel they have a vested interest in a show, but they're skilled and fast—one trumpet player even managed to keep up with the rehearsal while maintaining the light on his Tiparillo cigar.

Until the orchestrations are actually heard, there's a sense of uncertainty. Steve knew what he had written, and he'd had numerous conversations with Jonathan, but only Jonathan knew what they would sound like—and *he* had heard them only in his head. Mathilde and her copyists were musicians enough to have a sense of how each part would sound, but they, too, had never heard it all together, nor could they guarantee that no mistakes had been made. John Berkman, the dance arranger, had turned over his scores to Jonathan to orchestrate, and he, too, was curious to hear them. Although it's normal for something to come out sounding rather different from what was intended, in these experienced hands the orchestrations fulfilled everyone's fantasies. They were great. And there were minimal changes to be made—a few mistakes in the parts, an occasional wrong chord, a rare second thought. Hal Prince had a clever tradition of informing the principal actors about when the orchestra reading was taking place, saying that although they shouldn't feel under any obligation, they were welcome to come by, should they get to Boston in time, and hear what it sounded like. Who wouldn't take him up on that invitation? Both Alexis and Gene did, and when I brought one of Alexis's bags over to the Statler in the middle of the afternoon, I ran into them both, returning from the rehearsal. They were thrilled, and invited me to have a drink with them at one of the restaurants in the hotel. Gene then pulled out a small tape recorder that he had smuggled into the rehearsal and played me a very rough play-through of "Waiting for the Girls Upstairs." They were like two little kids, giddy with excitement. They also confessed that as soon as they'd arrived in Boston, they'd done pretty much exactly as I had: checked out the marquee, ventured

into the darkened auditorium, and asked the box office staff how ticket sales were going.

Michael called the dancers and Alexis and John onstage from six to seven P.M. to go over "Uptown, Downtown" and "Live, Laugh, Love" on the set, since both numbers had been staged only in the rehearsal room. The technical staff still had dibs on the stage, so the evening rehearsal was relegated to the large Bradford ballroom; but Michael insisted on squeezing in one hour of stage time during the tech crew's dinner break. Michael's patience was being tested. Not having gotten these two numbers until days earlier left him short-tempered, and occasionally he snapped at Alexis, whose own nerves were beginning to show. It was the first time she was on the set in the theater, and now she was doing her dance number on the various raked levels of the stage. The joy of the afternoon was now forgotten. She messed up a lot of movements and lyrics. When the dancers walked out onto the set they looked around the theater with a sense of awe. John McMartin wandered about, muttering how honored he was to be part of a production on a set as extraordinary as this.

I went over to the Bradford to help move Paul Gemignani's drum set from the rooftop ballroom down to the grand ballroom. There was some confusion about which ballroom we would be rehearsing in; Ethel Barrymore Colt snapped that I "was a terribly inefficient young man" when I told her the wrong one by mistake. Excitement, anxiety, and nerves were manifesting themselves in equal portions. Everyone was getting cranky. This was the last night we wouldn't be rehearsing in the theater and the only time we would be in the ballroom, so there hadn't been time to tape out the floor plan; the stage managers had to improvise with folding chairs. But there was an important job that had to be done: the chaos scene following "Live, Laugh, Love" wasn't finished. As a result, the musical accompaniment wasn't set either, and for that to be ready in time for Saturday it needed to be finished by John Berkman, approved by Steve, orchestrated by Jonathan, and copied by Mathilde and her people.

The dancers were sent home at eleven, as they had been working since six P.M. without a break. The rest of the company continued till midnight. Once the chaos scene was reasonably complete, Hal proceeded to stage the very last scene, which was still being tinkered with. He changed the staging for the young counterparts; they had always

been part of the scene, but Hal's new idea was to have them stay behind in the theater, making the final image the ghost figures watching their present-day counterparts leave. It looked very good. The ghost figures remaining in the Weismann Theater was a nice visual metaphor for the end; as the present-day characters try to go back to their lives, maybe they can leave their ghosts permanently behind in the theater that is about to become history.

Jim Goldman and Steve Sondheim snuck off to see *Prettybelle*; they weren't about to let a moment go by without taking in the competition. On their return they were joined at the bar of the Statler by Michael, Bob Avian, Larry Cohen, Paul Gemignani, and, later, after rehearsal, Hal. The conversation was interesting. Everyone was quietly relieved by their report: unsalvageable. Hal confessed that whenever he's working on a show, he loves anything he sees, but he hadn't seen *Prettybelle* and wasn't sure he was going to. The box office at *Company* was still sluggish, so Hal was counting on winning a lot of Tonys, including Best Musical, and wasn't interested in potential competition. The Tony Awards ceremony would take place in the middle of the *Follies* preview period. He didn't need anything more to fuel his anxieties. Right now, there was work to be done on *Follies*: Hal, Jim, and Steve adjourned to John Berkman's room at the Statler to go over the music for the chaos scene. The meeting lasted until four in the morning, a riotous and laughter-filled gathering that resulted in the completion of the final piece of the musical puzzle.

Since everyone had sensed Alexis's nerves and observed her screwups in the work-through of "Uptown, Downtown," it was suggested that the number be cut from the first preview on Saturday. Michael, smarting from the lack of time he had been given, was not about to let that happen. He knew somehow he would be blamed if the number wasn't performed, and he simply said no, the number would be in.

Wednesday morning the full company was back at the Bradford, this time in the rooftop ballroom, for the official read-through of the orchestrations. This is sometimes called a "sitzprobe," German for "sitting rehearsal," as the actors aren't onstage, although hardly anyone ever actually sits. The point of the rehearsal is to see how the voices and the orchestra work together. The onstage band was also in the room, off to one side, together. It was made up of piano, bass,

trumpet, and drums—players who had traveled with the company from New York.

The sitzprobe is one of the most exciting moments in the assembling of any musical. There is always a sense of discovery. For five weeks the cast had been hearing rehearsal pianists pound out the songs and dance arrangements. Suddenly to have twenty-seven players backing you up is thrilling, especially if the orchestrations are good. All eyes were on Hal Hastings, who was leading the rehearsal. He had been the one keeping tabs on everyone's progress, and he had the best sense of how everything was going to sound together. He was also the one who would have to deal with the nerves, the opinions, and the worries.

The cast gathered on the small stage at one end of the ballroom, a couple of steps higher than the floor. Hal Hastings was at his makeshift podium, perched on a stool in front of the players, his back to the stage. He would call each singer down to the orchestra when his or her turn came to sing. He conducted from the full scores, although during performances he would have a smaller and simplified piano/conductor score that would include orchestral and line cues, all the lyrics, and a piano-friendly reduction of the orchestrations. After a few performances he didn't need either. Most cast members brought small cassette tape recorders, which they surreptitiously lined up along the front of the ballroom stage. Michael and Bob Avian were off to the side, and the stage managers were making sure everyone was in the room and standing by, ready to come forward at the right moment. Hal Prince wandered around, showing everyone an article by Loudon Wainwright in the current issue of *Life* about the "nostalgia boom" that he felt spoke to exactly what he was trying to get across with the show. Perhaps Hal's attitude toward nostalgia was changing as the opening was approaching.

The task at hand was to see that everything worked musically. Does the orchestration work? Does it fit with the singer? Does it fit with the performance? Is the balance between orchestra and singer okay? Accustomed to a usually out-of-tune piano, everyone got swept away by the excitement of the violins, flutes, trumpets, and all the other instruments making the songs suddenly sound like real music. The energy in the room was palpable. As each song was played, the group listened intently and responded enthusiastically. The up-tempo dance numbers and the songs with a specific period sound were clear crowd-

pleasers. Everyone loved "Who's That Woman?" And when the full orchestra kicked in, MGM-style, after the last refrain of "Beautiful Girls," everyone cheered. The solo violin playing the melody of "Broadway Baby" was also a big hit. Ethel, needless to say, couldn't help herself and performed the song for the orchestra. "One lady violinist was looking at me every time she didn't have to look at her music! And all the musicians were laughing," she said afterward. Naturally, when "Ah! Paris" came along, Fifi tried to top Ethel. She couldn't. The response to some of the present-day songs, such as "Waiting for the Girls Upstairs," was more cautious. Some of the ballads were less showy. Everyone noticed and loved the cacophony of whistles and noisemakers throughout "Buddy's Blues," the Burt Bacharach brass in "The Right Girl," and the wa-wa trumpets in "Uptown, Downtown." The dancers tended to find an empty corner and mark through the dances as they were being played. The general feeling was very upbeat indeed. Some songs, including "Losing My Mind," weren't yet finished.

Follies was the third Broadway musical for which Jonathan Tunick had sole orchestrator billing. The other two, *Promises, Promises* and *Company*, were contemporary stories with contemporary scores that relied, to differing degrees, on electronic instruments and modern percussion. *Promises, Promises* was the first Broadway show to use pit singers and a true sound-mixing board, necessitated by the style of Burt Bacharach's music. *Company's* orchestra was based around a Roxichord, a state-of-the-art synthesizer keyboard capable of a percussive and slightly rock-and-roll sound. *Follies,* by contrast, was a show for acoustical instruments, both for the distinctive references to styles from the past—what Steve called "pastiche"—as well as for the songs in the present, which were very much in Sondheim's own theatrical style. Jonathan's task was, therefore, somewhat different this time.

Following the sitzprobe, it was time for the entire company to move into the theater. Dressing rooms had been assigned by the stage managers, with great care, of course, since billing plays a key role in who gets which dressing room. Each theater is different, and while the setup is never the same, there are always star dressing rooms, though never the same number. At the Colonial, there were two at stage level, and they went to Dorothy and Alexis; all the others were up a central staircase leading to five floors, each of which had seven rooms, providing more than enough space, even for a company this large. The stage

managers took a room as an office on the topmost level. Below stage were two large rooms, one used for the chorus and another already commandeered by the wardrobe department.

The actors found their assigned dressing rooms, dropped off their belongings, found their way to the stage, and wandered around. Partly they were reconnecting with something known, but everyone had to become familiar with a variety of new traffic patterns—how to get from

Barbara Matera adjusts one of the ghost costumes for
"Who's That Woman?" Marti Rolph is in the costume,
and Hal Prince watches.

the dressing rooms to both sides of the stage, where the crossovers were, etc. Mary McCarty walked down to her "Who's That Woman?" perch, saw that it was, as she had feared, just inches from the fifteen-foot drop-off into the orchestra pit. She took a deep breath and sighed. Fifi D'Orsay was praying as she found her way out onto the stage, which seemed even more terrifying than it had been in the Bronx.

The call was 7:30 P.M. for a full costume dress parade, onstage. By then, all the finished costumes had been hung in the dressing rooms by the wardrobe staff, along with the accessories—shoes, hats, gloves, coats, handbags. Most actors had more than one outfit, and the idea was to see everyone in every outfit during the costume parade. Dressers were in place to assist the actors when necessary, and to make certain all the accessories were put on correctly. Wigs were also to be worn, and it was the first time many of them would be seen. Hal, Steve, Michael, and Jim were out in the house with Flossie and a couple of Barbara Matera's assistants armed with yellow pads. Barbara was down in the wardrobe room working on some of the late additions to the Loveland costumes. Every actor had had a minimum of three fittings at the shop in New York, so their clothes were not supposed to be a surprise to them. And some changes had already been made along the way, occasionally to suit an actor's specific concerns: Alexis's original outfit, for example, was sleeveless, but after she made it clear, with a smile, that she really didn't think Phyllis would come to an evening like this in something without sleeves, they were added. The bust on Yvonne's dress kept being changed in order to "get a good separation." But no one had seen anyone else's costume, and none of the actors had spent any appreciable time wearing their own. None, to be sure, had worn them through the staging and dancing, all of which, by necessity, was created long after the designs had been approved.

Before the glamorous costumes that everyone knew would come in Loveland at the end of the evening, came the party clothes. The party was a reunion, and the guests represented a variety of social and economic strata, which their clothes reflected. Only one couple was clearly well off, Ben and Phyllis, and they were dressed elegantly in royal colors—purples and reds. Many of the others may just have pulled an old dress from their closet, or made it themselves, or merely dressed as well as they could, given their circumstances, which were probably modest. The women now lived all over the country, so their sense of fashion would not be the high urban fashion of the day. Some

might be inspired to wear clothing that echoed, or relived, the past. The palette had been decided early on: present-day clothes were all going to be in colors—dark, bold, or subdued; the ghost figures would be in black and white; the Follies sequence would begin in pastels. But no one had seen what all the present-day colors were and how, or if, they were going to work together.

Mary McCarty was the first out onstage, in an aqua-blue, long-sleeved, unwaisted dress; it had half of a beaded brown sunburst emanating from her left hip and going up, down, and across her ample front. The hem was uneven and slightly ripped—by design. There was also some beading at the end of the sleeves. She wore a wide-brimmed hat of a matching color with a pillbox center and blue feathers lying flat around the brim. Beneath her hat she was wearing a carrot-colored Betty Boop wig. The look on her face was matched by the one on Hal and Michael's faces. Within a moment, the wig was gone, never to be seen again, and the hat would be worn only at the very beginning of the show. Yvonne's dress was knee-length, sheer dark purple over silver, with mink trim along the bottom of the skirt and six-inch mink tails hanging off her sleeves. Alexis's outfit was bright red, one-piece, fitted, backless, and looking rather like a pantsuit, beads carefully and discreetly stitched throughout to give it some texture, with sweeping strips of fabric drooping down her back from the neck to the small of the back. Dorothy's frumpy dress had a skirt with lots of petticoats; pink, sleeveless, and full of flowers, with a stiff bodice ending in two hard points at her bare shoulders. Ethel Shutta stalked out in a little-old-lady suit of metallic green. She was pulling and tugging at everything, hardly disguising her disgust. Fifi came out in a high-necked, long-sleeved, powder-blue dress; beaded, sequined, and with a skirt of puffy blue feathers, the impression it gave was that of a giant feather duster. Her hat was the same color, small and round, with two long, dyed peacock feathers jauntily stuck in one side. Sheila Smith wandered onstage in a dark rosy-red, very long, very full, floor-length bias-cut dress made out of heavy fabric, with a large red feathered hat similar to the one Mary McCarty wore. Her wig was enormous and shockingly blond. Sheila was fair-skinned with very dark hair and features, so this get-up struck everyone as highly peculiar. The costume really was so oversized that it was hard to find the actress underneath.

The men were in suits of slightly different styles and different colors—John McMartin's was stylish, eggplant-colored, and double-breasted, while Gene Nelson's was single-breasted, medium blue, and plain. Other guests were dressed in various shades of dark burgundy, brown, olive, and blue. Waiters were in almost black trousers and white shirts, waitresses in short dark skirts and white tops.

The Young Four (Young Ben, Buddy, Sally, and Phyllis), as per the concept, were dressed in whites and grays—and were wearing powdery white makeup. The clothes looked quite good, but the makeup made the actors look as if they were in a freak show. There was much discussion about trying the makeup in at least one performance. When Harvey and Kurt came on in two very large and very white overcoats, Hal remarked: "I don't ever want to see *those* coats on *that* stage again." The costumes for the ghost figures with specific modern counterparts had interesting references. Young Hattie, the Broadway Baby, for example, had a dress with piano keys across the bust. Young Vanessa, played by Graciela Daniele, had an all-white full floor-length dress with multiple underskirts. Young Heidi Schiller had a short ruffled skirt with a large black hat with long white feathers. Young Stella was dressed in a dancer's tutu that flared out from the waist, a diamond-patterned bodice, beaded headdress, and gauntlets—all covered with small mirror chips for "the mirror number." For the Prologue, several of the chorus girls wore identical black or white scanty but feathered costumes with strategically placed beaded patches.

And the wigs. For some reason, Joe Tubens, the wig and hair designer, seemed to have gone completely over the top. He had been to rehearsals several times to discuss hair with the actors and with Hal and Michael. Some actors, it was decided, would use their own hair, while others needed wigs. As the rehearsals progressed, Tubens had sent some of the actresses to have their hair dyed or cut. But what came out onstage during the dress parade seemed excessive on almost every count. Both Alexis and Dorothy were to have wigs for their numbers in the Follies sequence—for Alexis, cascades of long, dark red Rita Hayworth hair, falling on one side to the shoulder; for Dorothy, a wavy, platinum-blond Jean Harlow wig. Young Phyllis and Young Sally had enormous concoctions on top of their heads, white-blond for Sally and dark-brown for Phyllis. They seemed as plainly wrong as Mary McCarty's carrot-colored wig and the blond one for Sheila Smith. Most of the wigs were quickly cut or modified, but both Dorothy and

Dorothy Collins—first attempt at a costume and wig for "Losing My Mind." Jean Harlow.

Alexis Smith—first attempt at a costume and wig for "Uptown, Downtown." Rita Hayworth.

Alexis wore their Follies-sequence wigs in a run-through documented by Bill Yoscary and Martha Swope.

Then came the black-and-white ghost Follies dresses, to be worn by the showgirls and a few of the taller dancers throughout. They were as fantastic and spectacular as anyone could have hoped, each one a near replica of showgirl costumes as seen in photographs in several books on the Ziegfeld Follies, some Erté-like in long, glamorous lines and totally fanciful. Although black and white was the rule, each of these was vastly different in look, in texture, even including variations of shades of gray. They were covered with beads, feathers, sequins of all sizes and shapes—shimmery, iridescent, and stunning. Ursula Maschmeyer, six feet two inches tall, walked out to create what would be the first living image seen by the audience at the very opening of the show—in a floor-length dress of white and black beaded fabric with two bold inverted "V" stripes of long black beaded fringe, patterns of black and white beads in circles and rectangles around the bottom, and a large headdress of black ostrich feathers rising from a beaded crown, cascading down her back. She was wearing platform heels, so she would top off at almost seven feet. Kathie Dalton, one of the taller dancers, came on in a white halter top, floor-length, flared-leg costume with an elaborately beaded neck and a fan headdress of white peacock feathers six feet long each, fanning out of a beaded brim framing her face and giving her somewhat the appearance of the show's poster. Margot Travers was all in black—a tight fitting, floor-length beaded black halter-top dress, turban, long gloves, and feather boa draped around her shoulders, both ends falling to the floor. Linda Perkins had a huge fan attached to the rear of her waist rising up above her head. Suzanne Briggs had a black-and-white beaded dress with enormous butterfly wings and a headdress with butterfly antennae rising straight up. Everyone in the company was astounded and overwhelmed. The women who had to move in them, however, found them somewhat challenging.

When those same dancers and showgirls changed from their black-and-whites to their "Loveland" costumes, everyone was blown away once again. The six dresses were entirely in pastel colors, with the hoop skirts so large that they had to be attached just offstage before the girls made their entrances. Each dress was themed with the spirit of a different kind of love—First Love, Young Love, True Love, Pure Love, Romantic Love, and Eternal Love—each of which was referred

"Loveland"—three of the showgirls (Linda Perkins, "Spirit of Romantic Love";
Suzanne Briggs, "Spirit of True Love"; Kathie Dalton, "Spirit of First Love")
and behind them, Dorothy Collins, Victoria Mallory, Julie Pars.

to, variously, in the song. Appropriate props were attached to each hoop skirt—cherubs, celestial instruments, violets, hearts, birds, and jewels. The skirts were open in the front, so that you could see beautiful legs underneath. The rest of the chorus were in eighteenth-century maiden and lad outfits, also pastel-colored, with large white shoes and hats with white wigs attached. They looked like something out of a Fragonard painting.

The costumes for the rest of the Follies sequence were paraded as well. Young Ben had an electric-blue sailor suit with cap and Young Buddy a bright-orange tailored military suit and hat. Gene Nelson came out in a bright-blue blazer and outrageously loud yellow-and-blue-plaid trousers. For "Live, Laugh, Love," John McMartin was dressed head to toe in white—tailcoat, trousers, bow tie, and top hat. Dorothy had a yellow bias-cut, floor-length dress with a low-cut, inelegantly draped front. Alexis had a pink, form-fitting bathing-suit top

with spaghetti straps, and, hanging from her waist, two-inch-wide, foot-long straps ending in little points. The front of her costume had what looked like a Christmas tree in sequins sewn on, and there were beads down the straps. For "Uptown, Downtown" and "Live, Laugh, Love" the chorus had bright-red outfits: red tailcoats, red pants, red top hats, and red shoes for the former, while for the latter the women stripped down to red hot pants and white vests and bow ties.

All in all, the costumes pleased. And the brilliant ones were so brilliant that worries about the ones that might not work were squelched for the moment. Of course, there were many slight adjustments to be made and some normal fitting problems to attend to, but for the most part the creative staff seemed more than satisfied.

Now it was time to put the entire show together.

7

"Everybody Has to Go Through Stages Like That"

FOUR FULL DAYS, THE TECHNICAL REHEARSALS,
FEBRUARY 17–20

ollowing the costume parade came the first technical rehearsal. Starting at the very top of the show, everything is worked through in sequence, with scenery, lights, costumes, props, and sound. No orchestra at this point—to have twenty-seven more people being paid to wait around while everything else is coordinated is unnecessary. They'll come in tomorrow, after the show has been stumbled through at least once. For now, the rehearsal piano will do fine, and it is rolled down one of the aisles of the theater. Phil Fradkin sits at the keyboard. For the dancers, Paul Gemignani sits in the pit, alone with his drums, ready to play along.

In comes the house curtain, and on go the house lights. The ragtag group of spectators out in the house remains the same: Hal, Ruthie, Michael, Steve, Jim, Bob, Boris, Tharon, and a few others. They scatter around, flopping down in whatever seat strikes their momentary fancy, but in predictable groupings—Hal and Ruthie, Michael and Bob, Steve alone. Tharon is still at her desk dead center, with assistants nearby. Fritz Holt is standing at his stage manager's desk backstage, immediately off stage right. He's wearing a headset and is in communication with all departments. George Martin is in charge of stage left. He has a headset as well. John Grigas is now in costume, doubling in his onstage role of chauffeur. He'll figure out how to balance his stage-

147

A conference in the Colonial Theatre: Hal, Michael, and Steve.

managing duties with his acting responsibilities once the show is running. Now he's on old-lady duty, keeping an eye out for Fifi, Ethel, and anyone else in need of a friendly arm. The onstage band members are, for all intents and purposes, actors: they're backstage, and they need to be ready to make a proper entrance on the proper cue. Hal Hastings takes his conductor's position at the podium in the pit, but until the cue is given to begin, he faces the auditorium, arms on the railing.

Voices seem to be coming from everywhere, some of them loud and from backstage. Fritz tries to get everyone quiet so the rehearsal can begin. He wanders out onstage in front of the curtain to make certain Hal, Michael, and the rest of the gang out in the house are ready. It's getting late—the costume parade has taken up the better part of two hours. There is no way the whole show can be run tonight, but it's important to begin.

"Places" is called. There is an eerie silence in the house, then the lights begin to dim. In the darkness, low notes come from the piano, sounding like a drumroll. The curtain rises and we see a tall showgirl at stage right on an upper platform, standing completely still. The lighting flashes, almost like strobe lights, then establishes a moody dark-

ness, yet there are enough stray shafts of light for us to see everything we need to see. Slowly, the showgirl turns her head and starts to move. From out of the shadows, other ghosts begin to move—slowly, eerily. The Prologue begins, and immediately the prerecorded segments are late. Everything stops. Fritz Holt comes out onstage from his backstage perch. Michael hops up onstage and adjusts the entrances slightly, and asks Fritz to get the cues coordinated. He wants both Hal Hastings and the sound man, Jack Mann, to understand what he's after. What will it take to get it right? Every question has to be answered, and some answers take time. It's slow going. Although each element is familiar, putting them all together is new. For the actors, wearing the costume is new, walking out onto a darkened stage is new, feeling lights in their faces while they go through the staging is new. Spacing the people is a challenge. Entrances and exits are confusing—in the dark the side towers and units are less distinguishable than they are in bright light. Maintaining equilibrium is a challenge. And the hour is getting late.

"Beautiful Girls" is a shambles. No one is comfortable with the entrances down the rubble/staircase, and almost every woman now has a floor-length gown. They can't see their feet—will they need to hike up their skirts to land on that first step? Are there things on the staircase that will catch the hem of the skirts? Is there enough of a railing to hold on to? By the time they hit the stage level to do the Miss America glide there won't be anything to hold. Even the timing of getting from backstage up the escape stairs to the top level of the tower and walking across behind the stage band to get ready for the individual poses at the top of the stair is tricky. The older women are in a panic; the younger ones are simply having their patience tested. Michael and Bob come right down to the front row of the theater, lean against the orchestra rail, and offer helpful suggestions. When that isn't enough, they jump up onstage and walk the women through their paces, slowly and carefully. When everyone finally gets down to stage level, walks around, and lines up behind Michael Bartlett in a Rockettes-like stance, it's clear that the stage picture will be wonderful. A more motley assortment of shapes, colors, styles, and ages would be hard to imagine. Each woman wears a gold banner off one shoulder proclaiming the year of her Follies. If this lineup doesn't convey who the people of *Follies* are, I doubt that anything will. When this gets pulled together, the moment will be golden.

The tech gets to "Ah, Paris!" and Fifi D'Orsay is in a complete panic. She is frazzled by where she is supposed to enter—she thinks her spot has been changed. She can't hear the piano accompaniment. The heels on her shoes are too big. She can't see the end of the platform. She flubs the lyrics. Hal Hastings, now standing at his perch at the podium, facing the stage and only a few feet away from her, treats her with kid gloves. He is standing where he will be standing from this moment onward, ever patient, there to help. He stops the piano, gets Fifi's attention, and assures her that he's here to make her comfortable, that she should just take a deep breath, get her bearings, look around, and see what the stage looks and feels like, and then move on.

But by now it's time to stop. It's eleven o'clock. Hal Prince comes down to the front of the stage, thanks everyone for a good day's work, and tells them to go home and get some sleep.

Hal had been remarkably quiet throughout the day. During tech rehearsals the boss is the production stage manager, since he's the one who has to coordinate everything behind the curtain. The producer can only sit and fret about how much everything is costing, and the rumor now going around is that Hal is personally covering any overages above the original budget. Every time some costume needs to be fixed or changed, and every time there's a problem with the set, it hurts the exchequer. And all the director can hang on to is the hope that his staging will work as well on the stage as it did in rehearsals. So Hal wasn't especially happy. Neither was Steve Sondheim. Jim Goldman remained very quiet, sometimes just standing at the rear of the auditorium, hugging one of the marble columns at the top of the aisles. This part is agonizing—so near, yet seemingly so far.

The subject of amplification in the musical theater is something about which everyone has an opinion. A strong opinion. It is a complex subject that has as much to do with the design of modern theaters and the placement of the orchestra as it does with manner of staging, style of performance, and sophistication of scenic design. There is a general feeling of nostalgia for the time before microphones, but really that takes us back before 1938, when the first microphones were used in a Broadway musical. Their use over the next decades was modest, mostly with foot mikes across the front of the stage. Modern audi-

Michael, Hal, and Ruthie conferring in the
Colonial Theatre's auditorium.

ences, whether they realize it or not, have grown accustomed to a more naturalistic style of performance in which actors can face each other in scenes as easily as they can face front, all the while being heard with clarity. In the days before microphones, actors with big voices got the parts, and they tended to come down front and sing straight out. The sets, when designed in "box" format, acted like scenic megaphones; but as sets became more impressionistic and sculptural, more open, they gave no help to the sound. In *Follies*, microphones were used, mainly across the front of the stage, on the floor. There were other microphones hidden within the set, often shotgun style, aimed at a specific area from a fair distance away. These were most useful when a song was sung by one person remaining in one place all the way through.

Although a body mike was first used on Broadway by Anna Maria Alberghetti in *Carnival* in 1961, using them with regularity was still a few years away.

Thursday began with a recording session, of sorts. Jack Mann, Hal Prince's chief sound man, had been a fairly invisible member of the team up to this point. He had been to a couple of the New York run-throughs, and had quietly made his notes. Earnest and humorless, he took his job very seriously and would say anything he wanted to anyone, often getting himself into trouble if he spoke too harshly to Steve, Hal, or Michael. He knew the sound needs of the show, and took over one of the boxes on the orchestra level of the theater, setting up his sound board and mixing equipment behind a makeshift black curtain, in such a way that he would be able to see the stage without the audience seeing him. The cables running in from the microphones and out to the speakers—there were mikes in the orchestra pit as well as onstage—were snaked into the box as subtly as possible, along the floor and over the railing.

Jack replugged the stage mikes and shifted dials in order to turn his makeshift sound booth into a recording studio. The reasoning behind the exercise was this: by the end of the big dance numbers, everyone will be winded. To prerecord these same people singing what they'll be singing onstage and to play the tape along with the live performers will allow the audience to hear the song clearly and take a little of the onus off the dancers. And no one will need to know it's happening. The biggest challenge was tempo: without actually singing the song and doing the dance, it's only a guess what the tempo will be. The cast assembled on the front of the stage and sang into the foot mikes. Two sections were recorded: the end of "Who's That Woman?" and, more for diction than for windedness, "Loveland." Hal Hastings made a best guess at the tempo for both, and counted off. Once recorded, the tapes were played back for the company to hear. Jack had made "Loveland" slightly celestial by adding some echo and reverb, as befitting the fantasy world of the song. The company was amused. (When Actors' Equity got wind of this, they slapped Hal with a bill for a week's salary for everyone whose voice was used on the tape.)

The other sound challenge was the tap dancing. If an audience sees tap dancing, it needs to hear tap dancing. Tap shoes, however, can be treacherous: the little metal pieces on the toes and heels make them awfully slippery. Cheater taps—two-piece metal tips for shoes that

make a loud tap sound—are even worse. And there were no flat floors on the *Follies* set. Gene Nelson damn near killed himself doing "The Right Girl" in tap shoes on the set in the Bronx, so it had been decided that no one would wear tap shoes during any of the tap choruses in the show. Jack Mann rigged up a microphone off stage left pointing down to a piece of Masonite. For "Who's That Woman?" George Martin and two other dancers would put on tap shoes, watch the stage, and dance the rhythm of every routine along with the dancers—but in place and on the Masonite board. The audience would see tap dancing and hear tap shoes and would assume they were coming from the same place.

The technical rehearsal continued, beginning where it ended the night before, still very much in stop-and-start mode. Many light cues were written and adjusted as the rehearsal proceeded. The actors who were confident and consistent had little problem adjusting to the stage. Those who had already taken up a lot of everyone's time continued to do so. When it got to "Who's That Woman?" the offstage tapping and the prerecorded "sweetening" were added for the first time. Nothing matched. The singing tape was much too slow, and the taps weren't remotely coordinated. In addition, during the costume parade, the chorus girls playing the ghost counterparts had complained that the mirror chips on their gauntlets were cutting into their skin, so now they were dancing in only partial costumes. Once they began their chorus, it was discovered that mirror chips on the skirts were also cutting into their arms. One by one the women just stopped dancing, and after Hal Hastings caught on to what was happening, he stopped everything while the girls went to change out of their costumes. The skirts were sent downstairs to Barbara Matera's makeshift shop to join the gauntlets, which were being sheathed in clear plastic.

Yvonne ad-libbed a line before "Can That Boy Fox Trot!" After "I had a number once all my own . . . a college number," she tossed off: "See, it's funny already," as she realized how preposterous it was for her even to mention college. Everyone laughed. It was a keeper; it stayed in the script. There was fussing about whether she should crash the cymbal of the onstage band to get everyone's attention at the top of the song, or whether it would be better for the onstage percussionist to do it. Everyone agreed: let the pro handle the drum.

Tharon was playing around with lights during "Could I Leave You?" Suddenly a blue wash came from stage left, and then a white

pin-spot backlight found John McMartin standing to one side. The two follow spots focused tighter and tighter on Alexis while she sat on the downstage corner of the second platform, delivering the song. She carried on, with an occasional look around, decidedly out of character, curious about what was going on.

Alexis finished the song, stood up, and continued with the dialogue as the others began to enter for the transition into "Loveland" and the Follies sequence. This had never been done before with the actual scenery and drops, so Fritz came out onstage and said, "Hold everything, please." He warned everyone to keep an eye on what was about to happen, explaining that the Follies drops would fly in, one at a time, and cautioned the company not to get hit by them as they flew in, and to mark through the transition carefully. No one, in fact, except the stage crew and designers had even seen the drops in the theater, as they had been the first pieces of scenery loaded in. Flying pieces are always hung before the floor is laid down, and this was especially necessary for *Follies* because the set was so complicated—who would want to carry a

Hal, Lisa and Boris Aronson, Ruthie.

large, rolled-up drop out onto a stage made up of so many levels? Also, because the Follies drops were so bright, they were hung as high as possible in order for them not to be seen during the rest of the show. The gray pieces of hanging flotsam were purposely designed to hang low enough to block out any hint of color above.

Fritz called for the scene to start again, and the actors picked up where they left off. The four principals continued, confronting each other and their younger selves, and the piano began playing "Loveland." Everyone onstage looked up, and one by one, from far upstage to downstage, the drops came in. First was a fan, then the oversized doilies, then, farthest downstage, a rich, silky, velvet-looking curtain, sky-blue and white, different in color and texture from all the others, which tabbed up as it flew in. As the dancers entered, they looked up to make certain the staging they had learned put them out of the way of what was coming at them from above. The company came sneaking out of the wings to gasp and applaud. Hal and Michael both nodded in approval. Fritz was proud of having pulled off the complicated transition. Steve Sondheim, standing in the auditorium, turned and said, "Not bad, Boris." Boris smiled. The drops filled about two-thirds of the width of the stage; there was no masking on the sides, allowing the side units to be seen lurking in the shadows. It worked brilliantly. Michael went over to Fritz to discuss the speed at which the drops should fly in. He felt they had all come in too slowly, and wanted to make certain they could be timed precisely, to fly in one after the other in perfect sequence, as if they were methodically taking over the entire place. He also wanted to synchronize the appearance of the two semicircular stair units from under the platform, although he didn't want their appearance to be noticed.

This was a difficult and important transition, so it was repeated several times. After five passes, it finally all came together: drumroll, fanfare, staircases, drops in, one at a time, coming to a stop right as the vamp began, tape synchronized with the onstage singing, chorus of pastel Dresden figures in position, and the showgirls ready to make their entrances. "No matter what audiences may feel about *Follies*, these Follies drops coming in is already one of the rare, glorious moments in the theater"—that's what I wrote in my notebook.

The hope was to finish the tech rehearsal in the afternoon and do a full dress rehearsal in the evening, with orchestra. But time ran out after "Love Will See Us Through" and "You're Gonna Love Tomor-

Marti Rolph and Harvey Evans, performing
"Love Will See Us Through."

row." As a result, the first portion of the evening rehearsal was used to get through the Follies sequence, into the chaos, out of it, and to the very end of the show. The tab curtain closed before "Buddy's Blues," then opened only slightly for "Losing My Mind" to reveal Sally standing in her slinky gown in a small opening only slightly larger than she was. The chorus was dressed in its reds for both "Uptown, Downtown" and "Live, Laugh, Love," but it was quickly discovered that the red translucent canes used in "Live, Laugh, Love" were rubbing off on the white vests. The rehearsal was stopped instantly, the canes disposed of, and the few vests that had already been stained were taken off and sent down to Barbara Matera's underworld.

One fascinating element of tech rehearsals for an outsider is that you get to see the actors both as the characters they portray in the show and as themselves. Whenever the rehearsal is stopped, usually to address some technical issue, the actors simply hang around while the problem gets solved. Sometimes they just stand there, caught up in their own world. Sometimes they wander over to other actors and

crack jokes. Sometimes they find a convenient place to perch. They may steal a moment to look at something on the stage that they don't get to see when the show is run. To someone smitten with the whole process of putting theater together, seeing the actors in these unguarded, spontaneous moments is both revealing and fun.

The more the actors became familiar with the backstage traffic patterns and how to get to where they were needed, the more they tended to sneak out into the auditorium through the pass door to watch other parts of the show. Actually, individual actors seeing the show they are in is something that happens only during these rehearsals. As soon as paying customers fill the seats, the actors have to stay backstage, either in their dressing rooms or in whatever areas become social gathering places during performances. Many will never again have any reason to go out into the house unless they're part of understudy rehearsals. They will arrive through the stage door, go to their dressing rooms, do the performance, go back to their dressing rooms, and go home. Technical rehearsals and dress rehearsals, when the whole theater belongs to the production, are really the last times the cast can watch each other work, look at the scenery and lighting from out front, and get a sense of what the audience will see. It's a very familial feeling. (Mary Jane Houdina took a week's vacation from the show during its New York run and decided to come by and watch a performance from out front. She was so impressed she urged her fellow company members to do likewise.) Of course, there are some hazards involved. First, the costume department gets frantic at the idea of actors sitting around in their costumes. Second, the actors have to be in position when they're needed onstage, and sometimes that is hard to judge. Just when they assume a scene is sure to be stopped, things will be going swimmingly, and then you see them racing down the side aisles to make an entrance they almost forgot about.

Finally, the first dress rehearsal began at 10:15. Back to the top, but now for the first time, instead of the piano the orchestra was in the pit. That was yet another exciting step, one more indication of completion. Since the orchestra was miked, the sound was out of balance from the start. Some sequences were still not yet orchestrated, so the piano simply filled in. Many of the usual mistakes were made, and by the usual suspects. In "Beautiful Girls," Michael Bartlett outdid him-

self with some entirely new words ending in "-able"—"nothing reflec-table half so injectable . . ." One exit for Phyllis and Ben was now obscured by Suzanne in her butterfly costume, which proved much larger than anyone had expected. Hal, who had been uncharacteristi-cally quiet, bounded up onstage to fix the moment. He moved Alexis and John around, then took off his glasses, put them on top of his head, looked out into the darkened auditorium and said, "Michael, I don't know what to do here." Michael joined him onstage, and came up with two good solutions right away.

In a line that has to do with asking for Ben's autograph, Hattie snaps out the name of her grandson—Jerome. "It's a perfectly good-sounding name," Hal said, "so please don't play it like you hate it. Besides, we sell a lot of tickets to people named Jerome!" The place-ment of the onstage band's piano had again become a problem, and attempts were made to get it positioned correctly. There were sight-line problems in "Waiting for the Girls Upstairs" that were adjusted easily. Then came Fifi's entrance for the Montage. She had previously been in an acute nervous state over it, and tonight was no different. The rosaries were now her constant companion. Not only was she a bundle of nerves, but word got around that she had had her agent call Hal to say that she would quit if she didn't get billing equal to Yvonne's, that she had demanded changes be made to her hat—that she was generally unhappy with everything. She came out onstage looking terrified. The Whitmans and Hattie were onstage, having fin-ished "Rain on the Roof" and "Broadway Baby." The orchestra played Fifi's vamp, and she sputtered, not sure of her words. She finally did get into the song, but in the second verse became flustered. "Oh, please forgive me, I don't know what to do. I'm so sorry." Hal Hastings stopped the orchestra. Here we were, ground to a halt at exactly the same spot as the night before. There was a moment of utter silence that felt endless. Every element of the show was poised—orchestra, company, scenery, lighting, costumes—and no one was sure what was going to happen next or exactly what to do. "Oh, forgive me," she mut-tered. Then a familiar voice came booming out from the auditorium: "Nobody needs to be forgiven. I know what to do. It's twelve midnight, let's all go home and get some rest." Walking down to the front of the stage, Hal repeated, "Just go home, get some rest. And, Fifi, come back tomorrow a changed girl." Fritz called for everyone to knock off, and

in a moment the work lights came on and the company wandered off to change.

Hal Hastings thanked the orchestra, gave them their call for the next day, then crawled over the railing and walked up to where Hal, Michael, Steve, and Jim were in a huddle. Once all actors had cleared the stage, Hal Prince turned to his group and said, "That was my best George Abbott imitation." "I know," said Hal Hastings, "I recognized it. But let's not forget that it's going to be tender for a while with Fifi. I think she'll pull through. She was terrified, and these rehearsals *are* for actors to get over their fears." Sometimes it was good for everyone to hear from the musical director, since he is the one who will be in constant contact with the company when the show is in performance.

There was a concern about one of the side units on stage left. Dorothy made an entrance sitting on this unit while it moved downstage, and she didn't feel she had a secure enough perch within the rubble. So Hal Prince decided to take a ride on it himself. After being winched downstage, he said, "Let's fix this piece of rubble so a human being can sit on it, please."

Friday afternoon saw the completion of the dress rehearsal, beginning where things had left off Thursday night. Because "Ah, Paris!" was where things broke down, that is where the rehearsal was to pick up. Ethel Shutta, standing in the costume she hated, but to which she was fast becoming resigned, was in place in the wings. She had no patience for Fifi's antics. She turned to me and said, "If that French bitch screws up once more, I'm going to go out there and sing 'Broadway Baby' in French!" This time Fifi got herself onstage where she belonged, sang her song, and seemed a little calmer and somewhat contrite.

Yvonne was now getting through all of "Can That Boy Fox Trot!" without messing up the words too much. Gene Nelson was mastering most of the words and all of the movements to "The Right Girl." The transition into Loveland went smoothly. The showgirls were allowed to do this run-through wearing only the headdress part of their costumes, and two walked out in blue jeans, one in green pants, two in black leotards, and one with nothing but a pink towel wrapped around her middle. Turns out that the last one hadn't gotten the headdresses-

only message and this was the way she would emerge from her dressing room before having the large skirt lowered on to her. More costumes were completed: the Follies dresses for Young Phyllis and Young Sally were bright and cheerful, with full, mid-length skirts with hints of the electric blue and bright orange of Young Buddy and Young Ben's suits. Heidi Schiller's costume was completed—white, beaded, and decidedly Germanic. She looked a little like a German drag act.

The chaos scene at the end was starting to come together. It was bold and complicated, beginning with the disintegration of "Live, Laugh, Love" into a visual and audio nightmare. John McMartin was almost scary at how well he played a man losing his grip, and it was chilling to hear Hal Hastings throw him a lyric. The orchestration hadn't been completed, but Hal was able to maintain order and tempo throughout. Then, as bits and pieces of the Follies scenery began to fly away, other characters were revealed standing at different spots around the set, each doing his or her own character thing. It was positively macabre, but it seemed to be working. At a designated moment, Ben cried out for Phyllis. That was the cue for the chaos to end. Once again, Fritz Holt stopped the proceedings to ensure that everyone knew how to exit safely. This was a very tricky sequence, since the company was perched on all available areas around the set and had to make their way off with care. Fritz was concerned that it be worked through precisely. Once the cacophony faded away, the lights went out, everyone exited, and the four principals were revealed standing on an empty stage in their initial party clothes. As with all the complicated traffic patterns, it took a couple of passes for everyone to straighten out who was to go where, but the company was getting accustomed to these moments. And the stage managers were always ready with a helping hand, a flashlight, and an encouraging and sympathetic word. This time, the actors couldn't go back to their dressing rooms, since the curtain call, not yet staged, would follow after the brief final scene. Once the lights came up on the last scene, the only difference to the set—and it was subtle—was that a street could now be seen through the upstage center panel. The night was over and the new day had arrived. But seeing daylight coming through also revealed that part of the wall of the theater had in fact already been torn down—something that was never made clear until that moment. And thanks to a curved element in the architectural detail, it looked as if the first thing that had been torn down was the theater's marquee.

This is where it all began, the famous shot of Gloria Swanson standing in the rubble of the Roxy Theater, as published in Life *with the caption: "Swan Song for a Famous Theater."*

TIME

That Old Magic Relights Broadway

Alexis Smith in "Follies"

Both Time *and* Newsweek *were planning to do cover stories of the show. However, they never liked to run the same "soft"-news covers, so when* Time *went forward with theirs,* Newsweek *canceled, but not before this cover was designed.*

Newsweek

Alexis Smith in
Hal Prince's 'Follies'

Here is the poster by David E. Byrd, this one from Boston and signed by the company. And here's what Forbes *did to it for an article on Hal Prince.*

Color finally arrived when the show was transported back in time. Here are the ghost counterparts to the four lead characters, singing of youthful love in Loveland. Kurt Peterson, Virginia Sandifur, Harvey Evans, Marti Rolph. Below: The showgirls from the past come fully to life with their "love"-themed costumes, each one depicting a different type of love.

The cool Phyllis finally lets down her hair and struts her stuff:
Alexis Smith and the ensemble in "The Story of Lucy and Jessie"—
red from one side of the stage to the other.

This was taken on the grand staircase of the Colonial Theatre, Boston, for the
Look *article on Hal Prince, which ran with the title "A Prince and His Follies."*
Here Prince is surrounded by several of the ghost showgirls, dressed in
black-and-white, who haunted the stage throughout the evening .

The final moment of "Beautiful Girls," as the stars from yesterday lined up downstage, with gold Miss America–style banners revealing the year they were Follies girls: Mary McCarty, Fifi D'Orsay, Alexis Smith, Yvonne De Carlo.

This was taken as the cover shot for Time. *The editors decided to go with a solo shot of Alexis Smith, and relegated this shot to the lead photograph of the story inside.*

After only a short break, Hal wanted another complete run-through without costumes before dinner. This went fairly smoothly, with some portions even beginning to look confident. It finished by the end of the afternoon.

There was to be a complete dress rehearsal after dinner with costumes and orchestra. This was Friday, twenty-four hours away from the first paying audience. A few New Yorkers had arrived to rejoin the family—Judy Prince and John Guare, several of the New York–based staff, like press agent Mary Bryant, with Louis Botto and Bill Yoscary from *Look* magazine in tow, general manager Carl Fisher with his wife, Joan, and others. The cast was energized at the prospect of performing for even a small and familiar audience. Hal wanted to show his friends and colleagues how much had been accomplished. It was also actually a clever way of preparing for what was coming. Confidence was building, but the show was still not technically smooth. Those who appreciated how bold in concept it was were slightly apprehensive about what Saturday night would be like. How the audience would react was anyone's guess, so letting the company play the show first for a theater-savvy "sort-of" audience who wouldn't be shocked by a technical glitch here or there was a smart notion.

Larry Cohen was also up from New York, and he and I went to dinner together, sharing stories and gossip. He told me that Weismann's first speech was being questioned—it needed to be clearer and more focused. There was concern that the setup of the young characters versus the older characters needed to be better established early on. A question had been raised as to whether having the showgirl ghost figures without present-day counterparts would confuse the audience. Were they just part of the scenery? Were they specific people from the past? Are they actually at the party? The question had been raised about why Ben and Buddy, neither of whom was ever a performer in the Follies, had songs in the Follies sequence. Everyone seemed to agree, however, that the set was brilliant, that although it was vast and complex, it was still able to isolate characters when they needed to be isolated. The jury was out on the costumes, especially the modern-dress ones. At least that is what had filtered back to Larry from Michael, with whom he had stayed in touch during the week.

The orchestra had been called before the rehearsal in order to go

over some late-arriving orchestrations from Mathilde's music-copying department. One was "Losing My Mind," which had been left for last. Of course, very little in the way of staging was required for the song; it was just one person making some subtle movements. Dorothy squatted down on the front of the stage and looked into the pit as Hal Hastings played through the song with the orchestra. Mathilde and Jonathan stood in the front row at the orchestra rail, scores in hand, listening. Dorothy beamed all the way through. Hal suggested they do it again with Dorothy standing in the approximate position where she would be. She quickly walked upstage and marked through her singing while the orchestra played it again. She was giggly with delight and afterward came back down to the front of the stage to thank everyone in the orchestra. Jonathan stood smiling, more than willing to accept the compliment. Then the orchestra played through the chaos, which was now fully orchestrated. Since it was meant to be chaos, there was a general sense of bemused excitement. It seemed noisy enough to everyone. Jonathan Tunick gave his characteristic shrug, as if to say, "Okay with me. Okay with you?"

The dress rehearsal went fine. In fact, it was really beginning to feel like a show. The actors were ever more confident, the scenic changes were getting smoother with the units hitting their marks with greater ease; the light cues were also getting smoother. Each time the show was run, it got more fluid. There was a certain giddy nervousness arising at the prospect of playing for the first real audience. What will they think? At this point, no one knows, and emotions run the gamut. They'll love us; they'll hate us. They'll be dazzled; they'll be bored. I'll win a Tony; I'll be fired. My song will stop the show; mine is the song they're going to replace. I'm the best thing in the show; I'm the only one who isn't any good. My career will take off; I'll never get another job. But there was one thing everyone knew: it was time for some honest-to-God audience reaction. And as a group, the audience doesn't lie; their reactions are genuine. Will they get the marvel of "Who's That Woman?" Will they make the connection between the lead characters and their Follies songs? Even the company-pleasers, like "Broadway Baby," aren't necessarily the things a paying audience will respond to.

When the rehearsal was over, a five-minute break was called. Little

groups huddled around the auditorium in different places. What were they saying? Hal, Judy, John Guare, and Steve made up one group on the stage-left side, talking softly enough that no one could make out what they were saying. Ruthie had been excluded, so she was pacing nearby. Flossie and Joe Tubens were huddled in another corner. Michael and Bob Avian were sitting calmly. Tharon was at her desk, resolutely going over notes with her assistants. The stage managers had come out into the house, but they were keeping a safe distance. Clearly, the five minutes were going to be filled by these little huddles, and when the curtain came up and the cast began assembling onstage for notes, they, too, congregated in small groupings—Harvey Evans with Marti Rolph, Michael Misita and Mary Jane Houdina wrapped in each other's arms.

The notes to the company were brief and simple. It was clear that energy needed to be preserved for Saturday, because there would be a complete, full dress rehearsal with orchestra, costumes, hair—everything—starting at noon. Then there would be a lengthy break before half-hour call for the first preview at 7:30. Hal simply said that he'd have a few notes before the run-through, and we'd stage a curtain call before the run as well. Then he wished everyone a good night's sleep.

Heading into Child's restaurant on Saturday morning for breakfast, I ran into Fred Kelly sitting alone at a booth and asked if I could join him. As I sat down, he asked how my journal was going. He taught theater in New York, he said, and would be very interested to see what I came up with when I was finished. I made a couple of overall comments about what an interesting experience I was having, and then, before I said anything about the show itself, he leaned over the table. "You know," he said, "nothing unusual has yet happened on this show." I couldn't believe my ears. My first thoughts were instantly defensive: "Are you crazy? Don't you get how amazing this show is? Has anyone ever assembled these wonderful old-timers together with such a gifted group of young performers? Can't you feel the tension between Hal and Michael? Don't you realize that Steve Sondheim is the most interesting writer of musicals to come down the pike in years? Can't you see what's being created here?" But I said nothing. Maybe he was right. Maybe this was the norm. Maybe by the very nature of the beast, the norm in the theater is indeed the kind of creative and emotional

mosaic that I had been observing. Each specific situation may be different, but is it always the same? To be truthful, I wasn't impressed by Fred Kelly onstage; he wasn't a particularly memorable performer and hadn't been given much of anything to do. He had a great name, but I really couldn't figure why he'd been hired, or even why he would want to be part of the company. And yet on the couple of occasions when he and I chatted, he was highly articulate, with a very distinct point of view. I left breakfast wondering whether maybe I was too caught up in everything to have any perspective. Maybe the show was more ordinary than I thought.

At noon, Hal and Michael staged a curtain call. Curtain calls rarely get attended to until the last moment, partly out of superstition and partly for lack of time. Choreographers and directors prefer to work on the show itself rather than on the portion of the evening where the cast gets congratulated. Since the curtain call for *Company* was brilliantly staged, I wondered if *Follies* would get a similarly clever treatment. For *Company*, the call was almost entirely choreographed, and at one point the entire company danced downstage so far that the curtain came in behind them. All of Bobby's friends took the call, leaving him alienated, behind the curtain. This clearly wasn't the moment when *Follies* was going to get a fully choreographed set of curtain calls. For now, the call was staged strictly according to the billing. After the ensemble, out came, in order, Ethel Shutta, Mary McCarty, Fifi D'Orsay, Yvonne De Carlo, John McMartin, Dorothy Collins, Gene Nelson, and Alexis Smith. The company walked through the blocking, rather businesslike, Bob Avian and a couple of others providing a sense of the applause that would greet them. In fact, *Follies* never did get a carefully conceived curtain call. The music was adjusted to reflect each actor, but that was it.

Then there was the final full dress run-through, with the works—costumes, orchestra, sound, hair, makeup, and lights. Still no audience—just us hangers-on. Things progressed nicely until "Don't Look at Me." At one tricky rhythm pattern, John McMartin got slightly behind, which then threw Dorothy off. Hal Hastings stopped the orchestra and said: "No, no, you keep doing that. You get so far behind, and by the end you get later and later." He told the orchestra to go back to a certain bar number and start again. It was just as bad. The pressure was on. These were two pros and this was a piece of music they had been performing over and over; there was no good rea-

son for them to be flubbing it. The tension was palpable. Hal asked if John and Dorothy could hear the orchestra. They tried again, this time with Hal singing along. It didn't help. Steve walked down to the front row. He was the calming influence that was needed. He stood quietly behind Hal Hastings and said to John: "In the first part, after Dorothy sings 'fat,' take two breaths, then sing 'turning gray.' At the end, listen to Dorothy and copy her rhythm *exactly*." He remained standing there as Hal Hastings re-cued the orchestra. This time the song was performed as written. Steve knew the problem was John's and knew what to say to solve it. Later he told me that Dorothy devised ways of squeezing whatever part of John's body was close by as a cue for him to begin his part.

After the Montage, one of the winches on stage left came to a grinding halt. Pete Feller and two stagehands came out onstage and pushed the unit back into position. "God," everyone thought, "what happens tonight if it gets stuck like that? We can't have stagehands walk out in the middle of a performance, let alone the man who owns the scenic studio." Aside from that, the rest of the run-through went smoothly.

Once the curtain came in at the end, the cast remained onstage, still in costume, for brief notes. Fritz gave the cue for the curtain to be raised, and Hal came up onstage to give a pep talk. "I know we haven't said this to you yet, but this is a slightly odd show. None of us can predict what the audience will think tonight. There will be laughs where none of us expect them, and there'll be many times where we thought big laughs would come when there will be none. Also, in the Prologue we can't tell who will get a hand and who won't, so keep the timing we've set and keep going through the applause. So everyone do your best, and we love you all." Michael chimed in with a good luck as well. The cast dispersed to their dressing rooms. The audience would soon be upon us.

8

"That's What You've Been Waiting For"

PREVIEWS THROUGH TO OPENING, FEBRUARY 20–24

Playbills had been delivered to the theater. For the Saturday night performance they would have to be stuffed with a purple insert from the organization that had chosen the date for a benefit. It began with a letter from Omar T. Pace, president of the Massachusetts Division of the American Cancer Society:

> *Dear Friends of the American Cancer Society:*
> *I want to wish you a very pleasant evening as we enjoy this production of "The Follies"* . . .

"The Follies." Well, I don't think so. In fact, Hal Prince had long been concerned about people thinking they would be coming to a Follies. That was one of the reasons he liked that crack in the austere face on the poster so much. He never wanted the show to be referred to as "The Follies" or "Hal Prince's Follies," but here it was, and at the first public performance, no less.

I doubt whether the 325 sponsors listed in the insert, including Senator and Mrs. Edward M. Kennedy, had a clue that as the first paying audience to see *Follies* they were about to become theatrical guinea pigs. Certainly if the head of the organization promised they were all in for a very pleasant evening at "The Follies," he didn't have a clue.

What would this crowd make of what they were about to see? If they were expecting Ziegfeld, they were in for a disappointment. (While the Cancer Society's party made up nearly the entire audience, there were a few normal patrons who got the insert as well.)

I had a gossipy dinner at the Union Oyster House with, among others, Hal Hastings. I took a ribbing about the women in the company who seemed to have taken a shine to me—in particular, the camp movie star (Yvonne) and the oldest member of the company (Ethel). There were jokes at Hal's expense about his acting moments in the show. Originally, the entire orchestra was to rise from the pit for the song "Loveland," Radio City Music Hall–style. For that to occur, an entire floor would have had to be built and mechanized, with enough space to accommodate the twenty-seven musicians and their instruments. The cost was prohibitive; it was decided instead to have a winched podium for Hal that he would control himself. He hated it and didn't think it was worth the effort. Furthermore, because of that one moment he was required to wear white tie and tails for the entire show. All he wanted was to do his job. He was also concerned that certain performances had already begun to deteriorate, even before they had been presented to an audience.

After returning to the hotel for a tie—it seemed appropriate—I walked into the theater, entering through the lobby. Once inside the auditorium, I was struck by the new look. It was now completely cleared of all evidence of technical rehearsals. Tharon Musser's desk was gone, as were all the wires leading to and from it. No coats were draped nonchalantly over seats, and all the briefcases, bags, and other paraphernalia had vanished. There was nothing but a sea of empty red seats, ready to be filled. And a new team was in charge: the front-of-house staff, which included, most visibly, the ushers. They were stuffing the Playbills and stacking them at the top of the aisles and chatting among themselves. I felt it was a good idea to cozy up to them, explain who I was, make some polite conversation. Establishing that you're meant to be there, that you're part of the show, allows you to roam freely around the auditorium during performances. And if you're on good terms with the ushers, you can get them to tell you what they think. They tend to have interesting, if blunt, opinions. And they have very good ears—they can tell you what the audience is really saying. (Interesting note: In order to help clarify that the Follies sequence was now entitled Loveland, the Playbill differentiated the segment

clearly—and listed the opening song "Loveland" and then the rest of the sequences as "The Folly of Youth," "Buddy's Folly," and so forth, listing each character song in its proper place; for example, "Losing My Mind" was in Sally's Folly. This was made even more elaborate in the New York Playbill.)

Backstage, the mood was a little weird. Because it was the first performance in front of an audience, it felt like an official opening night. There were flowers and telegrams to be distributed, but there would be no party afterward. It was a working night, though obviously a special one. There was a sense of nervous excitement. Were they ready? A few spousal visitors had joined the ranks, and they were sitting quietly and supportively in the dressing rooms. Craig Stevens, Alexis Smith's husband, had just flown in from Los Angeles, and Dorothy Collins's husband, Ron Holgate, had driven up from New Jersey. Others would be arriving shortly.

The creative team wandered about, talking to each other, then went out front to size up the crowd. Those of us who weren't provided with "locations" would have to find an empty seat or stand in the rear. Beginning at "half-hour," the auditorium doors were open and the audience was allowed in. There was the new sound of actual people, muttering, chatting. After they sat down, some looked at their programs, some went on talking with friends about anything and everything. It was a good bet they weren't talking about the show. I looked them over. These warm bodies, together in this one arena on this one night, were now the most important element in the collaboration. Who were they? What were they thinking? Before tonight, anyone who had watched any part of a rehearsal—a member of the press, a friend of the show, a staff person, or a family member—knew what they were watching. They were part of the greater *Follies* family. But now there were hundreds of people about to take in something few of them knew anything about. How many Sondheim devotees were there? How many Boston I've-got-to-see-the-very-first-performance enthusiasts who had bought their tickets the moment the first ad appeared? How many people just out on a Saturday night date who had felt that a show called *Follies* might be a good prospect? The company and the staff were about to learn how their show was going to play for an audience. What if those moments we knew were golden laid big eggs? What if the audience didn't get the connection between the past and the present? Would they favor one time frame over

another? Which members of the cast would they go for, and whom would they remember from old movies and shows? What if the Follies sequence doesn't feel like the result of a dramatic nervous breakdown? What if . . . ?

Members of the creative staff stationed themselves in what would become typical perches: Hal and Ruthie in adjoining seats in the orchestra, Ruthie armed with a yellow pad; Bob and Michael together in another part of the house. Steve wandered the rear of the auditorium, bottle of bourbon in hand. Jim had arrived early and taken his seat among the audience with his wife, Marie, a reserved and private woman, not particularly friendly, who kept her distance from everyone. Others—Jonathan Tunick, Tharon Musser, Boris and Lisa Aronson—were in assigned seats.

At 7:40 the house lights dimmed, the drumroll began, and the curtain rose on a wrong light cue. From a technical standpoint, it set the tone for the performance. Sloppy. The tape of the ghost announcers came in too early during the Prologue and the cast couldn't catch up. The orchestra played badly; there were lots of clams. "Waiting for the Girls Upstairs" was a mess—lyrics were dropped in the beginning, and the rhythm was so badly off at the end that Hal Hastings had to hum the beat directly to John and Gene. The audience was confused some of the time, but they seemed to stay with the story. They listened, they applauded, and they laughed. But certain parts seemed to mystify them. They clearly didn't get the point of "Can That Boy Fox Trot!"—and as a result it seemed interminable. Fifi wobbled but got through "Ah, Paris!"; Ethel delivered and they loved her; but putting the three numbers together in the Montage seemed shaky. Alexis got the most solid laughs of the night, including one on her seductive line to the young waiter: ". . . and I have thirty thousand dollars' worth of Georgian silver in my dining room." There were some definite positive signs: the numbers with clean "button" endings landed well, and "Who's That Woman?" stopped the show, cold. Mary McCarty's confidence had been building over the past couple of weeks, and she had begun to relish the number. In the process, she had made it her own, without anyone being aware. The fact that Stella was a secondary character and that the chorus behind her was made up of the stars of the show, made it all the more special. But since "Who's That Woman?" had taken up so many hours of rehearsal, and had been the cause of so much anxiety, everyone had been grateful for just getting through it.

The audience instantly got what the song was trying to do and say, and understood the brilliance of the staging. They loved seeing a plus-size middle-aged woman in a suburban party dress out there hoofing. And to have the stars back her up, dressed in their assortment (from glamorous to frumpy) of party dresses, made the number irresistible. The audience ate it up. They also got the brilliance of Michael's "mirror" staging, with a couple of oohs and ahhs when the ghost figures appeared upstage, lined up with their backs to us for the tap chorus in reflection.

For "Losing My Mind," Dorothy Collins appeared in a new dress, a body-hugging, floor-length gown with a slight train, covered with small silver bugle beads, which shimmered as the light played off it. This dress was originally intended for Alexis and then given to Sheila Smith. It didn't work for either, but worn by Dorothy, with a train perhaps longer than necessary for her height (both Alexis and Sheila were inches taller), it was perfect. The Jean Harlow wig was gone, and Dorothy's blond hair was coifed simply and beautifully. She looked and sounded radiant. The audience loved her, and she scored. The staging—simple, clear, and precise—had not changed from that first performance at Feller's.

The performance lasted over two hours, without an intermission. The audience stayed with it all the way through, the applause was more than polite, and there were several loud shouts of "Bravo!" during the curtain call. It went as well as anyone had a right to expect, and the audience's reaction was totally honest, pointing up what was good and what wasn't. The overall impression was favorable, but there were certainly problems. At various times during the course of the evening members of the audience were seen walking up the aisle, only to return several minutes later, having taken their own self-determined bathroom break. And one man was seen walking out after an hour and a half, muttering, "How *long* is this thing going to go on?"—never to be seen again. One disgruntled patron was overheard at the very end saying, "You just have to sit there for so long hearing about four people who don't like each other." Steve, staying within the safe anonymity of the rear of the auditorium, was depressed by everything that didn't work and felt that twenty-five minutes should be cut before the Boston critics saw the show, four days hence. Jonathan Tunick said he was often among the first to know when a show was too long, and he knew this show was too long.

Mary McCarty takes center stage for "Who's That Woman?"

Dorothy Collins, without wig and in the beaded dress, performs "Losing My Mind."

Hal and Michael bounded backstage as soon as the curtain came down to speak to the company before they dispersed to their dressing rooms. Hal was extremely bubbly and happy. He said he was thrilled with the show, and was thrilled that some patrons had walked out: it's a sure sign that a show is controversial, he said, and that's the kind of show he likes to produce. He had identified several spots where he wanted to prune and cut, and he couldn't wait to get to work tomorrow. Michael was also very buoyant, and far happier than he had seemed in a long time. He thanked everyone. There was a general feeling of relief that they had actually gotten through the first performance, that it didn't seem as if the show was a disaster, even if the technical side had been sloppy. It was a moment for hugs and kisses all around.

At this point, of course, no one knew how much work would take place over the next few weeks. In the abstract, everyone knew there would be some. But what opinions voiced over the past couple of months would come back to haunt us all? Which parts of the show that people had quietly complained about would prove to be real problems? To what extent would audience reactions dictate changes? The score was complete, but some of the songs were five years old while others were a week old; would they all gel? Would the "pastiche" numbers echoing the past blend well with the present-day book songs? As I sat there, watching and listening to the first audience, I saw the show take on a life of its own. None of these people knew where the laughs were, so no one could anticipate them. There, in front of me, was the show that we all had been contributing to. And instead of feeling proud, happy, or honored, I just sat there wondering whether the show was going to work. Some of the things I knew instinctively were good were proving to be good, and that was a relief—I wasn't surprised that "Who's That Woman?" received such a strong ovation. I knew it was a good song and well staged, and the reaction simply confirmed how good it was. Nor was I surprised that the audience didn't respond to "Fox Trot." All along, Steve had said it was a one-joke song, and now it seemed like a long pumped-up bad nightclub act. Yvonne just couldn't pull off the new middle section in which she sang all three parts. I had no idea what they were going to do about it, but I knew it was a problem. Ethel Shutta's "Broadway Baby" killed, as we all thought it would,

*"Broadway Baby": Ethel Shutta, a seventy-six-year-old,
stopping the show at every performance.*

Ethel Shutta.

but it was a scant three minutes out of two and a half hours; the show wasn't going to live or die based on Hattie. And the story of the four lead characters seemed boring. I wasn't sure the audience understood the Follies sequence: it seemed to be an awful long time coming, and when it arrived I didn't sense an overwhelming feeling of joy among those around me. That worried me. Watching those drops fly in was as thrilling to me as it had been the very first day; and now that the set was complete, when the curtain parted for "Uptown, Downtown," the silver fountains were all in place behind the company, who were all dressed in red. It was a spectacular moment, but it came at the end of a long evening. My sense was that the audience was almost numb by

then; they didn't react to the brilliance of this final burst of color as I had thought they would.

My personal response to the performance was one of almost sadness. I wasn't sad for the show, but sad because of what the beginning of public performances meant for those of us in support positions. We were soon to be obsolete. I was surprised that I had grown to feel so much a part of the company. Yes, there were those I considered friends and those I hardly had reason to speak to, but it had come to feel like some kind of family nonetheless. The experience wasn't over, but as I sat in the balcony watching the show, I realized that before too long I wasn't going to be needed. The stage managers knew that I would be useful enough through the Boston run to endorse the management's decision to pick up my hotel bill, but I saw an end in sight.

Even though there was no official party, everyone broke off into small gatherings. The bigwigs went to Trader Vic's in the Statler Hilton, and most of the rest of the company to the Tiki Hut in Boston's Chinatown. The difference between the two places was stark—the former heavily decorated and expensive, the latter very straightforward and unadorned. Both stayed open late. I went to the Tiki Hut, where Angela Lansbury turned up, fresh from a performance of *Prettybelle*. She was greeted especially warmly by two members of the *Follies* company who had been in shows with her before—Harvey Evans (*Anyone Can Whistle*) and Kurt Peterson (*Dear World*).

Sunday morning, the creative staff gathered on the stage to discuss the performance of the night before. Hal kept urging his collaborators to listen to the audience. Fritz Holt had heard several patrons say they didn't like the four main characters, who didn't seem to like each other. Hal responded: "Yes, we know that, and that's part of the point of the show. We also know that what we have to do is move the audience." Someone reported hearing an audience member saying it was "just god-awful," another that it was "longer than *Ben-Hur*." Others reported hearing that the costumes were good. Of the cast, Dorothy got the majority of the kudos. Overall, the mood was optimistic but also realistic. There was work to be done, but a panic had not set in.

Hal had learned from George Abbott the wisdom of playing the first performance on a Saturday night, leaving Sunday to make changes before a second performance on Monday. If Mr. Abbott felt something

didn't work, out it went—no hesitation. He didn't want a lot of talk; he just wanted things fixed. Hal wasn't quite that kind of director, and this show was too ambitious, and too conceptual, for that sort of approach. But there were things that concerned him greatly. First on the list was the intermission. No one was happy that the show ran so long in one act, but there was no agreement on how that should be remedied. Hal wanted an intermission; he felt that the audience would "savor the show by having a breather in the middle." Steve, on the other hand, wanted twenty-five minutes cut and no intermission. Someone had told him the show was like a banquet, and that by the time Loveland comes along, dessert has already been served. He himself didn't have twenty-five minutes of cuts to offer; he just felt instinctively that the show played better as one unit and wanted to avoid an arbitrary break. The producer in Hal didn't like seeing audience members wander up and down the aisles whenever they felt the need to take an intermission, and he was beginning to dig in his heels. He wanted an intermission. Michael was strangely quiet on the subject, but Hal felt so strongly that he persuaded everyone to give it a try.

Steve asked if anyone could figure out why Heidi Schiller got the biggest hand in "Beautiful Girls" when she made her way down the staircase. The consensus was that it took a while for the audience to catch on to the Miss America–style entrances at the top of the stairs, and when they did it just happened to be Heidi's turn. Hal wanted to know if one of Yvonne's lines was a joke: "When she tells the band to play in D minor, is that a joke? *Is* there such a key?" Steve said that, yes, there was, but that if Hal wanted the line to be a joke, she should say that she didn't sing the song in C-sharp minor but in D-flat minor. They're the same notes; *that* would be a joke.

The company was called for noon. Hal took everyone else to the anteroom of the ladies' lounge for notes. The late-nineteenth-century pedigree of the ornate Colonial called for a large and elaborate ladies' lounge. Just off the main lobby, it was as rococo as the lobby itself, with a beautiful carpet and a large oval onyx table in the center. The lavatory was discreetly through one of the four identical doors along the side walls. The gentlemen's lounge was on the lower level, and its anteroom was as workmanlike as the ladies' lounge was elaborate. Its marble floor and wooden benches provided a more conducive rehearsal space; it now had a rehearsal piano rolled into a corner. The ladies' lounge provided a more comfortable space for notes. Chairs were at a

*The company gets notes from Ruthie and Hal in the
ladies' lounge of the Colonial Theatre.*

premium, but Ethel Shutta, as senior member, commandeered a nice
one for herself. When she was called out of the note session for a message, Hal Hastings got up from the floor and took her chair. Upon her
return, she pointed right at him and said, "Out!" He obliged.

Hal Prince announced to the company that there would be an intermission on Monday. Although there was no perfect place for it, he had
decided, and Michael concurred, that it would come immediately after
"Too Many Mornings." From a timing standpoint, this made sense; it
came at about two-thirds of the way through the evening. The song was
a passionate statement of Ben's regret at having lost Sally many years
earlier, but the staging was simple and beautiful. It would make for a
quiet end to the act. Both Sally and Young Sally are onstage listening to
Ben, and during the course of the song Young Sally actually comes into
his arms and kisses him, while Sally mimics the embrace standing a few
feet away. Margot Travers, in her long slinky black gown, swept in in
front, while Buddy, from a perch high up on a platform, sees his wife in

"Too Many Mornings"—ghost and present-day characters interact.
Dorothy Collins, Marti Rolph, John McMartin.

Ben's arms for the first time. Hal said they would work out the logistics later on the stage, but it was definitely going in on Monday.

It was time for small fixes. Here are several:

1. Steve changed the first lyric in "Love Will See Us Through" from "Listen, dear" to "Sally, dear," partly to underscore the connection between the characters and the Follies songs.

2. "Madame" was added to the announcement of Solange LaFitte in the Prologue. (There was much amusement when Hal Hastings rerecorded this announcement and got unasked-for direction from all the French experts in the company about how to pronounce the word "madame.")

3. Everyone was given invitations to carry as they arrived at the party. This was to respond to a concern voiced by Steve ("This is a party—wouldn't they have invitations?).

4. Phyllis's line in the Prologue was changed from "It's not

right, Ben, to knock this down to build a parking lot" to "What this city needs is one more parking lot."

5. Phyllis's line after Hattie asks Ben for his autograph for her grandson—"Why don't they ever say, '*I* want your autograph'?"—was cut.

6. Heidi Schiller's line about Oscar Straus bringing her "white roses" (pronounced "vite rozez" by Justine Johnston) was cut.

7. Before the Montage, instead of several photographs taken of Emily and Theodore Whitman, there was to be only one, so focus could be given to Weismann's scene with the waitress, which ended with the line, "So you want to be a star, my dear . . ."

8. Solange's line about her perfume, Magic, being "available at all the best department stores" was cut. (Fifi looked panicked at the thought of a line being cut.)

9. Ben's line "What we need is a drink" after "Don't Look at Me" was moved inside the number, just before the final chord.

10. There was a new and smaller piano on the platform for the onstage band, since Hal had observed that the old piano looked like the star of the show.

11. The orchestration for "Waiting for the Girls Upstairs" was adjusted slightly to bring out the rhythm, and one staging moment was changed so Buddy ran only to the center platform in the middle of the song rather than to stage right and up one of the staircases.

12. Ben was to be seated on the rubble way downstage right at the base of the proscenium arch for "The Road You Didn't Take."

13. Young Sally and Young Phyllis were given a new entrance during the scene when Ben and Sally are looking through old photographs.

14. Six new lines were added for the women as they enter to get into position for "Who's That Woman?" including Carlotta's "I can't tap-dance anymore. I haven't had tap shoes on in thirty years," and Meredith Love, the role played by Sheila Smith, saying, "This number winded me when I was nineteen."

15. Slight choreographic changes were made to "Bolero d'Amour."

16. The end of "Can That Boy Fox Trot!" was changed so Yvonne could get offstage faster.

Michael took the stage, first to clean up "Bolero d'Amour" and then to go through "Uptown, Downtown" and some other moments that looked sloppy in performance. His nerves were short, and when people were talking too much for his taste he boomed out, "Look, if I'm going to take the trouble to rehearse you, then I think we should get something done. Let me remind you that you have played one, and only one, performance." Hal, too, had a moment of exasperation when he was working on the stage and there was a lot of noise backstage. From his rehearsal perch in the front row of the theater, he boomed: "Whoever is talking, shut up! I'm trying to get something done out here and if you don't shut up I will come up there and just see who's talking. Now for God's sake, shut up!" That's how the whole day went—little notes, little fixes, and little tantrums. The company walked through the new intermission, the stage managers standing by, scripts in hand. It was they, after all, who would have to coordinate any changes with the crew, who were not called in today. The logistics seemed fairly simple. One question was: Exactly where in the stage action to bring the curtain up for the second act? Should the showgirl cross again? Should she be onstage at all? Should Ben and Young Sally still be kissing?

The rest of the day was taken up with cleanups and walk-throughs of the moments that had been changed. Because "Waiting for the Girls Upstairs" had been a train wreck on Saturday, Hal Hastings called the orchestra before the performance so the cast could go through it. Jonathan Tunick made some adjustments, leaning over the orchestra rail and dictating them to the orchestra players for them to mark in their own individual parts. The idea was to clarify the rhythm that had proved to be so difficult on Saturday. (This was the first orchestration finished for the show, and Jonathan was never fully satisfied with it.) I found myself standing on the stage while the orchestra was playing, and was amazed to discover how little the actors can actually hear from the pit below. In another era, before true amplification, when orchestra pits were shallower and extended further out into the auditorium, it was easier for the actors to hear. But in order for the performers to hear the orchestra, speakers had to be placed behind the proscenium aimed onstage. Getting the balance right was tricky. How odd, I thought, even the actors need amplification to hear the orchestra.

Both the Monday and Tuesday performances were less successful than Saturday's. The Monday audience was very small. Alex Mohr, the house manager, blamed it on the late change in performance schedule; in any event, Monday night is a notoriously weak night in the theater, and the chances of our having had a significant presale or having sold this one as a benefit were remote. The mezzanine had patrons only in the first four rows of the center section, and they were scattered. Some appeared to be the first of the *Follies* groupies, however, since there was a small and vocal group who cheered certain things almost before they happened. Word had evidently gotten out. But their enthusiasm wasn't enough to make the performance anything but lackluster. Applause was polite. Things that had played well on Saturday continued to play well, but the reactions weren't as strong. The intermission made the show play in two parts, but that was about all it did. Reigniting the story after the intermission seemed an uphill fight, but since the performance lacked sparkle anyway, it was hard to tell whether that was due to the performance per se or to the show itself.

On Monday, unlike Saturday night, the creative staff was worried. When the performance ended, Hal came backstage and asked Fritz to clear the stage. He wanted an impromptu meeting with Steve, Michael, and Jim, and he wanted it without anyone hanging around. From the looks on all the faces, nobody was happy. Hal's biggest concern was "Can That Boy Fox Trot!" He felt they were doing the show and everyone a disservice by keeping the song and wanted a new number to replace it. This wasn't an entirely fresh sentiment, but it was the first time it had been voiced so adamantly. Steve was resigned to writing something new and made a half-joking move to get up immediately to go back to the hotel and begin writing. But he didn't have an answer as to what the new song should be, and he didn't want to start until there was agreement about what kind of number was wanted. Within the score, it held a unique position: although definitely a song from the past, "Fox Trot" was sung at the party in the present, performed specifically for the other guests. It never went into the past, Carlotta had no ghost counterpart, and its reason for existence was simply that the actress was determined to perform it once on this stage. Period. There was humor in the notion of a college song sung by an over-the-hill movie star, and one sensed that it might have even been

funny as a college song back in the days of the Follies. But it wasn't working. In the show's story line, Dimitri Weismann had cut it from the Follies in Philadelphia; now Hal Prince was about to cut it from *Follies* in Boston. This time, the chances were that it would be gone for good. Steve asked what Hal, Jim, and Michael thought a new song should be, and whether it should take place in the present or should it be another pastiche song from the past? No one had a clear idea, although Jim said that maybe it should be about survival, how Carlotta had been through a lot in her life and yet was still around. There was a sense of relief now that "Fox Trot" was going. More thought and discussion would have to go into the decision, but in the meantime everyone agreed to cut out the extended middle section as soon as possible. Michael had some staging thoughts about how the cut could be made easily. Obviously, though, Yvonne would have to be told that the song would be replaced before the cut could be made. And everyone wanted to wait at least one more day before dealing with her or with it. Uncut, at Monday night's performance, "Can That Boy Fox Trot!" had lasted seven and a quarter minutes.

Tuesday's rehearsal began, as all rehearsals were to begin from now on, with notes, this time onstage. The cast would sit around the set (there were enough levels and stairs to provide ample perching opportunities) and Hal and Michael would stand in the front row of the auditorium, facing up at the stage. Hal was now clearly in charge; he gave most of the notes. Michael and Steve would interject comments whenever they felt it necessary. Some of Monday's improvements were taken out, like the new staging of "The Road You Didn't Take." It turned out, although no one could have foreseen it, that having John McMartin sit on the proscenium rubble made it look like he was there simply to be near the floor microphones and to hear the orchestra better. There was a lot of gentle good humor about that, and the staging was returned to what it had been before. Mary McCarty raised her hand and asked if "Who's That Woman?" could be slowed down a little at a certain point where she felt she would get a bigger laugh if she didn't have to race through so fast. Politely but firmly Steve said that the number was written to go at a certain tempo and it should go at that tempo.

One actor was beginning to be a problem: Ed Steffe, who was playing Dimitri Weismann. Steffe was a very nice, polite man, with a perfectly lovely voice. He always addressed Hal as "Sir." But his acting was wooden, and Hal wasn't making any headway in shaping his perfor-

Yvonne De Carlo, belting it out.

mance. Notes were received graciously, but little change was evident. Granted, Weismann wasn't a large role, but it was crucial—not unlike Cap'n Andy in *Show Boat*, who provides the "motor" to the play. It's his party around which the show is based, and he must give the audience the sense that he was once a force to be reckoned with. Florenz Ziegfeld was the clear inspiration for the character, and history tells us he was not a bashful man—it was, after all, the Weismann Theater in which the Weismann Follies once played. Steffe wasn't understanding the role of the congenial host, and he seemed particularly uncomfortable with the lecherous side of the character; nor did he have much authority onstage. He still carried the cigar that Hal had given him in rehearsal in the hope that a prop would help him take command of the character, but the performance wasn't improving, and Hal found himself giving the same notes over and over.

Arriving for the performance on Tuesday night, I ran into Alexis and Gene, who were in the lobby looking at the new photographs. Alexis was in a good mood, and while we talked she explained

how detrimental she thought it was for actors to try to shape a show to their own needs, especially to get a bigger reaction, as Mary McCarty had suggested earlier in the afternoon. Of course she was relishing her new first line ("What this city needs is one more parking lot") because she was using it to establish that "this lady is going to say funny things." But there seemed to be a clear dividing line in her mind between an actor finding the right way to say lines—and get proper laughs—and one who wants things around her to be changed so she can get bigger laughs. It didn't sound as if she was complaining about the competition; she just seemed like a very aware performer. And she was starting to get a good reaction from the audiences. She had a real sense of humor. With relish she related that when she and Gene had gotten into the cab together to come from the hotel, the driver wasn't sure where the Colonial Theatre was. After they described it, he said, "Oh, yeah. That's where that Yvonne De Carlo show is playing." And she let out her nearly guttural laugh.

The performance on Tuesday was a slight improvement over Monday's. Now it was Michael's turn to get depressed. "It's a disaster," he muttered. Hal wasn't much happier and ordered the onstage band unit to be lowered by two or three feet, as his eye was still distracted by seeing the piano so prominent. Fritz asked whether this had been okayed by Boris, and Hal replied, "I have just decided it, and Mr. Aronson need not be consulted." (Note: that was the last we ever heard about lowering the platform, which remained as designed and as built.) The lighting came in for some criticism. It was complicated and not yet finished, but Tharon knew it was going to take several performances of adjusting and fiddling to get the cues right. She had made it clear from the outset, once she saw the technical schedule, that it was going to be very tight for her. She would simply continue to fix, change, and set cues right through the previews.

The Wednesday note session was as pleasant as possible. Tonight all the Boston critics would be in attendance, so the creative staff did their best to appear cheerful. Michael gave Ethel Barrymore Colt a new line before the song "Who's That Woman?": "I can't tap-dance; I never could." Ethel smiled oddly and said, "I know someone is trying to tell me something." A decision was made to repeat a section of "Too Many Mornings" when the curtain rises on the second act, to help get

back into the story. Michael asked Hal to give a pep talk on energy, and Hal promptly fell to the ground in mock exhaustion. It was a nice moment of levity. Hal then called for a final run-through, without costumes or orchestra, just to make certain all the small changes that had been made over the past few days were smooth and clean. He said that this was one of his traditions, and that it always helped put a company in the right frame of mind for the opening performance. He explained that he didn't want to stop, but that if he needed to, he would blow on a new small shrill police whistle that someone had given him, and he held it up for the company to see.

The run-through went off without a hitch, although with performances that were not at peak level. Hal didn't use his whistle once. When it was over, he gathered the company onstage. He had no notes; he just wanted to wish them well. This wasn't a time for gushing; everyone knew that tonight mattered. He was straightforward and businesslike. He told them to go out there and enjoy the performance.

Backstage now looked like a real opening night. Telegrams were posted on the company callboard, many from friends of the company, but also from cast members of *Company* and *Fiddler on the Roof* in New York. Of course, theatrical tradition dictates that you never actually wish actors well, so instead you wish them the opposite, "Break a leg!" being the most traditional comment. Steve Sondheim, who had accidentally kicked a piece of the set one night at Feller's and had broken his toe, wrote simply: "Good luck. Break a toe."

The portion of the New York contingent necessary to a Boston opening was up in force. First and foremost: press agent Mary Bryant, who was scurrying around making certain everyone was being taken care of. While all the critics needed to have prime locations, it was known that some preferred certain seats, and it was in everyone's best interests to see that those requests were fulfilled. There was also a little gentle skulduggery at work. When *Company* played in Boston, *Variety* had sent a reviewer who, according to rumor, had once worked for Hal but had been fired. He certainly had it in for the show, and concluded his nasty out-of-town review with this: "As it stands now, [*Company*] is for ladies' matinees, homos, and misogynists." A different critic was being sent by *Variety* to review *Follies*, but Mary nonetheless seated him way off to one side and behind a pillar. It turned out that he liked the show and wrote quite a favorable review despite his seat location. You never can tell.

Not surprisingly, the performance was the best so far. Mary Bryant spent the better part of the first act cursing some unknown audience member who was, annoyingly, clapping at *everything*. At intermission, word started to spread about which critics seemed to be liking the show. Kevin Kelly liked what he saw, it was rumored. He had been an early champion of *Company*, so it was assumed that he would also go for *Follies*. Pat Collins, a television critic for WBZ-TV, had hated *Company*, so she was all but written off. Elliot Norton, dean of American critics, had been too long at the game to let on to anyone what he was thinking. He sat with a poker face. They were the three critics who were of most interest.

Michael made his way to a neighborhood bar for most of the first act. When he returned he ran into Steve in the lobby. "Are you going to watch the second act?" "No," Michael replied, "I've already seen it and I'm sure I'll see it again."

Before the end of the performance, Hal and Michael were already backstage, standing at the stage managers' desk at stage right. They watched the curtain calls as their cast received a warm response from the audience—with the reaction beginning to fit a pattern. The first big cheer was for Ethel Shutta. There was a moderate uptick for Yvonne, a nice cheer for Dorothy, and the, by now, largest reaction for Alexis. Once all the solo bows had been taken, there was a company bow, and the curtain was brought in, passing in front of everyone's face with what looked like an inch of space to spare, effectively muffling all the cheering from out front. Then when the curtain went up again, the cheers could be heard again. A nod to the conductor, who nodded back, another company call, and the curtain was lowered once again. As soon as the final curtain was lowered (it's the stage manager's decision how many calls to have), Hal and Michael rushed out onstage and hugged as many cast members as they could grab. There was a general sense of euphoria. Another milestone had passed.

In the back of the house I ran into a woman I knew, a friend of the family. I had no idea she was seeing the show, or why she was there. I didn't even know she was a theatergoer. But, naturally, when I saw her coming up the aisle, I greeted her, and asked, "So, how did you like the show?" "Get rid of the football hero in De Carlo's number, cut Gene Nelson's dance because it's just too long, and tighten up the beginning. Then it'll be fine." I guess that's why producers bring shows to Boston.

Tonight there was an official opening night party. It was being

thrown by Capitol Records, which would be making the original-cast album. There had been a lot of interest expressed by various record companies for the album of the show, and Capitol had won the bidding. Hal was upset with the way Columbia had promoted their album of *Company*. He wanted them to commit specific money for promotion if they were to do *Follies*, and they refused. So the show went to Capitol, which had been the label for *Forum*. They were pleased to have another Steve Sondheim/Hal Prince show for their catalogue, although Steve wasn't altogether happy with the choice. They had taken over Charley's Saloon, a small English pub on Newbury Street, and, typical of all opening night parties, the place was too small for the number of people invited. Executives from Capitol Records were circulating and greeting everyone. Interestingly, the one person from Capitol who wasn't there was the producer of the album itself, Richard C. Jones. He would be coming to see the show in a few days, but I was curious as to why he wasn't there now. Once he showed up the reason became clear: he was engaged in a tug of war with his

Chorus girls and showgirls at the Boston opening night party.
Enough eye makeup? Margot Travers, Rita O'Connor, Ursula Machsmeyer
(hidden), Suzanne Briggs, Linda Perkins, Suzanne Rogers, Kathie Dalton.

187

bosses. He felt the show deserved and needed two discs, but the company was adamantly opposed to it. There were very few cast albums of more than one LP, and all the departments at Capitol felt that a two-disc set would cut into the sales potential enormously, although they were more than happy to squeeze as much *Follies* onto one LP as possible. In the end, Dick Jones lost the fight. The *Follies* original-cast album did indeed come out on one LP, truncated, and the unfortunate result of a variety of technical glitches on the day it was recorded. To add insult to injury, the show that beat out *Follies* for the Tony in the Best Musical category, *Two Gentlemen of Verona*, had a two-LP cast album, albeit on a smaller label.

Everyone in the cast showed up at the party, as did anyone connected with the show, including visiting family and friends. The drinks flowed and the food was quickly devoured. The standard groupings held forth: Hal and Judy sat with Steve and John Guare. Michael Bennett was at a table with several of his gorgeous dancers, all of whom had dolled themselves up for the party. Alexis was joined by her husband and a few California friends; Dorothy sat with her smaller retinue of family. Mary McCarty gathered with some of the older members of the company; I sat at a table with Yvonne and her agent, Ruth Webb, who had flown up from New York.

Of course the moment everyone waits for at an opening night party is when the reviews come out. It's a weird feeling when all the critics have seen the show but you have no clue as to what they thought. Tradition dictates that if a major review is good, the crowd is hushed and the producer reads it aloud. This was 1971, and the routine remained what it had been for decades: all the press see the show on opening night, rush back to their offices, and pound out a review for inclusion in the late edition of the morning paper. The television reviewers, a new phenomenon, rush back to their stations and prepare to go on as part of the eleven-o'clock news. At the party, the show's press team finds a room with a TV and a telephone, there to await word from the newspapers, and sometimes, rarely, from the critics themselves. If the news is not good, chances are the party will keep going until most of the guests catch on to what's happening and the party winds down in a hurry.

At an opportune moment, Hal called for quiet. "Well," he said, "that TV blonde loved us!" Cheers erupted. That was precisely the opposite of what was expected. "If *she* loved us, we may be in trouble!"

Hal Prince reads the rave review from Samuel Hirsch.

Laughter rippled through the room and the party continued. Then Hal hushed the crowd once again and read a review out loud. It was not, surprisingly, by any of the major critics—it was by Samuel Hirsch, from the less important *Boston Herald Traveler,* but was enthusiastic and intelligent. Hal read it in its entirety. It began:

> There's a magic feeling [that] comes over you when a new musical opens and lets you know all's well within the first few minutes. You sense it's going to be a special evening because the talents of the men and women who conceived it and who put it all together and are playing it with sure skill and good taste let you know immediately that you're watching something extraordinary take place. . . . It happened last night at the Colonial Theatre, where Harold Prince's new musical opened, a show called *Follies,* and it has a magnificently complicated and sophisticated book by James Goldman, sensational and rueful sentimental lyrics and music by Stephen Sondheim, and brilliant choreography by Michael Bennett. These men are at the top of their talents—and in superb form. This is a smashing show.

That was the kind of reaction everyone was hoping for. Later on, Hirsch acknowledged that there was some tightening and pruning to be done, and that "there's an overstatement here that needs to be brought under control before the Technicolor fantasy style [of Loveland] works properly." He called the black and white ghost figures "effective because the tall show girls are like living scenery," and said that the joint staging by Michael and Hal "boldly and brilliantly and with exquisite taste binds the fabric of this superb musical together in what surely must be their masterpiece." At one point Hirsch described John McMartin's voice as weak, but it was too late for Hal to stop. He was on a roll. "Well, sorry, John," he said, and he went on. Hirsch's comments showed that he "got" the show. He ended by saying, "*Follies* is going to change our musical theater the way *Oklahoma!* ushered in the new American lyric theater." A big cheer erupted.

The party crowd continued to celebrate in a jolly mood. "The other reviews haven't come out yet," was the excuse offered to those who asked, and the fact that one critic in a prominent Boston newspaper had liked the show was encouragement enough for the moment. Anyway, it would be rare for a producer to read more than one review to an opening night party. So what if the one he chose to read wasn't from the expected source? And, to tell the truth, it wasn't *all* love and sunshine in the room for critic Samuel Hirsch. As Fifi D'Orsay left the party, she walked past the table where I was sitting, where she could be heard to say, to anyone who would listen, "And that man Hirsch, he didn't even mention me." No, he didn't, and the fact that he did mention Ethel Shutta and Mary McCarty must have annoyed her. Out she went.

The next morning, the reviews proved to be decidedly mixed. Kevin Kelly, as some at the party had feared (Hal's not reading the *Globe*'s review couldn't have been a *good* thing), didn't like *Follies*. The man who had been arguably the earliest and most influential champion of *Company* and its collaborators acknowledged none of the innovations of *Follies*. This time out he simply didn't get the show. (Interestingly, although Kelly had been quite enthusiastic about *Company*, Steve said that he felt he actually hadn't gotten that show, either.) He seemed to fumble over his own words as he tried to express his inability to figure out why he was so unaffected by the show. "At the moment in its pre-Broadway tryout at the Colonial, *Follies* is in trouble. Intrinsic in its fascinating format (and the format is fascinating) is a difficult problem, a series of promises made and, if anything, only partially kept."

He understood that the lead characters' "life is a pretty bleak routine," and that "there is certainly a predictability to Goldman's final outcome." Dorothy Collins gave "the truest musical performance of all, and she's dramatically credible as well." He felt that "since there are so many persons of passing interest in the plot it takes a while to sort them out and know them." He longed "for the past to rise up and claim the stage"; but when the Follies numbers come, "they turn out to be surprisingly repetitive." He concluded by saying that "it has the makings of a solidly entertaining musical, and that's what a Boston tryout is all about." Solidly entertaining? That's the kind of comment one might expect to hear about *Hello, Dolly!* But *Follies*? And from the man who said that *Company* was "destined to become a classic"?

Elliot Norton, whose comments were always taken seriously, was very direct: "When it sings and dances, Harold Prince's new *Follies* is generally exuberant and exhilarating, ingenious and extraordinary entertainment. When it talks, however, when its four principals thrash out the follies of their love lives, it is bitter and shallow." That was the harshest public comment yet about the book. Norton respected the style of the musical numbers, saying there were "any number of wonderful songs . . . by Stephen Sondheim, in a sustained burst of inspiration." The dances "are grand, too . . . Bennett has marshaled his dancers, young and old, in patterns that reflect the old styles and make them live in new glory, with skill and wit. Some numbers are slick, some hilarious. Some are ingeniously tied into the story of the former 'Follies' girls and their boys." He had nice words for the old-timers—"It is one of the sights of the season to see Ethel Shutta, who sang once with the great bands, belting out a new song about a 'Broadway Baby' "— and felt that while the four principal actors "act, sing, and dance faultlessly in roles that are not attractive," he called Alexis Smith "a revelation: coolly beautiful, entirely at home with the barbed lines, bitter but believable—and wonderful in the song-and-dance numbers."

The "blonde from TV," Pat Collins, called the show "beautifully staged, a dazzling and fine musical. Spectacular!" It was good enough to be used in the newspaper ads in the coming weeks.

Some of the other reviews had interesting takes on the show. The *Christian Science Monitor*'s Roderick Nordell said, "If *No, No, Nanette* was nostalgia imported from the innocent past, *Follies* is nostalgia reconstituted with the sophisticated wit of the present." His reservation was for the book and the leading characters: "Too much time is

spent on these characters without telling us enough about them. . . . The deficiency . . . is that the central characters in James Goldman's script are not fresh or interesting enough for the innovations around them. They are like two couples left over from Mr. Prince's *Company*, dissatisfied with their marriages, failing to find themselves through 'playing around.' "

Boston After Dark's review, by Larry Stark, was titled "Fantastic Follies," and although he had some concerns about the show's length and the quality of the songs ("there is a sort of nostalgic sadness—the same sort of sadness that is evoked when grandparents or an old maiden aunt does a stiff-limbed polka at a wedding"), he felt that Prince "will be hailed for making another significant advance beyond *Company* in the field of the 'new' musical."

Steve Vineberg in the *Justice* observed: "*Follies*, in a pre-Broadway run at the Colonial, may be the most frustrating show I have ever seen. In some ways it is the most mature musical in about five years; in some ways it is awkward and overproduced. But whatever else it may be, *Follies* is arresting; it is provocative; it provides food for thought. And I firmly believe that what is good and important in the play and production is almost too good to be true, even when half buried by the banal dialogue and endless repetition."

The critics are nothing if not unpredictable. They all saw the same show, yet their opinions were so different. As an example of how their observations can vary, here is what some had to say about Yvonne De Carlo and the song that the creative forces already knew was going to be replaced: "[she makes] a happy evening's entertainment out of 'Can That Boy Fox Trot!'" (Elliot Norton). "Yvonne De Carlo amiably essays a complicated number that's a lark because she's doing it, though it still needs work" (Roderick Nordell). "Yvonne De Carlo has a good time with a showy number called 'Can That Boy Fox Trot!' " (Samuel Hirsch). "[Sondheim] has written a fiendishly difficult number for Yvonne De Carlo . . . [who] is simply unable to master Sondheim's involved lyrics and, for that matter, I doubt if Callas could" (Kevin Kelly). Callas? Was she ever known for performing intricate lyrics? I don't think so. As it turned out, the Boston critics of 1971, taken as a group, proved to be a pretty good indicator of the overall critical reaction this show would continue to get over the next thirty years. The ones who liked it loved it and got it. The ones who didn't care for it dismissed it and never saw beyond the details. What was odd about

Boston was that the "enlightened" critic missed the point and obviously didn't enjoy much of anything about the evening, while both a fairly standard newspaper critic and a cheerful blond television reporter got it.

But the most interesting review was yet to appear. Several days after the opening, a member of the company wandered into the theater at noon for the daily note session with a copy of the *Crimson*, Harvard University's student newspaper. He had happened upon a copy of the paper, which, he said, contained an interesting piece on the show. Someone on the production staff had also picked it up, and soon the paper was being passed around for everyone to read. Hal was fascinated by it, and Steve was absolutely intrigued. Many in the company had no idea what to make of it, and were dumbfounded. Titled "The Last Musical," it seemed almost more of an essay inspired by the show than a review—at least that's what everyone thought. Written by a Harvard senior named Frank Rich, it began by describing the women making their entrance for "Beautiful Girls," the first recognizable musical number in the show.

> These are old women coming down the staircase. They are dumpy, their hair is dyed, they don't exactly keep time with the music. They are not very secure, and, for that matter, neither is the staircase they are descending. It is ratty. But it doesn't make any difference. The staircase is on the stage of a theatre that is about to become a parking lot, and the women—well, the women don't have much farther to go before they die.

He went on to say that the show "is about what has happened to these women since their golden moment and, more importantly, what has happened to the American dreams they symbolized for a generation." He praised the form in which the show was conceived: "It is a measure of the show's brilliance (and its brilliance is often mind-boggling) that it uses a modern musical form, rather than the old-fashioned one that the Follies helped create, to get at its concerns." He understood that Prince "has thrown out the time-honored musical convention of using songs to advance a simple-minded script in favor of letting the music add new levels of meaning to a sophisticated libretto." He captured the mood of the production and articulated it better than anyone:

Sondheim's score uses old conventions of songwriting as well as new ones, and it is in his music and lyrics that *Follies* puts across its extraordinarily upsetting point of view. Almost cruelly, we watch old performers of yesteryear relive their greatest moments on the stage, singing melodies that sound as ancient and scratched as our parents' old 78 records, dancing steps proclaiming a kind of spirit that has long since passed from their lives as well as our own. The world of the dead Follies and the reality of the present intermingle constantly in Sondheim's work. No sooner does a performer do her old soft shoe than the tin-pan-alley trumpet fades into a somber and often dissonant piece of music Sondheim has written to capture the mood of disintegration that hangs over the ongoing celebration.

The most stunning part of Rich's review—and it certainly stunned everyone connected with *Follies*—were its two closing sentences:

> In the playbill for this show, the setting is described as "a party on the stage of this theatre tonight." They are not kidding, and there is no getting around the fact that a large part of the chilling fascination of *Follies* is that its creators are in essence presenting their own funeral.

It was not the intention of the creators of *Follies* to present a funeral. And if it had been, it wouldn't have been their own funeral they were presenting. That part of Rich's piece stymied everyone. Pathos, resonance, pain, memory, reality—those were the ideas and emotions everyone was going for. But not the death of musical theater. So one of the first decisions made in reaction to the review was to alter the line in the program indicating where the show took place, from "this theater tonight" to "the Weismann Theater." (Amusingly, several patrons arrived at the stage door following some of the early performances because they took the description of "a party" quite literally and wanted to join in the festivities onstage.) At least if the show proved to be a funeral, let it be Weismann's funeral and not that of the newest band of innovators of the American musical. And please let it not be the funeral of the musical theater as a genre.

Fortunately, it turned out not to be. There were *A Chorus Line, Pacific Overtures, Sweeney Todd,* and many other innovative musicals to

come from this collection of artists. But for a new and original musical, trying out in Boston with the best of intentions, hoping to be a hit, to have touched a nerve so profoundly that it prompted such an eloquent and articulate essay was almost overwhelming for the company of *Follies.* The intellectuals in the group were absolutely fascinated and wondered how Rich's review augured for the New York reaction. And who was this guy Rich, anyway? No one knew anything about him except that he was an undergraduate at Harvard. Hal remarked that "there's a key sentence I don't understand yet, but I have a feeling that man understands the play better than anyone else." Steve sought him out and invited him to lunch. Most people in the company just hoped it was a good review.

9

"The Choices That You Make Aren't All That Grim"

THE FIRST TWO WEEKS OF THE BOSTON RUN,
FEBRUARY 25–MARCH 7

I can't understand it. It must be a subject that just doesn't interest him." Hal was talking with Jim Goldman. Kevin Kelly's review came as a blow; it was the one review that Hal had felt reasonably sure was "in the bag." Not having his support was going to hurt; the question was how much. The advance sale had been building, which is always a good sign, but if it tapered off, the commercial prospects for the future life of the show would look grim. No matter how good other reviews were—and some were very good indeed—at this moment the commercial producer was focused on the *Globe*, Boston's largest and most influential paper. He didn't get that one, and he was worried.

The creative staff gathered in the ladies' lounge to discuss the aftermath of the reviews and decide on a game plan. The decision about replacing "Can That Boy Fox Trot!" had already been made, but how much the reviews were going to influence other edits and changes remained to be seen. I had been told by Steve that Hal really comes to life out of town, and now was his moment to shine. He had been here before, and he thrived on rolling up his sleeves and getting to work. One challenge, of course, was to make certain his collaborators agreed as to what needed to be done. Michael had begun to remove himself slightly from the rest of the creative staff, but he was constantly refining and questioning his work, and everyone else's as well. He was ready

Hal—out of town with a new musical.

to do whatever was necessary; he had even mentioned, quietly, to those close to him that nothing he was unhappy with would come to New York.

One subject that did come up at the meeting was the Prologue. Everyone felt that it wasn't quite working, that it was somehow too fragmented, yet there wasn't general agreement on exactly how to fix it. Michael said he had an idea, and that he would take one more crack at it, but he didn't want to discuss it with anyone; he just wanted to be left alone to do it. He was persuasive, and since no one else had an alternative, they agreed. The first thing he asked was for Steve to play him all the songs ever written for the show in the hope of finding some music around which to base a more cohesive Prologue.

Before discussing what should be done among themselves, Hal,

Steve, Jim, and Michael met with Steve's agent, Flora Roberts, a brilliant and perceptive supporter of Sondheim's work whose opinions were valued. She had come up from New York for the opening, as was her tradition, not having been to any of the preview performances. Other colleagues would make their way to Boston over the next few weeks and deliver an armada of opinions, only some of which would be helpful. But Flora was different, and the doors to their meeting were closed to all outsiders. What was discussed at the meeting was never disclosed; chances are she confirmed many of the decisions that were being contemplated.

Hal was revved up by the time the company arrived for their pep talk before the matinee performance. Yes, Boston still had Thursday matinees, and despite a late night partying, everyone had to get back to work. Since performances had begun on Saturday night, this would be the first matinee. *Follies* by daylight, what a thought! Somehow it seemed like such a nocturnal creature.

As the full company assembled onstage, Fifi went over to anyone who would listen and said, "I was not even mentioned in a single review. You know why? Because the song is no good, and I've known it all along. They will have to change my song or I'll leave the show." She was correct, as far as the daily newspapers were concerned; none of them mentioned her, although several did notice both Ethel Shutta and Mary McCarty, whom Fifi had earmarked as her direct competition. Fifi was not bashful, and in some ways it was healthy to have one member of the company so vocal with her own self-serving opinions; it made the rest of the company keep their thoughts to themselves. And while there was no talk about changing "Ah! Paris," there were concerns about its position as the final song in the Montage. When Yvonne arrived, she confessed quietly that Hal had told her they were going to build up her part and give her a new song. She was both thrilled and terrified; she knew "Fox Trot" was not going over very well, but since it had taken her so long to learn it, she was nervous about having to learn something new.

Hal addressed the company: "Well, we know what we are going to do and it will entail a lot of work from everyone. We will all be busy until we leave this town. Every time this show is played—here, in New York, and all over the world—there will be people who will hate it. It's about age, which some people feel is audacious, but the Shuberts love

The cast gathers onstage for notes, fountain and Loveland drops still in.

the show and it's going to run for a hell of a goddamn long time! Nevertheless, you will all be working your asses off in Boston." Michael, who had been standing alongside, echoed the thought: "You bet your ass!" The reference to the Shuberts was something new: it was important that the Shubert Organization, as landlords of the Winter Garden Theater, be supportive. Otherwise, they might well begin to think of another tenant for their theater, since their primary interest was to keep their theaters filled: taxes, staff, and maintenance are continuing expenses even when a theater is dark. At this time, the titular head of the Shubert Organization was Lawrence Shubert Lawrence, Jr., but "the Shuberts" were fast becoming a new team consisting of two lawyers (Bernard Jacobs and Gerald Schoenfeld) and one questionable businessman (Irving Goldman) who had recently taken control of the business. There was no one named Shubert currently in sight.

Hal thanked the company for all their hard work, told them they would triumph, and set them off to prepare for the matinee. "Give a good show," he said.

Follies was now settling into a routine. There were to be twenty-nine more performances over the next three and a half weeks, and since the show was the only reason everyone was in Boston, the schedule revolved around performances and rehearsals. Each performance would be slightly different, reflecting not only notes given by Hal, Michael, or the authors, but also including whatever changes, cuts, and additions were being implemented that day. New things would be tried, found wanting, and the previous version would be quickly restored. Some changes took only a moment: a new line could be given to an actor at five P.M., run at half-hour on the stage behind the closed curtain, and put into the show that night, to stay there forever. On the other hand, an entire new number would have to be discussed, written, rehearsed during part of every rehearsal day available, orchestrated, and then put into the show at a performance planned days in advance, to allow for the coordination of new orchestrations, new lighting cues, and new set cues. Most of the changes fell somewhere between those two extremes, but changes on every level were going on at all times. Audience reactions would prove as valuable as anything in helping Hal, Michael, Jim, and Steve figure out when the collective attention span was waning, which jokes worked and which didn't, and which musical numbers were landing. To know how to listen to an audience is an art in itself, and to balance what an audience can tell you against individual comments made by friends and colleagues is even trickier. Despite the many years of experience represented by the collaborators on *Follies*, they were always in danger of making missteps at this most vulnerable of times. It's nearly impossible both to keep perspective on the whole and to attend to the details. The best one can hope for is that all the creative people discover that they are, in fact, working on exactly the same show. Then and only then can the back-and-forth of a theatrical collaboration result in a work with a unified point of view.

The actors were still feeling their way into the routine and rhythm of performing the show—after all, the opening night performance attended by the critics was only the fourth time the company had ever played it before an audience. Just finding and timing the traffic patterns was hard enough for the old-timers. Sometimes they weren't at the right places, and entrances were occasionally made from peculiar

and illogical spots. The actors were constantly making slight adjustments of their own onstage, either reacting to lines and modifying moments that didn't seem to be working, or simply trying to see how much leeway they had to place themselves where they felt they would come off best—or be seen best. This happened most often in the party scenes, where the staging wasn't precisely marked out. The partygoers had been asked to behave as if at a party, standing around tables of food, chatting. Some of these actors just worked the tables until they found the light and a spot for themselves, usually as far downstage center as possible. Occasionally notes would be given about this tendency, but some stalwarts tried to find other ways to be noticed.

Of course, there were already several golden moments that everyone knew worked. The most obvious was the mirror number, "Who's That Woman?" Audiences loved it, and almost every review singled it out as not only a great number but also one that was deeply in keeping with the themes of the show. Michael would tweak it (he once said that when he went in to fix a show in trouble—*How Now, Dow Jones*—he first improved the number that was working best before trying to fix

In "Who's That Woman?"—the mirror number—
old and new come together as one. Brilliant.

those that were not), but for the most part, "Who's That Woman?" was a solid hit. Other moments worked, but would elicit different reactions every night. Applause on the women's entrances during "Beautiful Girls," for example, never happened the same way twice. The principal actors had already made entrances in the Prologue, although in overcoats, and audiences were never sure whether they should applaud again for stars they had just seen, even if now they were in their evening dresses with their gold Miss America–style banners across their chests. In addition, many of the supporting actresses hadn't yet been introduced, so audiences weren't sure whether they knew, or were supposed to know, Sonja Levkova, Ethel Barrymore Colt, Justine Johnston, or Helon Blount. The ambiguity of knowing or not knowing who the women were was part of the point, but it made for curious reactions from different audiences.

Certain moments, both in the score and in the libretto, had been identified as problems. "The Right Girl" was one, but it was hard to tell whether the difficulty lay in the performance or the material. It had been a struggle for Gene to master the dance, and Michael had already simplified many of the steps, but he was eager to keep pushing Gene right up to his choreographic breaking point. "Waiting for the Girls Upstairs," for some reason that was hard to fathom, wasn't working. This seemed to have happened gradually, and no one was sure why. The rhythms were sloppy and the song seemed to confuse the audiences. Since it was a core moment in the show, it was imperative that it be fixed. And the big worry was whether audiences made the proper connection with Loveland, whether they grasped the psychological state of mind of the whole sequence, which, of course, affected their reaction to the songs. Some got it, some didn't, and no one could tell why. "Bolero d'Amour" was too long, but it was unique enough to be left alone. Michael and Bob would tinker with it when they had the dancers to themselves.

Actors' Equity rules specify how much time can be spent in rehearsal during out-of-town tryouts. They allow five hours in a one-performance day and two hours in a two-performance day. A dinner break was sacrosanct, beginning at 5:30 P.M. for a 7:00 P.M. half-hour call. Actors could be called in early before a performance in order to run specific things that were to be changed or inserted into that particular performance. While every week was supposed to include a day off,

Gene Nelson, relatively happy.

under some circumstances actors could be called in on that day, only with specific permission from Equity, with proper overtime pay, of course. On the days prior to first performances there are "ten-out-of-twelve" days in which the actors can work ten hours out of a straight twelve and without a day off. These are reserved for the period of technical rehearsals, since everyone acknowledges that assembling the elements of any show takes a lot of time and a lot of patience. They're grueling, but once audiences start coming in, they're over. Technical problems get taken care of at crew calls during the day, and they, of course, have to be coordinated with the director or choreographer's use of the stage for rehearsal. Whenever possible, a minor technical change would simply be explained to the performers before a performance; but if a change involved actors on moving units, or new hanging pieces of scenery that they'd have to watch for, then time had to be made around half-hour to run the changes with the actors.

Being out of town is an adventure. Everyone is away from home. For the actors, it's a surreal world of hard work mixed with boredom and fatigue, all the while never knowing if they will have this job for the next month, six weeks, six months, a year, or beyond. Socializing takes place mostly in restaurants or bars. The opportunity presents itself to get to know the other actors. New friendships are made, new romances happen—for the most part discreetly. Dramatic love affairs can mess things up, and while that certainly does happen on some shows, it didn't seem to on *Follies*, unless I was just too naïve to know. Wives, husbands, and lovers occasionally made visits. There are also unavoidable jealousies, both professional and personal. The camaraderie of actors together in a rehearsal room is changed as soon as everyone gets onstage. The jokesters, the recluses, the boisterous ones, the caring ones all take on new dynamics when everyone gets to do what they were actually hired to do in the first place. Every actor wants to be noticed; those who aren't are instantly disappointed. If one actor shines above the others, particularly if that comes as a surprise to the rest of the company, a "victim" can be created. This, too, didn't seem to happen on *Follies*. (Boris Aronson was known for saying, in his thick Russian accent, that there were two rules in the theater: "One: There is always a wictim. Two: Don't be the wictim.") Friendships made during the rehearsal period can become strained as the natural artistic pecking order becomes established. Some actors are generous and gracious to their fellow actors; some are not. The ones with experience help the new ones through the inevitable boring stretches and the inevitable homesickness. When an actor is replaced, it's devastating to a company. *Follies* had already seen one person leave for good and another have his role reduced. Were more heads being readied for the chopping block?

For the creative staff, the pressure was on. The gambling mood was becoming intensified. The ticking of the clock became louder. Three and a half weeks may seem like a long time, but it can feel like no time at all when big changes are needed. There was also no time to waste—a wrong change could take far longer to recover from than just leaving something alone that is working only moderately. And of

course, there were endless discussions. And everyone had opinions. The creative staff had ample opportunity to meet in small groups in out-of-the-way places—hotel rooms, bars, restaurants, and even walks around Boston—and to meet at any time of day or night that wasn't taken up with other show-related business. As a result, some of the decisions that were made public to the company appeared to have come out of nowhere, yet they may well have been contemplated and discussed for some time in private. Suddenly a plan is announced: a new song is being written, a number is going to be restaged, new dialogue is going to be inserted. Whether a decision is right or wrong won't be known until it gets tried.

The biggest job for Hal, at this point, was to create uniformity and agreement among his collaborators. Fred Ebb once observed that what was great about working on a Harold Prince show was that "You're all working on the same show." He explained that all too often you get to the place in the development of a new musical when you start discussing what you think does and doesn't work and are shocked to discover that some of your collaborators are envisioning a completely different show. With Hal Prince, said Ebb, you have been forced into so much discussion, argument, contemplation, experimentation, examination, and opinion before rehearsals start that you can't help but share the same vision. That way, when trouble comes and things need to be attended to, you are all at least starting from the same vantage point. At no time is that more important than when the show is out of town, and at no time was it more essential for *Follies* than right now. Many an ambitious new musical has gone up in flames at precisely this moment, with people freaking out in one way or another. The stories are legendary, with the kind of experiences that once prompted Larry Gelbart to say that he hoped if Hitler were alive he'd be out of town with a musical.

But what about perspective? Did anyone still maintain perspective on the show? Hal clearly needed to know if his collaborators agreed on the status of *Follies*. Did they agree on what worked and what needed to be changed? Would pet peeves influence rational thinking? Would instinct guide the creators along the right path? It's a slightly schizophrenic time—having to be realistic about what needs to be changed or cut in order to bring the piece into focus yet never losing sight of the core of your creation. The authors have been living with this work for years, most intensely for a number of weeks, and it isn't the show they originally conceived. Steve had already said during rehearsals that

Hal Prince and his leading ladies. Above: Alexis Smith; right: Yvonne De Carlo; below: Dorothy Collins

he missed *The Girls Upstairs*, but how would that affect his thinking? Jim seemed to be in a relatively constant mood, always watching, always conferring, and always changing small things. But if major rewrites were needed, would he agree? And what about Michael? He had behaved slightly differently from everyone else all through the rehearsal period. He was younger, hipper, more overt, and no less creative. He had made his annoyance clear about the quantity of songs that came late in the process. His past experiences had shown him to be a thorough professional, and he was clearly capable of doing whatever work was needed out of town.

I was as uncertain about where things stood as I ever was. Nothing that was earmarked as a problem surprised me, yet I had no idea how things were going to be fixed. I also knew that a certain strangeness had begun to seep into the process for the simple reason that the public now had access to our show. Who knew where an idea would come from? Already remarks overheard in the lobby had been taken seriously, and it was clear that outsiders were making their opinions known. Whereas earlier the show would be discussed only at a central location—the rehearsal studio, or at Feller's—now there were any number of places where it might be a topic of discussion. I knew this would be an interesting time.

The good news was that word of mouth was positive and business at the box office was growing. The box office grosses rose every week, from $57,924 in week one to $78,255 in week two, $93,798 in week three, and then, for what *Variety* reported was "a sell-out and a house record for the 71 year old Colonial Theatre," $98,485 for the final week, with a house scaled from $9.90 for Friday and Saturday night to $3.00 for the second balcony at the midweek matinees. Hal wanted to break the $100,000 mark, previously achieved in Boston only by Pearl Bailey touring in *Hello, Dolly!* (By the middle of the final week, general manager Carl Fisher broke the news that although we would come close, we wouldn't quite break it.)

Once the routine was established, each day brought slight variations of activities.

Thursday, February 25

Michael Bennett went back to New York; he had decided to take a couple of days off and was scheduled to return on Saturday.

The first matinee went well: a house full of gray-haired matinee ladies enjoyed the show far more than many of us thought they would. A holdover of sheer post-opening energy got the company through without a hitch. By the evening performance, however, things were beginning to fall apart. Fifi's entrance for "Ah, Paris!" had been changed a couple of days earlier, and she came charging on from the correct spot but suddenly forgot what she was doing. As the orchestra played on, she smiled and wandered around, saying to the audience, "I may be an old girl, but, ooh-la-la, I'm willing!" Hal Hastings coaxed her back into the second chorus of the song. Following the end of the Montage, as she came offstage, Fifi apologized to Ethel, who shot back, "Oh, Fifi, you always have some goddamn excuse." Fifi said she was hurt and that Ethel shouldn't say such mean things. But Fifi wasn't the only one who lost her way; when Alexis got to the interlude release in "Uptown, Downtown," she began the tongue-twisting lyrics and got completely lost. She just kept dancing away, threw her head back, and laughed until the second chorus, where she found her way back. You might even have thought she was singing the song as written. John McMartin went up completely on the lyrics to "Live, Laugh, Love." This was truly bizarre, since that was the whole point of the song when performed correctly. But for the actor to lose his place was unnerving, most of all to John. After the performance, as he was making his way out the stage door, he muttered, "God, what a strange night. Sweet Jesus!"

I spent the evening performance in the orchestra pit. This was fascinating. First of all, the only feeling I got of being connected with the stage was the thumping overhead during energetic dance numbers. It felt as if a dance class was taking place on the floor above. Most of the time you could barely hear the actors or the audience. The pit is an area large enough to accommodate twenty-seven players with their instruments and music stands and a podium for the conductor. The floor is lower than the floor of the orchestra level of seats, which itself is lower than the level of the stage. The pit is partly covered, the back half tucked underneath the front portion of the stage. (Stage floors have been moved slowly in front of the proscenium arches over the years so the actors can be closer to the audience.) The musicians are fanned out, all facing the conductor, who is placed in the middle of the wall away from the stage. The players face the audience; Hal Hastings faces them and the stage. The podium gives the conductor a mid-level

"Live, Laugh, Love"—John McMartin, in the middle of the line.

position, so that his head is visible both to the actors onstage and also to the musicians below. Strange though it may sound, there is no standard size and shape of an orchestra pit. The one at the Colonial Theatre is large enough to accommodate the *Follies* orchestra but would have trouble fitting in any more players. (Theatre owners are always trying to create a new row of high-priced seats at the front of the theater, thereby decreasing the size of the orchestra pit. They've become all too successful at doing that.) Each player needs an amount of space dictated by his instrument: the string instruments need room to bow, violins and violas at shoulder level, cellos and basses at knee level. The harp, with its tall lyre, needs to be at one of the far ends so it won't obscure the view of the stage. Percussion tends to take up a significant amount of room, dictated chiefly by the instruments called for in the orchestration, plus a place for the player to stand amidst them all. For *Follies*, it was a trap set, xylophone, two timpani, and a couple of small triangles hanging from a music stand. One of the traditions of Broadway orchestras is for the woodwind players to play more than one instrument throughout the course of the evening. Called "dou-

bling," this procedure allows the orchestrator to use, for example, clarinets at one point in the evening and saxophones later on, provided there is enough time for the players to shift from one instrument to the other. The flutist almost always doubles on piccolo, used sparingly but necessary when the orchestration demands a high-pitched sound. Woodwind players tend to be surrounded by stands and poles on which to rest their instruments. The brass section has its own particular needs: trombones need space in front for the slides to move freely, the tuba takes up considerable room, and trumpets need to be placed where they blend in with the overall sound, but also where they won't blast into the ear of a fellow orchestra member. Brass players also need places to put their mutes, which often have to be put in and taken out during the course of a song. Tradition dictates that the strings usually fan out to the left of the conductor and the woodwinds to the right. And if there is a keyboard, it usually stays close by the conductor as well. There wasn't a keyboard in the *Follies* pit, but a piano was part of the onstage trio.

Hal Hastings's baton of choice was a Scripto mechanical pencil, chosen because it was short, about six inches long, and had a metal tip on the end that caught the light. His stool sat on a mechanized podium that was raised slightly off the floor. He could sit or lean on the stool when he wasn't conducting. In front of him was a music stand, lit from the sides and large enough to hold a stack of bound copies of the full orchestral score for each individual song. By now he hardly ever referred to the full scores, since this was the sixth performance and he knew the orchestrations pretty well. He never referred specifically to a score when the orchestra was playing; occasionally, while a scene was taking place, he might check on something, make a note, or shift to the next score. He had a script nearby in case he needed to refresh his memory about how much time he had until the next song. He could speak to the orchestra quietly, and even though his rising up from his stool signaled that a number was coming, he would sometimes have to remind one of the players to get his or her instrument poised. He could also give notes during the course of a performance when the orchestra wasn't playing, but most often his comments were simple and direct, like the one he made to a bass player who almost botched an entrance: "*Watch* me." One of the extraordinary things about Broadway orchestras, and about the specific orchestra for this particular

Thursday-night performance, is that the players assigned to and hired for the orchestra have the right to send in substitute players. There are rules under which a "sub" can be used, and it isn't uncommon, as was the case this evening, for there to be eight substitute players out of twenty-seven. Since the part for each specific instrument is always on the music stand, it is the responsibility of the man or woman assigned to the original orchestra—they're called the ones "with the chair"—to make certain the books of music are up-to-date and accurate. The conductor has no say over when a sub can be in the pit, and often he isn't even informed. He steps into the pit, looks over the orchestra, and sometimes sees a sea of strange faces. It's his responsibility to guide them through the performance as proper members of an ensemble. After the one performance the conductor can decree that a sub isn't good enough, but if he doesn't speak up then, he is stuck with that player as a sub for as long as the show runs. It doesn't take long for a conductor to sense which substitutes need specific attention and which are able to hold their own with everyone else. Surprising though this system sounds, it does allow for first-rate freelance players to work in the pit of a musical while maintaining other jobs.

Once the performance began, Hal's concentration was focused on the stage. Much to my surprise, he conducted every song differently. Different actors needed different things from their conductor. When Fifi was singing, both his arms were pointed right at the stage so he could follow her precisely and throw her whatever lyric she might miss. When she messed up, he pointed right at her and said, fairly loudly, "No, wait," and put his finger up until he knew the orchestra had caught up to the verse. He understood that when the chips were down, it was the actors who needed his guidance more than the orchestra, that they usually looked at his downbeat and then played their part instinctively. Most of the time he would mouth the words carefully, especially for those in the company who were still somewhat on edge, like Marcie Stringer. On occasion he would cue an actor with his left hand, but for the most part he let his right hand gently beat the rhythm. For "Losing My Mind," he simply looked at Dorothy and made the smallest casual movements with his Scripto pencil for the orchestra to follow. At times he didn't do anything; he was clearly following her, and the orchestra just played along. Dorothy's career had been almost entirely singing with an orchestra, and she knew how to

take the stage and "lead" the conductor. Most of the time he cocked his head slightly to one side, smiled, and waved his arms in a way that looked fairly nonchalant.

Orchestrations are deceptive. They're meant to sound complete and whole, yet it's surprising to listen to the individual pieces that make up a whole. For example, during "Waiting for the Girls Upstairs" I heard things in the flutes and piccolos that reminded me of *Bye Bye Birdie*. They came during the women's chorus, adding a playful punctuation to the ends of four of their descriptive lines. I hadn't noticed them before, and they reminded me of the flute passages in "Put on a Happy Face." I asked Jonathan Tunick about them, and he said, "Ah, yes, the Ginzler flutes." Robert Ginzler was the orchestrator of *Bye Bye Birdie* and had been one of Tunick's mentors. Obviously, the homage wasn't meant to call attention to itself, and Tunick would not have done it had he not thought it right for the song. But since the whole of an orchestration is made up of hundreds of details, in the hands of a good orchestrator there's room for appropriate musical quotes or references. Little ornamentations or even jokes can be added that really are invisible except to anyone fairly knowledgeable about musical-theater orchestrations. In the documentary film of the *Company* cast recording session there is a moment during "Another Hundred People" where the camera is focused on the trumpets, which are echoing the "Bobby baby" theme—something that I never heard in the theater or on the recording until it was pointed out visually. Fascinating though the quotes and references are, the most important job for theater orchestration is to support the singers and serve the work.

Friday, February 26

Today, Michael Bartlett, the silver-haired septuagenarian who played Roscoe, decides that he needs to be introduced more fully in the show. This is a concern that has never been raised before, and it smacks of influence by some friend who has seen the show and rendered an opinion. This kind of interference can't be avoided, but it tends to be less than helpful. The request seems out of character: Michael has been a quiet and diligent member of the company, working hard to remember his lines and his blocking. He has also been saving his high B-flats at the end of "Beautiful Girls" for the actual performances, and has hit them every time since Saturday. He cer-

tainly looks the part, and sounds it. Yet now he is complaining that "The character of Dimitri Weismann just *says* my name once. How are people supposed to know who I am?" He puts this question rather generally to whichever of his fellow actors will listen. He won't dare, however, ask anyone in authority. (Nothing was added; he continued to be introduced by Weismann's line, "Here, as always, the inevitable Roscoe. . . .") Virginia Sandifur (Young Phyllis) is becoming a slight irritation to some members of the company because she is behaving like a star. Harvey Evans and Kurt Peterson (Young Buddy and Young Ben, respectively), who share a dressing room, joke about how Harvey liked "his" (Marti Rolph) better than Kurt liked "his" (Virginia). There is also a rumor that she's having an affair with Jim Goldman. Changing the subject slightly, Gene Nelson remarks that when Virginia first appeared onstage during the dress parade in a black wig and black-and-white dress she reminded him so much of his first wife that it was positively scary.

Before rehearsals, the "sweetening" tapes for "Who's That Woman?" and "Loveland" were rerecorded. As the company gathered around the foot mikes for a brief rehearsal, Hal Hastings reminded everyone of the notes in the final chord of "Who's That Woman?" Ethel Barrymore Colt lost her note and, reaching into her past as a recitalist, asked, "What was the penultimate note of that chord?" It seemed so in character. There wasn't time, unfortunately, to test the new tape with the orchestra before the evening performance, and, of course, the synchronization was chaotic. Everyone kept on dancing, and much of the audience probably had no idea anything was amiss.

Since Michael Bennett wasn't around, Hal could rehearse whatever he wanted. He chose to run the Prologue and to try a slight rearrangement of the dialogue around "In Buddy's Eyes." Jim and Steve also took the opportunity to work with the actors directly. Jim had brought a new line for Yvonne for her entrance. He had two ideas, both of which were tried at different performances: "This reminds me of alumni day at Forest Lawn" and "I got my start on this very spot, four score and seven years ago." These were to replace her lines "Act? Me, act? I just go out and let fly and heaven help the leading man." This became a pattern with Jim—bringing in small line changes, many of which were tweaks to make lines land better. Large-scale libretto changes didn't seem to be under consideration. Steve took Hal Hastings, Phil Fradkin, the Old Four, and the Young Four into one of the

lounges for a rehearsal of "Waiting for the Girls Upstairs." Steve was unhappy with the performance, which had gotten musically sloppy. He said he wanted "to hear the downbeats" and told Gene, "It is important that the first section be as square as possible. You tend to be a little off the beat." Hal corroborated the places where Gene and the others tended to get sloppy. The second section, conversely, was "too sharp. It should be more of delight and not as if someone is challenging you—it shouldn't have the feeling of recollecting a blow." Steve said that as soon as Gene sings "I remember, me and Ben . . ." the audience "should feel that the song is an 'up.' " He wanted Alexis more wry when she sings "One of them was borrowed and the other was blue." Then he wanted them to anticipate the "down in a minute" section, not to do it square but rather with anticipation. His direction was precise, detailed, and brilliant—he knew exactly what he wanted. The session may have gone a bit over the heads of the performers, but they were game.

Saturday, February 27

The matinee was nearly sold out, with only a few seats left in the extreme corners of the house. A good sign. I stayed backstage to watch the routines that had developed during the running of recent performances. Starting at the half-hour call, the stage turns into a veritable gymnasium. Dancers and actors are stretching against parts of the set, using the levels as supports and the pipes in the movable units as ballet barres. John McMartin marked through his number, muttering to himself. Going up on his lines on Thursday had spooked him, and he wanted to pace himself ahead of time. Ursula, the tallest showgirl, the one who is preset when the curtain rises, walked through some of her blocking trying to figure out how best to deal with the heavy, beaded train to her dress. She has to maintain a ghostlike aloofness, but at one performance the train had gotten caught on some of the rubble in the set. Freeing it up while remaining in the ghost reality wasn't easy. She was trying to find a foolproof path that would minimize the possibility of its happening again. Hal Hastings sat on one of the levels of the set in his white tie and tails, talking with the stage managers. Several members of the company wandered out on the stage, said hello, asked the stage managers some questions, and wandered off. John Grigas, as stage manager number three, went around

to all the dressing rooms collecting "valuables"—wallets, jewelry, whatever—that needed to be put in a safe during the performance. Once "places" was called, Fritz Holt stood, headphone on, at his desk immediately off stage right, and George Martin manned his desk on stage left. John Grigas was now arching the occasional eyebrow when escorting the same older women to their same entrance spots.

During the performance, most actors kept to themselves as they prepared to make their entrances. Alexis and John were of this school. In fact, Alexis preferred to stay in her dressing room until right before entering, and she preferred everyone to be quiet around her. One night she said she must have scared one of the showgirls to death by turning around and telling her to shut up. Dorothy, on the other hand, had no problem socializing right until the moment she was to go on, whether the scene about to be performed was comic or emotional. At one moment when she finished a scene with Ben and wandered upstage to one of the party tables, I could see that she huddled right in with the rest of the actors, giggling along with them.

An intercom system brought sound to all the dressing rooms on every level. In addition to piping in the show, the "squawk box" system allowed for announcements by the stage managers, who would give warnings and cues, and sometimes specific calls to actors who might not be on the "deck," ready for their entrances. Wardrobe people were stationed at strategic spots backstage, either for quick changes or, in the case of the showgirls, to assist with the large costumes. Mostly those actors with costume changes had enough time to go back to their dressing rooms. On *Follies*, only Alexis and Dorothy had individual dressers.

During intermission, some costumes were taken from the stage to the dressing rooms or down to the wardrobe department for cleaning or repair. Since the set didn't change between acts, there wasn't a lot of activity during the intermission—a good thing, since by the time the show opened in New York, the intermission was gone.

In between shows I went to dinner with Yvonne and an actor who had done *Hello, Dolly!* with her on a tour. With two young potential gigolos on her arms, she downed two large martinis before dinner and generally enjoyed being the center of attention. That night, however, when it came time for her entrance for "Fox Trot," she forgot to step onto the platform that brought her onstage. I was in the stage man-

agers' office on the fifth floor, typing some script changes and listening to the performance over the intercom, when I heard some very odd ad-libs—"Hey, Carlotta, come on out here, we want to hear your number!" Later I learned that she turned offstage to Pete Feller and yelled, "Hey, I missed the boat! Bring it back!" And so he did, reversing the platform until she could step easily on. Apart from the missed cue, her good spirits made for a carefree rendition of the song, which she sang correctly for the first time in several performances.

Sunday, February 28

Rehearsal call was for "Waiting for the Girls Upstairs." Out of concern for how the song was coming across, Steve changed the last four lines of the lyric. The original lines:

> Though we know now life is immense,
> Full of wars and marriages and things that make sense,
> Time was when one of the major events
> Was waiting for the girls upstairs.

were changed to:

> Life was fun but oh, so intense.
> Everything was possible and nothing made sense
> Back there when one of the major events
> Was waiting for the girls upstairs.

There were people in the company who couldn't understand why the change was made. The change placed the lyric in the past instead of the present, and it had been pulled off deftly. Another example of the puzzle man at work.

The Young Four were not called at the beginning of rehearsal. After the new lyric had been run and Hal had adjusted the staging of the dialogue going into the song, including cutting four stinging chords that had introduced the number, the Old Four got up onstage to run the entire song, with fixes. When they got to the transition section when the young counterparts appear, the Young Four were just arriving in the theater. As they heard the transition, they started

singing from wherever they were while making their way to the stage—Virginia Sandifur and Harvey Evans dashing in from the wrong side of the stage, Marti Rolph running down the aisle of the theater and crawling over the orchestra pit, and Kurt bouncing on from stage right. Somehow, they all made it to their spots right on cue. Everyone laughed; it was one of those spontaneous moments that could never have been rehearsed and would never be repeated.

Michael showed up back from New York, refreshed and ready to work. He had watched the show on Saturday night, and was poised to get started. His first order of business was to cut the middle section of "Can That Boy Fox Trot!" Despite Yvonne's efforts at portraying the low-voiced football-playing jock and the high-voiced poet, and despite her game attempt at singing a trio all by herself, the middle section now became her simply pointing at two different men in the company, dancing with each one briefly—a box step only—and rejecting them both. It needed only a simple line change, from "I can't find him" to "I find him—*you*!" and then she plucks two guys from the party. Michael had her choose John J. Martin and Dick Latessa, who were still playing "Sally" and "Margie" in drag in "Buddy's Blues," and it was suspected they were picked because it was doubtful they would remain in the "Buddy's Blues" number much longer. By this time, Yvonne had discovered there was a big laugh to be gotten in the line "Remember when they used to dance at college?" by emphasizing, for all it was worth, the word "dance"—and waiting for a reaction. She got it every time.

Another fix made and rehearsed was the rearrangement of the Montage. Clearly, "Broadway Baby" was the hit, and one of the high points of the entire show. To sandwich it in between the throwaway "Rain on the Roof" and Fifi's "Ah, Paris!" was to put it at a decided disadvantage. "Rain on the Roof" was never intended as much more than a vignette—the stage direction from an early script says: "the number goes as quickly as it came, almost as if it never happened." As the older characters emerged in the various early drafts of the script, the sequence saw "Broadway Baby" added as well as a new song for a French chanteuse, titled "Hello, Doughboy." The latter only got as far as one version of the script. The lyrics were about a French tart imploring her GI beau to take her back to the good old U.S.A. now that the war was over:

Cheri,
Now the war is finis.
Hail the land of the free!
Pin your medal on,
Take me back to Oregon,
Pin your medal on—
(By the way, my name's Yvonne)—
Pin your medal on
Me!

That song somehow turned into "Ah, Paris!" As the Montage was assembled and rehearsed, the ending with all three songs together never quite worked. Now the task was to switch the order, placing "Ah! Paris" in the middle (and cutting its first verse) while moving "Broadway Baby" to the end. Steve, Michael, and Hal Hastings devised a new ending, in which the three songs would appear to come together, building to a rousing trio finale. This was rehearsed on both Sunday and Monday so it could go into the performance Monday night. Obviously, it made both Fifi and Ethel nervous, but they had no choice. Somehow when Fifi became aware of the shift of order and the elimination of the first verse of her song, she grew very quiet. Ethel simply did what she was told. But despite this strengthening of her song, she was troubled once again, about her salary. She hadn't acted on her urge to ask for a raise while the show was in rehearsal, but now she was bothered enough to speak up. She told me what she was making— $225 per week plus an additional twenty-five dollars to cover out-of-town expenses. Somehow she had found out that Fifi was making $400 per week, and that galled. (To put this in perspective, Alexis was making $1,500; Gene, $2,000; Dorothy, $1,000; John, $1,250; and Yvonne, $1,000.) She decided to go and speak with the company manager and say that she needed a fifty-dollar-per-week increase or she would have to leave the show—she would stay until a replacement was found, but she just couldn't remain, it was too insulting. After she had approached company manager John Caruso and asked him to take her request to the general manager, Carl Fisher, Ruthie came over to tell her that Hal had overheard the conversation and that he was giving her a raise effective immediately, not the fifty dollars she had requested but a hundred. That pleased her. On the lighter side, she mentioned that both Soupy Sales and Jack Cassidy had been spotted in the audience on Sat-

Fifi D'Orsay—a feather duster in sensible shoes.

urday night and that she'd heard a rumor Hal was not happy with John McMartin and was thinking of replacing him with Cassidy. That seemed unlikely; Cassidy was an old friend of the Princes, and I was sure that that was the entire reason for his being in attendance. Ethel also said there were rumors that Soupy Sales was having an affair with one of the dancers, and she wondered aloud if Sales couldn't just replace Fifi.

Monday, March 1

Hal began the rehearsal by addressing the full company. "We've got a lot of text that's going to be changed, and I've just seen six to eight pages which we'll try to get staged tomorrow. What I want to say, though, is that we are in a grace period during which we can take out the flab by really performing the material that is there and pruning what isn't essential. I'm going to ask the stage managers to be on top of the lines in the script and make you pick up any lapses."

He then ran some small changes in the Prologue, once again trying to coax a stronger performance out of Ed Steffe. Michael changed a few steps at the end of "Uptown, Downtown," gave some notes for "Live, Laugh, Love," telling the dancers not to react to Ben's breakdown, and announced that Suzanne Rogers and Rita O'Connor were going to be taking over the roles of Sally and Margie in "Buddy's Blues." No longer would the two roles be played in drag.

Monday was busy. I had no access to a Xerox machine the way I had in New York, so I had some serious typing to do to produce enough copies of revised script pages. I could make around ten good copies from one fat batch of carbons, but because I often had to distribute copies to more than ten people, I would have to type the pages out again, sometimes as many as three times. Late in the afternoon, Gene Nelson asked me to send an urgent telegram authorizing his wife to be admitted to a hospital in Los Angeles for a routine but necessary medical procedure. I had to find a Western Union office in Boston that stayed open after six, and then when I returned to the theater I was asked to take Mike Misita, one of the dancers, to the hospital because he was ill and no one could tell what was the matter. Knowing that he wasn't going to be able to perform that night, Bob Avian made adjustments to the dances and made the decision that the Vincent and Vanessa dance team would have no ghost figures in "Bolero d'Amour," since no one knew Mike's role as Young Vincent well enough to attempt it. Graciela (Young Vanessa) was relieved. Simple adjustments were made in other places where Mike had solo bits—mostly in the Prologue and in "Loveland."

The performance went well, for the most part. The shift in the Montage worked better than anyone could have expected. And "Can That Boy Fox Trot!" was at least shorter, although Yvonne wasn't happy with the hand she received at the end; she sensed it was measur-

ably less enthusiastic than what she was used to. Alexis slipped and fell in the dance section of "Who's That Woman?" She picked herself up, kept smiling, and went on dancing. Later, she explained that she feels it's vitally important for a performer to get right up if something happens onstage that might make the audience nervous. Keep smiling, keep going, and then once you're off, look to see if you're hurt. She seemed to be uninjured, but she did admit that she wasn't feeling well in general, which may have contributed to her concentration not being at peak.

I had an interesting test in my role as gofer. Richard Avedon was scheduled to do a *Follies* photo shoot for *Vogue* at the Ritz-Carlton Hotel after the performance, so I was dispatched in mid-afternoon to rent a panel truck large enough to hold several of the ornate showgirl costumes. The only place I could find to park it until the end of the performance was an indoor parking garage that turned out to be so tight that I came within an inch or two of getting the truck stuck in the circular ramp going from one level to another. After the performance, I had to back the truck into "Allen's Alley" and wait until a rack of showgirl costumes and wigs were loaded in. The call was for six of the women—two of the real Vegas showgirls and four dancers from the ensemble. As all these expensive costumes were loaded in, with my help, George Green, the show's Master Propertyman and quite a character, laughed and said, "United Truckers better not find out you're doing this." I wasn't sure how funny that comment was meant to be; I was simply doing as I was asked. But it did strike me as a little odd that with all the union jurisdictions around every aspect of the show, here I was driving a truck full of costumes to a photo shoot. I did, however, get to stay and watch the shoot, which was fascinating. A large roll of white paper, maybe fifteen feet across, hung from one side of the room to the other, allowing enough space for the dancers to stand in front and Avedon and his assistants to move freely in front of them. First, he had Suzanne Rogers and Rita O'Connor dress in their "Who's That Woman?" ghost costumes and go through the dance steps in place. Avedon kept snapping photographs, and when he came to the end of a roll he simply handed the camera to an assistant, who handed him another camera. As Avedon kept going, the assistant detached the removable film-back from the first camera and replaced it with a new one. Next, Kathie Dalton and Margot Travers, two of the Bennett dancers who also played showgirls, were asked to strike various poses.

These two women had great style and they looked gorgeous in their dresses, one white and one black. It was harder going with the two actual Vegas showgirls, who seemed to have no idea how to pose. Avedon had to be unusually precise with them—"Now, can't you do something with that arm?" Because they were both so tall and were wearing such large headdresses, there were problems with height as well. At the end, Avedon expressed surprise that they were such trouble, since he had assumed they would be the easiest to shoot.

The photo shoot over, I got to return the costumes to the theater, park the truck once again, and wait for the next morning, when I could return the truck and retire from my shady role as a teamster fink.

Tuesday, March 2

I was sent to Hal's suite at the Statler Hilton to pick up new pages for a reorganization of what was called scene 6, which included the songs "The Road You Didn't Take" and "In Buddy's Eyes." The order of the two songs was to be reversed, and they were no longer going to be separated by "Bolero d'Amour." Hal and Michael were sitting and talking, waiting for Jim to arrive with the new pages they had obviously all discussed. When Jim came in, he handed the pages to Hal, who read them, made a couple of notations, and handed them to me with the request to type them out and get them ready for the noon rehearsal. It was about 11:10.

When the cast assembled, Hal announced the new arrangement of scene 6, but said that he had decided to wait until tomorrow to rehearse it and put it in the show. Michael did some cleanup work on "Loveland," changing some of the entrances so more of the dancers would enter upstage and sweep downstage with the sequencing of the Follies drops coming in. Because the offstage tap-dance "sweetening" was never in sync with the dancers, the Masonite board was moved to a spot underneath the stage, just outside the orchestra pit but well within sight of the conductor. It was hoped that things would be better coordinated if George Martin and his tap-dancing associates could watch Hal Hastings directly instead of watching the dancers from one side of the stage. Since the taps would be put through the sound system, it didn't matter where they came from. And as long as the tappers had time to get to the floor below, it would work. It did.

Among the industry people who ventured up to Boston to see the show were my parents. At the time, my father was working with Leonard Bernstein, who was composing a theater piece for the opening of the John F. Kennedy Center for the Performing Arts in Washington, D.C. With the opening scheduled for September, only seven months away, no stage director had yet been chosen; Jerome Robbins, everyone's first choice, had passed. Hal was on the list, and so my father decided to come to see *Follies*, at least partly to report on his work. I had dinner with my parents before the show, then as they filed into their seats, I returned to my lair on the fifth floor to get going with the job of retyping copies of the new version of scene 6 to be ready to hand them out at the end of the evening's performance.

When I finished, I went down to watch the end of the show, which seemed very low on energy. The audience was awfully quiet; in fact, it was the first time the "reveal" for "Uptown, Downtown"—the entire dancing ensemble dressed in red tailcoats and hats and a silver fountain set at the rear—got absolutely no applause. "I could absolutely kill you!" Hal exclaimed when he saw me coming across the lobby. "Why did Betty and Schuyler come tonight? This is the worst performance yet! I thought they were coming on Wednesday, and I had a hunch this was going to be a lousy performance." He added that they would probably tell him they loved it no matter what—so I pulled them aside after the performance and told them to be honest. They were, even to the extent of saying that they didn't feel Ed Steffe was effective. My father had worked with Steffe in his days with Columbia Artists Management, and liked him, but he zeroed right in on the problem, which was also being felt among the staff: Steffe lacked the presence to play such a commanding role. Hal asked Michael to come over and listen. My parents were quite positive about the rest of the show, but I got the feeling that they weren't entirely taken with it; they had been big fans of *Company*, but this one seemed to leave them a little cold. Dorothy met them both and was very cordial, hugging me and telling them that she thought I was great. And Hal did listen to the Bernstein Mass (as it ended up being called), but Gordon Davidson was ultimately chosen to direct the piece.

Word got around that it was now official: *Prettybelle* would be closing this weekend and wouldn't be coming to Broadway. *Company*'s odds at the Tony Awards had suddenly improved.

Wednesday, March 3

Hal began rehearsal by handing out the new scene 6 and telling everyone involved how he intended to work on it: read it through, block it, then break for an hour so everyone could memorize the new lines, then do it onstage. He dismissed those members of the company whose roles were not affected by the change. Generally, everyone took the new scene well, and its staging didn't look as if it was going to create too many train wrecks. There was work on other bits and pieces: cleaning up the beginning of "Beautiful Girls" with Michael Bartlett; a little adjustment and rehearsal of "Who's That Woman?"; and the beginnings of some understudy rehearsals in the lower lounge with Peter Walker, understudy for John McMartin, going over Ben's music with Phil Fradkin.

Larry Cohen arrived, full of the New York gossip on the show. From Mary Bryant he had heard that several new publications were now interested in doing feature stories, along the lines of the "Prince of the Theater" story that Louis Botto had been working on for *Look.* That meant good word of mouth filtering back to New York, a very good thing for the show's prospects. The impression in New York was that the show had gotten great reviews in Boston. Business at the box office had started very strong, and there were hopes that it would continue. One curiosity: Larry had been in the Prince office one day when Joanna Merlin seemed to be on the phone with the agent of one of the lead understudies, and the agent was telling Joanna that he didn't think his client should ever go on in the role. He had been to Boston, seen the show, and frankly didn't feel his client was up to the rigors of the role.

At half-hour, Ethel was nowhere to be found. Fritz called her hotel; she answered the phone and said that her clock must have stopped at six o'clock, since that's what it read. She got to the theater as quickly as she could.

Alexis was in great spirits, though she confessed in a quiet voice that she had no idea what her singing would be like tonight. She had been fighting a cold all week, and no one had seemed to care, but now it was beginning to affect her voice. Once the performance began and she spoke her first line, it was apparent she had a problem. You could sense everyone clutching as they wondered what was going to happen when she had to sing.

*Alexis Smith—cool, sophisticated, soon to become the
real star of the show.*

There is never a good time for people to get sick on a show. And
out of town is the worst time possible. Leading actors being sick can
mean either Ruby Keeler–like *42nd Street* moments when unprepared
understudies go on, or in the worst case, having to cancel a performance. In the case of *Follies*, although understudies—actors already in
the show who learn other roles—had been assigned, there had been no
time to rehearse. (There were no standbys—actors who are not in the
show but cover leading roles—yet hired either.)

In addition to Alexis's obviously deteriorating condition, the audience seemed to be the stoniest one yet—no one in the Prologue or "Beautiful Girls" got a hand—and the orchestra must have been filled with subs because there were wrong notes all over the place. As soon as Alexis tried to sing the line "Waiting around for the boys downstairs," it was very clear she was in big trouble. Pitch was nowhere to be found, so she simply spoke her remaining lines. Even so, the song was still having problems landing. And everyone onstage seemed suddenly to get nervous. Little mistakes were made. Ethel missed one of her lines in the party scene, John McMartin seemed unclear of the staging in the newly restructured scene 6, and the Montage was very low in energy. Alexis barreled through until intermission, but it was obvious that she'd never be able to make it through "Could I Leave You?"—one of the few moments in the show that had come to be rock solid. At the start of the intermission, Hal was standing at Fritz Holt's desk looking at the script and trying to figure out what cutting the song entirely would entail. His mood was strained; it was almost as if he couldn't believe anyone would have the audacity to get sick. Fritz went out into the auditorium to find Michael. All three looked over the script and worked out how to adjust the cues to allow for the song simply to be excised from the performance. Agreeing that this was the best thing to do, they summoned Hal Hastings, who went over it with Fritz. As Fritz canvassed the crew and told them about the change, Hal summoned the Old Four and the Young Four to Alexis's dressing room to go over the changes with them. They were attentive and focused. Fritz then made a special announcement backstage over the sound system, alerting everyone that "Could I Leave You?" would not be performed. The audience would have to take the show as it came—they knew that when shows are out of town, the listing of musical numbers may not accurately reflect what is performed onstage.

The second act went off without too many problems, although Alexis sounded pretty grim in "Uptown, Downtown." When she came out for her curtain call, the entire company applauded her. Then once the final curtain came down, the company applauded her again. Company manager John Caruso had phoned a doctor, and as soon as she was out of her costume and into her street clothes, she was taken off to see a specialist. She was amused that no one had paid any attention earlier in the week when she announced she wasn't feeling well, but now that she'd lost her voice it was a crisis. As she was whisked off to the

doctor, Hal told Sheila Smith to begin learning the role. Sheila Smith was listed in the program as the standby for Yvonne and Fifi only, but no one was listed as either understudy or standby for Alexis. The original notion had been for Yvonne to cover the role of Phyllis, but I think that began to fade as soon as rehearsals started. No one had paid much attention to the whole issue.

The company rumors were that Yvonne's new number was going to be a Harold Arlen–style blues song and that Steve was also fiddling with "Uptown, Downtown." Steve hadn't been seen in a few days, so it was only natural that rumors would get started. In this instance, however, they were true. Michael was never happy with "Uptown, Downtown," felt that because it came late, he never had proper time to plan for its staging. It had been shoved at him at the last minute, and he asked for a new number. Judy Prince was said to be in favor of a new number as well. Steve was willing to oblige.

Larry Cohen watched the show, sitting next to an old couple who just loved it. They were so grateful to be seeing a musical with old people in it—and couldn't fathom why anyone young would have the slightest interest in the show. In the old days, you see, people had talent—not like today. Of course, they had come to the show with no idea it was a musical.

Thursday, March 4

Despite this being a matinee day, Sheila Smith was called at 10:30 A.M. to go through Phyllis's material. She pointed out to Fritz, nicely but firmly, that she believed Yvonne had a contract to cover the role, that she did not, and that if she were to go on, technically she would be violating both her own contract and Yvonne's. Fritz said he would call Carl Fisher and see that it got straightened out. Hal, realizing there was now a strong possibility that Alexis would have to miss some performances, spoke with Yvonne about her no longer covering the role. The report that filtered back was that Yvonne was relieved.

First Sheila went through all the music in the lounge with Hal Hastings and Phil Fradkin. Hal said she was fine but that her singing was one-dimensional. Then she went onstage, where George Martin took her through the staging. John Grigas remarked, "That girl is terrific." I was sent to the music copyists' suite at the Bradford to pick up copies of Phyllis's songs so Sheila could have her own set. Of course, the decision

whether she would fill in for Alexis had not yet been made, but everyone knew that they had better be prepared for the possibility. In the end, Alexis played the matinee, using a speak-sing style with whatever voice she had, still not attempting to perform "Could I Leave You?"

Yvonne, concerned about her new song, went to Steve's hotel room at midnight, in tears. She was convinced "Fox Trot" was being replaced because she was incompetent, that she was performing it badly, and that no one was telling her the truth. Steve tried to assure her that there was nothing wrong with her performance, that the reasons for replacing the song had to do with the song itself. He didn't think he was totally convincing, although what he said was the truth. Maybe just unburdening her woes made her feel better, but Steve was already hard at work on the replacement.

At noon Gene was called for a rehearsal of "The Right Girl." This number wasn't landing the way Michael wanted and hoped it would. He kept working at it, trying to find steps that Gene could execute well and that would make the staging exciting. He knew the set gave him ample opportunities for Gene to fly around, leaping from platform to platform, but he also knew that Gene was still nervous, and that his nervousness was coming across in performance. Michael seemed to have more patience with Gene than with some of the other performers, but he was still pushing, trying to find a balance between something that Gene could execute well and that was still exciting and energetic. He knew it wasn't there yet.

The matinee performance was energized, partly because the entire cast of *Prettybelle* was in the audience. Since their closing notice had gone up, and because they played their midweek matinee the day before, on Wednesday, Hal had issued an invitation to the whole company. Angela Lansbury was in "house seats"—good locations held back from public sale to be purchased by people connected with the show, but since the box office wasn't prepared for the number of people who took Hal up on his offer, the *Prettybelle* company manager, Seymour Herscher, worked with John Caruso to find locations for everyone. Not only would Angela Lansbury be in the house (audiences are always atwitter when a celebrity is spotted), but so would Jon Cypher, the originally cast Ben Stone who had taken the lead in *Prettybelle* after dropping out of *Follies*. He had the grace to write a note to Hal after the performance saying what a wonderful show *Follies* was, and adding that he would have had a nervous breakdown if he had

stayed with it. (He also penned a very cordial fan letter to John McMartin.) Lansbury came backstage after the performance and congratulated everyone. She was very cordial to all, and told Yvonne she was marvelous and asked if she had ever been on the stage before. A somewhat nonplussed Yvonne concluded later that Angela must have been in a state of shock since her show was closing.

Graciela Daniele fell at the beginning of "Bolero d'Amour" and did the rest of the number with a sprained ankle. At intermission she was sent to a doctor, and Bob Avian gathered the dancers to discuss the

"Bolero d'Amour"—The young ghost figures,
Michael Misita and Graciela Daniele.

changes needed in the second act to compensate for her absence. To keep the pairings equal in "Loveland," one dancer was taken out and his line given to someone else. With Michael Misita now back in the show but looking wan, Young Vincent and Young Vanessa seemed to be the cursed roles so far. But Graciela would bounce back by the evening performance, Ace bandage securely in place.

I had dinner with Larry Cohen and Paul Gemignani at the Union Oyster House, a Boston landmark on Stuart Street. Mainly we gossiped about the show: Larry hadn't seen it since the opening and questioned whether a lot of the new changes were taking the show in the right direction. There was a lot of tinkering going on, and we all wondered whether some wholesale changes weren't more in order. It seemed clear that the libretto was going to stay as it was—any notion Michael may have had about bringing in someone to write jokes or spruce up the dialogue seemed to have vanished. We all agreed that the opening needed to be fixed, but Michael did seem to be working on that, although we couldn't tell how much fixing he was actually doing. Paul had some specific criticisms of his own, but as he and his drum set were in the pit for performances, his vantage point was not ideal. And he was annoyed by something else: he wanted to conduct; he wanted the job as assistant conductor on this show. The man who had been hired, but who wouldn't join the company until New York, had fine credentials. Paul Cianci by name, he had studied with Pierre Monteaux, had conducted several Broadway shows, and perhaps most important, had been the assistant on *Funny Girl*, where he had kept Barbra Streisand happy. Paul was annoyed that he wasn't being considered for the position. (He did stay with the show, and must have played his cards right because he ultimately did take over as conductor, and has gone on to become Sondheim's number-one musical director to this day.)

After the performance, Larry Cohen met with Steve, who hadn't been seen around the theater for days. Steve played him the new song he was writing for Carlotta, which he was quite pleased with. Larry liked it and felt it would be perfect for Yvonne, but Steve was disheartened because neither Hal nor Michael had reacted favorably to it, and he couldn't see starting over again. They also discussed some current company rumors: that both Fifi and Ed Steffe would likely be gone before the show got to New York, and that Hal was considering postponing the Broadway opening. Steve felt that Hal was on the right track with changes but that Jim was proving to be obstinate.

Friday, March 5

Hal was in an agitated mood. He had a lot of little line fixes he wanted to follow up on and was annoyed that some of them hadn't yet been given to the actors. There did tend to be a certain level of confusion between Hal, the stage managers, and me about what was to be typed and what was to be handed out to the actors—and when. Hal wanted to keep working on little improvements in the dialogue, which now included a speech for Roscoe in the very beginning in which he talks about feeling useful—"so many of my friends have given up." The speech lasted only for a couple of performances.

Michael worked with the two dancers who had gone into "Buddy's Blues." They had basically been thrown into the number on the day the decision was made to replace the men in drag. Since both Rita O'Connor and Suzanne Rogers were accomplished dancers, putting them in the number had been a cinch. But something was bothering Suzanne: she hated her costume. She behaved as if she just didn't want to be in the number. Michael explained the tone of the number to them, that it was a vaudeville, pure and simple, and wasn't really any more complicated than that.

Alexis got through another performance, but her state of health was still a major concern. And she still didn't do "Could I Leave You?" Bob Avian and the three stage managers worked with Sheila Smith on the stage, going over all of Phyllis's blocking and musical staging until 1:30 in the morning.

Saturday, March 6

Saturday was another matinee day, and the limited rehearsal time was used for the understudies. Ethel Barrymore Colt, Peter Walker, and Dick Latessa worked through Sally, Ben, and Buddy. I was confused enough about when new pages were and were not supposed to be given to the actors that I hadn't a clue what to distribute to understudies. George Martin did most of the understudy blocking rehearsal, with Bob Avian and Fritz focusing on Sheila. She wondered what her wardrobe would be—for most of the show she could wear her own dress, but she would have to wear either Alexis's dress or something else that was conducive to the choreography of "Uptown, Downtown." (She was already in "Who's That Woman?" so she knew she

could handle that choreography in her party dress.) Fritz wanted to be prepared, so although no decision had yet been made about whether Alexis would be going on for either or both performances, he found an old *Hair* poster backstage and wrote on the back of it, in big bold letters: "AT THIS PERFORMANCE THE ROLE OF PHYLLIS STONE WILL BE PLAYED BY SHEILA SMITH." Actors' Equity rules require that if an understudy or standby goes on for a lead actor, two of the following three steps must be taken: an explanatory slip inserted in the program, a sign put up in the lobby, an announcement made before the performance begins. A slip in the program and a sign in the lobby are the preferred methods, but it takes time to print a slip and stuff copies into all the Playbills. If Sheila went on, she would have to be announced and the sign would have to be hung in the outer lobby before the house was opened. As it turned out, Alexis did perform at the matinee.

I went to see *Prettybelle* at its final matinee. It was pretty bleak— some interesting moments and performances, but it felt thrown together. The set looked cheap, the costumes looked like they came off a rack at a store, and the story was unbelievable. Angela Lansbury, with a thick Southern accent, did her best, but with her musical highlight a song entitled "When I'm Drunk I'm Beautiful," you knew it was doomed. Alexander Cohen and his wife, Hildy, were standing in front of the theater, talking with anyone they recognized. They were gracious enough to say that they had seen *Follies* and felt that it was "a dream realized." Luckily, *Prettybelle* was short, so I could get back to the Colonial to catch the end of the matinee, making a stop to get some more medicine for Alexis. It's interesting how you can walk into a show midway through and within thirty seconds know exactly what kind of performance the cast is giving and what kind of audience it is. This performance was fine, but Alexis was still croaking her way through "Uptown, Downtown." When the performance was over, she burst into tears and said, "You'll be lucky if you see me tonight" as she disappeared into her dressing room.

Barbara Matera was going crazy. She had been quietly shuttling between her New York shop and Boston, where she was now constructing a new costume for Alexis for "Uptown, Downtown." Few knew this was taking place; so many in the company had voiced displeasure with their costumes that it would have been suicide to let word get out that changes were even a possibility. Alexis's Follies cos-

tume was revealing and sexy, but it wasn't particularly flattering, either to Alexis or to the choreography. Phyllis was so repressed that to see her come out with her shoulders exposed and her great long legs was a surprise and a delight. Alexis's entrance in the Follies sequence usually got gasps, but just because a moment appears to be working doesn't mean you should stop fine-tuning. That was the thinking behind the new dress. Alexis had broad shoulders, and her spaghetti straps made them look even broader than they were. And although the strips hanging from the waist moved when she danced, they weren't very graceful. Barbara needed a fitting with Alexis before she could finish the new dress, but because everyone was hovering around the ailing Alexis, there clearly wasn't an opportune time. Ruthie had accosted Alexis to plead for her to try the new dress on, and in her raspy, coldy voice she said, "What do you want, a performance or a dress?" Later she apologized to Ruthie, saying she often says things that make no sense when she's stressed.

The evening performance, the last one for the week, was quite spirited. Alexis performed, again without "Could I Leave You?" She had learned how to make her way through "Uptown, Downtown." Dorothy, in her demure way, was beginning to get tired of all the attention being paid to Alexis. She knew Alexis was sick, but she was starting to feel overlooked by everyone, and Alexis had started to be a little standoffish with Dorothy anyway. Dorothy had tried to be friendly with everyone, and the rest of the company clearly adored her. But she felt the Californians weren't friendly. She loved Ethel and wanted to applaud her every night at the curtain call, standing off in the wings as she waited for her entrance. But so as not to insult anyone else, she clapped for everyone until the moment came for her to come out onstage.

Henry and Mary Guettel were in the audience, along with Bill and Jane-Howard Hammerstein. They all went out to dinner with Sondheim afterward, and Mary said some unflattering things about the show. She regretted her candor later on, and was far more enthusiastic at the opening in New York.

Sunday, March 7

This was the official day off for the company, but a few things had to be dealt with. Flossie finally prevailed and got Alexis to come in and

try on her new dress. Hal and Michael were both in the theater when she came walking out on the stage with it on. It was still red and pink, but this one was a complete, floor-length, form-fitting Marlene Dietrich evening dress with a high collar, long sleeves, and a skirt of overlapping long fringe going to the floor—and slit all the way up the right side. And it was clearly very heavy. Alexis looked quite unhappy. Flossie and Barbara Matera stood nearby. Michael said, "Okay, execute some of the steps." She began, and it was immediately evident that the choreography for her number in no way agreed with a heavy long skirt slit up one side. At one moment when she executed one of her moves, a large red bead flew off the dress and rolled off the stage. I picked it up; I still have it.

"Well, I would have to rechoreograph the whole number," Michael said. Alexis remained quiet, but clearly hoped the dress would simply disappear; she hated it. Luckily for her, it was never seen again. A new one would be made, but that was still a week away.

Michael went over "The Right Girl" with Gene on the stage. It seems that Gene had become very upset with the number, and with the show. Gene's frustration with the number had spilled over into a general malaise with everything. He had exploded in front of Hal and Michael. Hal had experienced this before with Dean Jones in *Company* and had a premonition that something would go wrong with Gene shortly after the New York opening, at which time he would ask to leave the show. Hal's premonition was only slightly off the mark: it was a family crisis that nearly prevented Gene from opening the show in New York, yet he remained with it throughout its New York run.

Jim Goldman met with Hal in the lounge to go over some more changes.

Steve Sondheim, who hadn't been seen in several days, showed up, manuscript in hand. It was Yvonne's new song, finished. There had been very little gossip around the company about the song, so I didn't know what to expect, but at least it was finished, and Hal was pleased about that. Steve handed me his manuscript, warning that it was the only copy. Knowing that the stage managers would be anxious for the lyrics typed out, I climbed to the fifth-floor dressing room/office, where the red IBM typewriter awaited. By this time I had a pretty good idea of how Steve liked his lyrics transferred to script format, so I was confident I could extract them from his musical manuscript with few

mistakes. I rolled the nine carbon sheets into the typewriter, and began:

I'M HERE

Carlotta

Good times and bum times,
I've seen them all and, my dear,
I'm still here.
Plush velvet sometimes,
Sometimes just pretzels and beer,
But I'm here.

The lyrics were precise and well crafted, so it was easy to figure out where the line breaks were. And they were evocative, with wonderful images from American history—breadlines, Beebe's Bathysphere, the WPA, Greer Garson, Amos and Andy. Herbert Hoover and J. Edgar Hoover were lyrically linked, probably for the first time ever. There was even a line cribbed from dialogue, in the fine tradition of the musical theater. Carlotta once had a line: "Used to be I played the vamp. Now I play somebody's hot-pantsed mother, stinko by my swimming pool and all my kids are acid heads." That had become:

Been called a pinko
Commie tool,
Got through it stinko
By my pool.
I should have gone to an acting school,
That seems clear.
Still, someone said, "She's sincere,"
So I'm here.

I was astounded. The song just kept delivering brilliant images, of events and people from the 1930s and forties, all woven into a passionate and dramatic statement of survival. Wow, I thought, and this from a fairly simple-minded character who had previously sung a clever song with one big double-entendre joke and some tossed-off quips about being a has-been. Now we're learning who she was, and it was

really good. There were a couple of references I didn't get—Brenda Frazier, Wally and George (later changed to Windsor and Wally)—but I did know about mahjongg, since my grandmother had taught me and my brothers the game that went with those beautiful ivory cubes. Certainly, though, I had never seen it used in a lyric before. Line after line continued to amaze me:

> I've gotten through "Hey, you remind me of whoozis.
> Wow, what a beauty you were."
> Or, better yet, "Sorry, I thought you were whoozis.
> Whatever happened to her?"

After these lines came a key change. Just typing these words, without hearing the music, it seemed as if the song had reached a different plateau and that a key change would probably be effective. Lyric after lyric was clever, perceptive, harsh, sad, piercing, funny, and honest. And perfectly crafted. In some ways the song seemed to be as much about Yvonne De Carlo herself as it was about Carlotta Campion, and I wondered whether Steve figured that Yvonne would probably not make the connection, which would add a layer of pathos to the performance that couldn't have been planned. He had been observing her, I thought, and he must have taken in a lot of who Yvonne was to create a piece of material that would give such depth to her character in so emotional a way. (Steve later claimed that Joan Crawford, not Yvonne, was his inspiration.) When I was told that Yvonne's audition song had been "Ten Cents a Dance," I wondered if there wasn't a reference to that in the lines:

> Danced in my scanties.
> Three bucks a night was the pay,
> But I'm here.

The song would exist very much in the present—a personal statement by a character who had exhausted her repartee for the evening and was now revealing the truth about herself. Steve was replacing a comic turn with a from-the-heart statement. "Fox Trot" was a throw-away expanded beyond its resources. Now it was gone, and it was just possible that in the process *Follies* was going to gain a powerful moment that would strengthen its emotional center. I couldn't wait to

hear the music that went with these words, especially as I got to the last page:

> I got through all of last year,
> And I'm here.
> Lord knows, at least I was there,
> And I'm here!
> Look who's here!
> I'm still here!

Keeping a clean copy for my files, I brought the copies and the manuscript down to Steve. The next step was for Mathilde to create a piano/vocal copy. Then the song could be circulated. This one was definitely a keeper. Little did I or any of us know then that it would become one of Sondheim's most performed songs, and one whose sentiments, first typed that day by a twenty-year-old gofer, would continue to have resonance for years to come.

10

"I'm So Glad I Came"

THE LAST TWO WEEKS IN BOSTON, MARCH 8–20

Monday, March 8

Hal Hastings called Yvonne in early to teach her "I'm Here." They disappeared down into the men's lounge, where the piano was, and spent the better part of the afternoon going over the song. Hal had to explain some of the references, since Yvonne had a tendency to sing "Amos and Randy" instead of "Amos and Andy." She was excited about the song, but anxious about just how soon the powers that be wanted it in the show. She had a big job in front of her, and she knew it.

Gene's blowup had somehow energized Michael, who attacked "The Right Girl" with a new sense of excitement. He came up with new ideas, including additional swings around poles and an astonishing leap from one high platform on stage right to another. He was also determined to devise an ending that would both act as choreographic punctuation and get a huge hand. Gene seemed to have gotten over his frustration and was excited as well. The number was starting to cook.

Some new material from Jim had the company somewhat taken aback. Alexis was given new opening lines that she did not like. Dorothy was given some new lines for her "mad" scene following "The Right Girl," and she wasn't happy with hers, either. That scene was being tinkered with to get the tone right—it was when Sally thinks that Ben will marry her and is as crazy as she ever is—but one new line

in which she speaks about cold corpses had the company actually gasping at the first read-through.

The evening performance elicited the best audience reaction so far. For some reason, this Monday-night Boston crowd was out for a good time, and they loved it all. Strange that two weeks ago the Monday audience was a total bust, and yet here was a riotous group. They laughed at lines that had never gotten laughs before; they applauded every number; so it was hard to figure out whether the performance itself was any good. Gene, with the new changes for "The Right Girl" on his mind, flubbed the second chorus of lyrics to "Buddy's Blues." "Rain on the Roof" was a disaster, while "Ah, Paris!" was in a holding pattern and generally doing fine, and "Broadway Baby" continued to knock 'em dead. The Young Four performed their Follies numbers very peculiarly; apparently they were spooked by a rumor that both songs were about to be cut.

Tuesday, March 9

Notes began with Michael's announcement that the new version of "The Right Girl" would be put into the show on Friday. Then Hal took over, yellow pad in hand. "Not a bad show last night. Pretty good . . ." Ethel, feeling frisky, replied, "Yeah? That what you thought?" "Well," he replied, "I'll tell you where I didn't like you. Were there any places where you didn't like yourself?" Michael took over: "Hattie, I think it looked like you knew how funny you were last night." Ethel said: "Well, yes, I did." "Please don't *tell* us—just *be* funny." He was similarly concerned about the women in "Beautiful Girls": "All you girls who come down those stairs are coming down for *yourselves.* Do not make eye contact with the audience. You are coming down those stairs for a last time. You are not at a performance of the Ziegfeld Follies, so do not play to the audience." Hal and Michael huddled over a few notes they weren't sure who should give. Michael said "Who's That Woman?" was getting sloppy. "When I have fixed everything else in the show—next week, maybe, although I know that's optimistic—then we'll clean up the mirror number." Hal inserted two new lines before "Waiting for the Girls Upstairs"—"because I would hate for a day to go by without doing something to that number"—and had a few new line readings. To Michael Bartlett, regarding one of

Roscoe's lines, Hal said, "Just relax, will ya? The key is to throw the whole goddamn thing away." Alexis questioned one of her recently added lines, and Hal told her she could simply cut it. At that, Jim Goldman, who had been lurking out in the house, piped up: "The line should stay as written. It's needed to make another reference in the speech make sense." Hal, stealing a glance in Jim's direction, turned back to the actors. "We'll take five and talk, and then I'll have a note for you, Alexis. Cool it." A compromise was reached; the line remained, but with one minor edit.

Gene remarked later that he didn't like the way Hal talked to the actors.

Wednesday, March 10

Steve showed up to watch Michael rehearse "Buddy's Blues" with the two dancers. They were still unhappy with the number. "Act like two of the dumbest showgirls ever," Steve coached. "Play it absolutely straight. You've both been to acting school and have had exactly one lesson . . . any emotion you show is simply what you've been taught. But be careful—nothing in the song must ever sound like contempt. The fact is, both Sally and Margie *do* love Buddy, and he is torn between the two."

It was a matinee day. Celebrity sightings: Phil Silvers, who was about to open in a new comedy titled *How the Other Half Loves* at the Wilbur, was at the performance. Robert Goulet and Carol Lawrence attended the evening performance, along with Gene Kelly, who was there to cheer on his brother, Fred. Tharon Musser, her assistant Spencer Mosse, and Boris and Lisa Aronson were there, having been gone for several days. The matinee was pretty sluggish, the evening performance more spirited.

In between shows, Hal wanted to hear Yvonne sing "I'm Here." After everyone had cleared the stage, Hal Hastings climbed up to the onstage piano and played, while Yvonne, clinging to her lyric sheet, sang it twice. It was the first time I had heard the music all the way through. It was, as I had been told, in the style of a smoky Harold Arlen blues number, and the key change three-quarters of the way through was great. It felt like a big change but was actually only a half-step up. Yvonne didn't have it mastered, but it sounded as if she would be able to deliver it well. Dorothy sneaked into the wings from her

dressing room in her bathrobe to listen and gave Yvonne a comradely hug when she was done. Hal was apparently so pleased that he cried— at least that's what Yvonne told members of the company, who were beginning to hear good things about the new song. She was concerned about when it would go into the show. Staging hadn't even been contemplated. It was Wednesday, and although she didn't know it, Hal and Michael wanted it in by the weekend.

Steve was now deep into the new Follies number for Alexis that Michael had requested. This came out of nowhere, at least to us on the periphery. "Uptown, Downtown" was the second-to-last song finished, and it was going over well. But people were still worried about the audience making the connection between the main characters and all the Follies numbers, and Alexis's song did seem to be the hardest for the audience to grasp. According to Hal Hastings, Steve had come up with some very funny ideas for the new song.

Thursday, March 11

"This is going to be a big day. There are lots of changes, seemingly small but they mean a lot of rearrangements, which will mean a lot of coordination," Hal began, and then proceeded to do what he had been doing for days: make small changes to scenes, mostly to the same ones that had been worked over before. Big fixes were clearly not going to be made. Yvonne's new number was being rehearsed, and everyone now knew Alexis was going to have a new Follies song. Michael was redoing the Prologue and was still intent on making "The Right Girl" a showstopper. The libretto was pretty much what it was going to be, and Jim continued to be the slightly aloof figure he had been from the beginning. He watched every performance, and made only slight changes. People treated him with kid gloves, but there was a growing feeling that he wasn't holding up his end, that the changes being made were strictly cosmetic and, in some instances, less good than what they were replacing. Had he lost all perspective? Audiences were watched and paid attention to, but since there wasn't a consistent response it was hard to take coherent direction from them. Work was taking place, but where was it all heading? Members of the company were confused—were they in a big, splashy musical comedy, or were they in an innovative, conceptual work the likes of which had never been seen before? When audiences were silent, were they listening or bored?

Reaction varied from performance to performance, and reaction varied from friend to friend. No one seemed to have a clear notion as to whether the show would be a big hit or a big flop. Some audiences seemed to leave *Follies* enchanted; others seemed to leave disappointed. The emotions of everyone involved with the show swung similarly between two poles. We were right smack in the middle of the Boston run: there was a week and a half left, followed by a week and a half of previews in New York. Then opening.

Even though the news of a new number for Alexis had made its way around the company only the day before, Steve brought it in today, finished. It paid homage to a song from *Lady in the Dark*, "The Saga of Jenny," with its title "The Story of Lucy and Jessie." It covered much the same territory as "Uptown, Downtown," but in a more Cole Porter way—sassy, and at a bit of a clip. If audiences were unable to make the connection between Phyllis herself and the hypothetical "hyphenated Harriet" of "Uptown, Downtown," perhaps they would make the connection with this new verse:

> Here's a little story that should make you cry
> About two unhappy dames.
> Let us call them Lucy "X" and Jessie "Y,"
> Which are not their real names.

When Michael got around to staging it, he even had Phyllis point to herself at the end of those four lines. As a big fan of "Uptown, Downtown," I wasn't wild about the new song, and my ear kind of balked at the idea of someone wanting to be "juicy," even as I was fascinated by some of Steve's wonderful rhymes:

> Lucy wants to be dressy,
> Jessie wants to be juicy,
> Lucy wants to be Jessie,
> And Jessie, Lucy.
> You see . . .
>
> . . . .
> Poor sad souls,
> Itching to be switching roles.
> Lucy wants to do what Jessie does,
> Jessie wants to be what Lucy was.
> Lucy's a lassie

Brush-up rehearsal in the men's lounge, Colonial Theatre.
Phil Fradkin at the piano, Hal Hastings in charge.

You pat on the head.
Jessie is classy
But virtually dead.
Lucy wants to be classy,
Jessie wants to be Lassie . . .

It was hard to fault the creative flow of this creative mind. Michael intended to stage it very much along the lines of "Uptown, Downtown," although it was an entirely new song and needed an entirely new dance arrangement.

Having now finished all the songs, Steve sat and watched the show for the first time in nine days. He was genuinely excited and came backstage and said to everybody, "I haven't seen the show in over a week and I am absolutely thrilled." That was meaningful praise, and it gave everyone a boost. As he went off to the dressing rooms to speak to the actors individually, Hal, relieved somewhat by Steve's enthusiasm, sat on the stage with Jim Goldman. "Jim," he said simply, "this is a

wonderful show." Company manager John Caruso wandered out on the stage to give Hal some good news: the remainder of the run in Boston was virtually sold out, with only a few balcony seats left for the Monday, Tuesday, and Wednesday nights. Hal was thrilled to hear that audiences were embracing the show.

Michael and Bob Avian began taking Yvonne through some basic staging; they would resume working with her at the start of rehearsals on Friday.

Friday, March 12

Everyone felt that it was important to concentrate on "I'm Here," get it staged, make whatever changes were necessary to the dialogue before and after it, and get it in the show. The goal was for it to go in at the Saturday matinee. Because it was a book song, the introduction had to be changed; "Can That Boy Fox Trot!" had some silly lines introducing it that were now completely inappropriate. Steve sat in the auditorium, watching the stage intently. When at one point Yvonne went up on a lyric, everyone turned to Steve, who was, himself, momentarily flummoxed. "I was so involved in the song that I forgot what the next line was," he confessed.

Hal took the rest of the company to the ladies' lounge for notes. He characterized the day as "kind of a funny one" since it consisted primarily of making whatever adjustments needed to be made to accommodate "I'm Here." But the new version of "The Right Girl" was going in tonight, and it needed stage time as well. Michael would have to turn his attention to "The Story of Lucy and Jessie," since it was hoped that it, too, could go in the show soon.

When time came to work through "I'm Here" onstage, Yvonne performed it for the rest of the company sitting out in the house. She messed up a few lyrics, but when she finished, they cheered. She was relieved. Fitting the song into the context of the show went quicker than anyone expected, and it was run without incident a couple of times.

Michael began "Lucy and Jessie." John Berkman and Paul Gemignani sat at the onstage piano and drum set. Michael climbed up to the platform as John played the song over and over. He was listening and marking his way through, thinking about how much of the choreography for "Uptown, Downtown" could be retained or adapted.

When Alexis came out of her dressing room and heard what was going on, she said, "Well, *his* Lucy and Jessie are certainly faster than *my* Lucy and Jessie!" She liked the song, though, and mentioned somewhat sardonically that she was hoping she would be given enough rehearsal time before it went in. Michael came down on the stage, Bob Avian and George Martin on either side of him and the dancers behind, and began to work his way through the song. Steve watched, at one point reminding Michael of a step he had liked that had been discarded; Michael was grateful for the suggestion and promptly put it back in. John Berkman gave Michael the counts and the "feel" that he was asking for. The song seemed to please everyone; it seemed closer to the character of Phyllis, who, in Jim Goldman's words, "was open and alive at twenty and is now closed and dead at fifty." This new song established the two sides of her personality better.

Hal had a new concern about "Too Many Mornings": he wasn't sure that Sally's line "And my fears were wrong" was clear enough. He wasn't sure whether the problem was in the performance or in the writing itself. Since Steve was nearby, he went over to Dorothy and talked her through the moment that was the musical climax of the song. The lyric was an expression of joy. He could zero in on any problem with precision and without hesitation.

Hal had a new task for me. Word got to him that since they knew they wouldn't be eligible in the "Best Musical" category, *No, No, Nanette* had requested a Special Tony at the awards ceremony, which was only a few weeks away, and that the people who ran the Tonys were seriously considering the request (this was before the Tonys had categories for revivals). He was livid, and dictated a letter that he wanted to send "to whom it may concern": "Special awards should not be given to people simply because they ask for them. In the event that you should feel the desire to acquiesce, I will withdraw *Company* from the competition in all categories and, in order to be consistent, I shall withdraw all future shows of mine from the Tonys." (Interestingly, the first draft of his letter also included a disparaging comment about their plan to honor Elliot Norton: he said it was "lunatic" to grant a special award to a critic—but they did.) As it happened, there was no special award for *No, No, Nanette*; still, it won four Tonys. *Company* had an unprecedented thirteen nominations and won seven awards.

"The Right Girl" changes went into the performance—luckily, without a hitch. It was decidedly better, the audience responded in

kind, and Gene felt a boost of pride. Now the challenge was to keep it up, since, as Michael had hoped, it pushed Gene's skills right to the edge.

After the performance I went out with two of my faculty supporters from Connecticut College. They were pleased for me that I had been able to pull off the independent study, and were determined to come see what it was I was so passionate about. They smiled the whole time, thrilled that I had hooked up with something obviously so exciting. As theatergoers, their take on the show was fascinating. They liked it, but when pressed, found it a little bleak, and didn't like "Fox Trot" at all. I was able to explain that they had seen a bit of history, because they had just witnessed that number's final performance. I told them the new number was looking very good, but that tomorrow would tell. I walked them back to their car, and again they said what a thrilling experience this was for me. And after the show opened and made it to the cover of *Time*, the whole administration took notice.

Saturday, March 13

The call was 11:30 Yvonne, noon the rest of the company. "I'm Here" was going in at the matinee. The orchestra was called early to run through the orchestration, which had been created and copied only days before. Jonathan Tunick and Mathilde Pincus were in the house, as usual, wandering back and forth along the orchestra rail, making certain all the players had their parts. Once through without the singer; everything seemed fine. Next, the company was brought out onstage and placed in their positions so it could be run with Yvonne. It went well, and when it was over the cast gave her a healthy ovation. As she was walking offstage, the applause started dying down, and she turned back to them, giggling: "No, don't stop clapping!"

Alexis had been nursing her cold all week and hadn't missed a performance but hadn't sung "Could I Leave You?" at any of the performances. She now felt her voice was back enough to try for the matinee, but wanted to go through it once with the orchestra first. She was fine, except for the high notes—"Sweetheart, I have to con*fess*"—and she asked Steve if it was okay for her simply to punch the note. He said it was fine, under the circumstances. Dorothy and Gene went through a slight rearrangement of lines around "In Buddy's Eyes." Luckily,

Dorothy's "corpse" line in the mad scene had been excised before ever making it to rehearsal.

Hal was called away for a phone call. The night before, David Burns had dropped dead onstage in Philadelphia during a performance of the Broadway-bound musical *70, Girls, 70*. Not only was David Burns a beloved actor and one who had worked for Hal in *A Funny Thing Happened on the Way to the Forum*, but the show he was in was a new musical comedy that celebrated old people. *70, Girls, 70* had a very different tone from that of *Follies*; it celebrated life with older folks singing and dancing up a storm, and the cast included many old theater veterans. Apparently Burns had finished a song, stepped behind a bar on the set, and collapsed. At first, the audience laughed, thinking it was a part of the show. It was all too macabre to contemplate, and Hal knew it would have a devastating effect on the *Follies* company. After making arrangements to send flowers, he asked those of us who had heard the news not to spread it around. It was too late; Bob Avian had already mentioned it to some of the dancers, and everyone was soon aware. Hal then decided to speak with the lead actors personally. The older members of the company took the news especially hard.

"I'm Here" went into the matinee as planned, and the reaction was very strong. It was a sold-out and enthusiastic house, and although Yvonne made a couple of nervous mistakes with the rhythms, on the whole she nailed the song. Even the candy lady from the lobby—a tough critic—who had sneaked into the back of the house because she'd heard a new song was going in, gave her approval.

Alexis performed "Could I Leave You?" with enormous emotional conviction, and it reminded us all how good that song was and how well she performed it—and how much it had been missed.

Larry Cohen and I were standing in the rear of the auditorium when a foppish English producer by the name of Peter Bridge came over to us. He had seen the very first performance, and, although he was a big fan of both Hal and Steve, he had left the theater thinking they had another *Anyone Can Whistle* on their hands. Then he came back for this matinee, performance number twenty-four, and was just amazed at the changes, every single one of which was decidedly for the better. "I'm Here" just blew him away; and he gasped when Gene did his swings around the poles in "The Right Girl." The book seemed tighter, too, and he was just delirious.

At dinner between shows, Yvonne was as high as a kite. She had a new song, and she knew all the words and all the staging. On top of that, pretty much everyone agreed that "I'm Here" was just what the show had needed. She was on, and she felt like a star.

The evening performance was very strong, although this audience particularly loved anything that remotely smacked of double entendre. They were a Saturday-night crowd with one thing on their minds. I realized that audiences were now liking the show with more consistency; very few people left at intermission, and "bravos" had become commonplace at the curtain call, if not always for the same people. The biggest hands went, consistently, to Ethel Shutta, Yvonne, Alexis, and Dorothy. The men were treated respectfully, but Boston seemed to go for the gals. And whether the loudest applause was for Dorothy or Alexis changed at each performance. The box office was virtually clean for the rest of the run. There was no reason not to be pleased by the status of the show. There were still things to be tweaked, but there was reason to feel confident. In the week left in Boston, two revised numbers—the new Prologue and "The Story of Lucy and Jessie"—were to go in, and minor revisions were expected elsewhere. There were still sloppy moments at almost every performance: Yvonne messed up the end of "I'm Here," although the audience still loved it; "The Right Girl" seemed tired, but then it had been an exhausting week for Gene; a piece of a yellow feather boa ripped off one of the "Buddy's Blues" girls, which prompted George Martin to run out onstage to grab it before Alexis made her entrance for "Uptown, Downtown." But at this Saturday-night performance, the show felt awfully good.

Alexis's new dress for "Lucy and Jessie" was somewhere in the ether. It was promised, but no one knew its status. Clearly, she had made her feeling about the Marlene Dietrich dress known to her confidantes, one of whom was now Joe Tubens, the hair and wig designer. Tubens had a good sense of fun, and he decided to play a joke on her. He went to a Goodwill thrift shop and bought an awful red dress, to which he had attached every odd piece of fringe and every stray bead he could find. Then he found a box from Matera's, some fresh tissue paper, and wrapped it all up so it looked like "the new dress." Tubens roped Michael Bennett into the scheme, since he knew that Michael, too, hated the Dietrich dress, and at intermission, Michael came across the stage saying, "Alexis, your new dress has arrived from Barbara

Matera." She opened the box and shrieked with laughter. She was game—she went in and put it on and paraded around the stage. It actually fit pretty well, so Michael suggested she wear it for the first technical rehearsal in New York at which time he would tell Flossie, "Okay, Alexis has decided to wear the fringe dress."

I sat in the balcony, way to the side. Watching the stage from that high up revealed patterns of movement that weren't readily apparent from the main floor, especially in the dances. Then I noticed something late in the show that floored me. It was a subtle shift in the scenery during "Could I Leave You?" While Alexis sat on the middle platform delivering the song in what now seemed like almost a catatonic state, tight spotlights focused in on her. John McMartin stood in the shadows on the side, and the overall lighting was very dim. At some point in the song, my attention was caught by the most solid piece of hanging scenery, the one that looked like a broken-off piece of a proscenium arch. Slowly—very slowly—it was being raised up into the flies and out of sight. The audience was completely unaware of this; I had been watching the show for the past couple of weeks and hadn't seen it. But now that I did take notice, I understood what was happening: while all the focus was directed to one spot and one performer, every bit of atmospheric goods hanging from above was taken out, so that when the lights came back up for the confrontation scene before "Loveland," the stage would seem strangely bigger, emptier, and more filled with shadows. That was because it actually *was* bigger and emptier. Doing this also cleaned up the top of the set so that when the Follies drops flew in, nothing would be hanging in their way. This was so subtle, and yet so brilliant. (It was so subtle that years later neither Lisa Aronson nor Frank Rich noticed that one shot in a sequence of photographs detailing this very transition into "Loveland," in their book *The Theatre Art of Boris Aronson*, was from some other moment in the show: all the hanging pieces were still in place.)

Sunday, March 14

The cast wasn't called on this day off, but the production team gathered to discuss strategy. Steve said he had been "zonked" by the show on Thursday night when he sat and watched. He was overwhelmed within the first forty-five minutes, and just stayed with it right to the end. His work was finally done, so now he was casting a careful eye over

the whole show, looking for ways to make more connections between the characters and the events. One of his ideas was to have the four leads perform their Follies numbers in their street clothes rather than in their Follies costumes. They would watch "Loveland" from the edge of the stage, and then simply step up into the scene when their song came along. Steve suspected that might clarify the connection between the characters and the songs. And he thought that taking those four costumes out would make the show less "rich," which he felt would be beneficial. He was also interested in exploring the possibility of shifting the order of "I'm Here" and "One More Kiss," which would move Carlotta's song to the "eleven o'clock" position.

I had dinner with Hal Hastings, who was worried about how long the show could run in New York. He said the critics have influence only for the first three months after the opening; from then on, it's all word of mouth. He was worried in the realistic way of someone who had been there through countless triumphs and failures. He noted that Clive Barnes, the chief drama critic for the *New York Times,* had taken a swat at Jim Goldman in a recent review of *Abelard and Heloise,* a modern English play based on a twelfth-century story. Barnes had written that the writing was "often effective, particularly in that slickly anachronistic way characteristic of James Goldman's *The Lion in Winter.*" Few in the company had seen it, and Hastings wasn't about to spread it around. Hal Prince knew of it but chose to ignore it.

Monday, March 15

The dance music for "Lucy and Jessie" was pretty much finished, and clustered around the piano were John Berkman, Jonathan Tunick, Hal Hastings, Michael Bennett, and Paul Gemignani. Berkman played it while Michael marked his way through. Before passing it on to Jonathan to orchestrate, Michael wanted to go through it with his dancers. It looked wonderful—reminiscent of "Uptown, Downtown," but more spirited and edgy. At one point Michael stood in the aisle of the theater, doing Alexis's steps while listening to the arrangement. Because the number was faster than its predecessor, the dancers complained that their top hats were unsteady; they had been measured for hats with their own natural hair, but because they were now all wearing wigs, the hats were small and would probably fall off doing this new,

faster choreography. The number definitely had shape, and everyone signed off on it. The plan was to put it in the show on Thursday night; that meant three days to get the music orchestrated and copied.

Hal told the principals about having them perform their Follies songs in the costumes from the rest of the show. They were not pleased. Alexis was the most unwilling, but Hal asked her to put on her red pantsuit and go through the staging of "Uptown, Downtown" with the dancers. She did, but not happily. All four performed in their street clothes—dispiritedly—for the next few performances, but none of them could believe that this change would stand, and they prayed to get their beautiful colorful clothes back.

Michael took everyone onstage to do more work on the new Prologue. He had been making small changes throughout the Boston run whenever he had a moment with his dancers, but now that every other number seemed pretty much mapped out, he wanted to focus on completing this new version, which was going to be more atmospheric, using bits of songs long ago cut from *The Girls Upstairs*, starting with "All Things Bright and Beautiful." (When he had Steve play him all the material cut from the show, this is the song he pounced on.) The ghostlike announcements weren't going to be used anymore; instead, the Prologue was going to be turned over completely to the world of the ghosts, who would evoke the general world of the Follies in slow motion. The principals entering the party would be the first hint of the present. Michael turned to Steve and asked him to give the dancers the words to "All Things Bright and Beautiful" so they could mouth them while dancing; Steve said they were mostly words of one syllable and would therefore probably not give Michael the effect he was looking for. Michael tried using the words of "Who's That Woman?" slowed down to fit the music of "All Things Bright and Beautiful." That seemed to work. An entirely new Prologue struck some in the company as a bit mad, but Michael was focused—there were only a few days left in Boston to make changes.

Everyone knew this was the crunch week. The adventure of being out of town was wearing thin, and everyone longed to be home. Hal had expected this, so he threw a party for the company following the performance on Tuesday night. He announced we would "keep it sloppy—some drink and food and entertainment—but know that we all have a matinee on Wednesday."

Tuesday, March 16

Monday's performance had gone uneventfully, but Hal wanted to tinker with "I'm Here." He had plugged it roughly into the staging for "Fox Trot" and now he was having second thoughts. Was it right for Yvonne to stand surrounded by partygoers on one of the stage-left units as it rolled downstage? Would she sing this new song to the same group that had been interested in "Fox Trot"? He was wondering whether the new song demanded a less showy staging and suggested she just come downstage, but he wasn't sure whether that would solve the problem. He tried cutting her opening monologue so she would just start by singing. That didn't work so he left it alone. He agreed to think about the staging, saying that he'd leave it alone for a day or so. Steve decided to change the title of the song from "I'm Here" to "I'm Still Here."

The pre-party performance was fine. Afterward, everyone headed over to the Statler Hilton. The room had a sunken dance floor with a small stage area at one end. A piano and microphone stood waiting for any impromptu performance. The open bar was well attended all night, and tables sorted themselves out in the usual groupings. I sat with Alexis, Craig Stevens, Suzanne Rogers, Michael Misita, Larry Cohen, and the entire entourage of hair and makeup: Ted Azar, Charles La France, Michael Gottfried, and Joe Tubens (in red hot pants). For some reason I never quite understood, Tubens and Alexis had struck up a friendship that would continue through the run of the show. Ruthie, who had obviously done the planning, urged me to play the piano. I don't know who had told her I played, and although I wasn't very good, I felt the path of least resistance was simply to sit down and get it over with, so I played through a couple of the short piano pieces I remembered from grade school. Dorothy came over, followed by Ethel Barrymore Colt, both surprised to see that I could play. And as soon as I could, I left the keyboard to others. When it seemed that everyone was finally present, Hal called for attention, pointed to the food, and quoted a Dimitri Weismann line from the show: "Are there any hungry actors in the house?" It was a nice gesture for an exhausted company that needed a little fun. Alexis regaled our table with stories about Ann Miller and other Hollywood dames, assuming the role of hostess with delight. After a fair amount of eating and drinking, various members of the company were coaxed to the

microphone. Some needed no coaxing. Mary McCarty did a brief nightclub routine that went over pretty well, and Ethel Shutta brought down the house with some old dirty songs. Fifi was unusually quiet, choosing not to perform. Elaine Stritch was visiting from New York, and after several people had made their way to the mike, shouts of "Elaine! Elaine!" were heard. She finally agreed, reluctantly, and grabbed Steve Sondheim to accompany her. After making a few jokes at Hal's expense—"He never likes to rehearse, you know"—she started singing some old nightclub number of little consequence whose lyrics she warned us she'd never be able to remember. Sure enough, she forgot some, but Steve calmly threw her the words. This was exactly the sort of situation Steve had said was an inspiration for "Can That Boy Fox Trot!" All in all, it was a very happy, lighthearted evening.

Wednesday, March 17

Dick Jones arrived for the matinee. He was the producer of the cast album, which was to be recorded on the Sunday after the opening in New York. He would stay for the rest of the run in Boston to see the show several times, take timings, and plan the recording. For him, the matinee was "to see the show for emotion's sake." Since he was an old family friend, he invited me to dinner between shows at the Ritz, where he was staying.

His observations were interesting. "You really have quite a show there," he started, "as much of a theatrical experience as *Cabaret*." He said he could tell that a lot of research had gone into the showgirl costumes; he thought he recognized some as exact copies of Ziegfeld originals. A lot of the show hit home with him, since it reflected the period he grew up in. He loved the opening image. He thought the score was remarkably good. He then went on to detail some of his concerns. He didn't like "One More Kiss"; he thought it was the one song that added nothing to the plot, and he felt that having it come right before "Could I Leave You?" was a mistake, since that put two songs in three-quarter time back to back. He found Ben's line "I haven't cried since childhood" too stiff, even for Ben. "People just don't talk like that," he said. He had already come up with an idea for the end of the album—a bit of the cacophony dissolving away to Phyllis saying, "Ben, I'm here." He was still upset about Capitol's decision to force it on to one LP, worried about what would have to be cut, and

hopeful that his bosses might still change their collective minds, but he wasn't optimistic. The album jacket was already designed—the Byrd poster, the top half on the front of the album and the bottom half on the back. It would not be a gatefold-opening album—again, a decision from the marketing department—but would include a six-page insert with photographs and production notes. (The insert ended up a mere single folded sheet.)

Follies would be Jones's last cast album before retiring. For decades he had been the senior cast-album producer for Capitol, and as such had made many much-loved albums of musicals of the 1950s and six-ties: *The Music Man, No Strings, Funny Girl, Fiorello!* among others. For Hal Prince, he had made *Forum* and *Zorbá*. He was erudite and elegant, and he had great stories to tell. One of the early experiences he often spoke of was teaching the score of *Porgy and Bess* to the Harlem instru-mentalists Gershwin had hired for the original band, none of whom could read music. He was most eager to meet the company, and asked if I would make the introductions. A student of musical theater history, he wondered whether Justine Johnston could possibly be the same actress who had appeared in Jerome Kern's *Oh, Boy* in 1917 (the answer was no—that was an actress named Justine Johnstone); and he was looking forward to meeting Michael Bartlett and Ethel Shutta, both of whose work he had admired through the years.

The company was ready to get home. Morale was sagging. Boston audiences were generally positive about the show, but most every per-formance had its naysayers—and it would be those people whose com-ments would sting, and whose comments would end up being passed around the company. Harvey Evans described being out of town with Sondheim's innovative *Anyone Can Whistle*, when everyone kept say-ing, "They're not getting it here, but wait until we get to New York. This is really a New York show." It came to New York and ran for nine performances. There was also a general flop feeling going around Boston: *Prettybelle* was on the way out as *Follies* pulled into town; then it died, and now *Lolita, My Love* was coming to the same theater, hav-ing already closed in Philadelphia and gone back into rehearsal. Word was bad on that one as well. As *Follies* was assured of a New York open-ing, some members of the company were joking that they should con-sider themselves lucky because it looked as if their show would at least get out of town alive. (*Lolita, My Love* closed forever four days after opening in Boston.)

The end of a very long day—a few notes before calling it quits for the night.

Thursday, March 18

The dancers were starting to get testy about "Lucy and Jessie." It was going in tonight, and no one felt prepared. Alexis was especially nervous—she had a lot of tongue-twisting lyrics to spit out in addition to having to adjust to a new dance that was similar to the old, yet different. She had performed "Uptown, Downtown" for the last time the night before, and was feeling under-rehearsed and tense. Dick Latessa mentioned that the dancers would look great in white gloves to go with their red tailcoats. The idea took hold, so I was given fifty bucks and sent out to two local department stores, Filene's and Jordan Marsh, to find gloves.

Michael had the stage most of the afternoon for "Lucy and Jessie" and the new Prologue. He was determined to put the Prologue in for the final performance in Boston on Saturday night, and that meant a lot more work—and fast. John Berkman was keeping up with him, helping him find places to insert as many of the cut songs as possible. Michael liked them—to him they were new—and loved their ghostlike atmosphere. He had already taken "All Things Bright and Beautiful,"

and was now working with "That Old Piano Roll," and "Can That Boy Fox Trot!" now a reject. Some of the songs still in the show—like "Broadway Baby" and "Rain on the Roof"—would be used as well.

Hal was working with Yvonne in the men's lounge on "I'm Still Here." He was determined to make it work even better; he wanted to place it in its own unique time frame, not quite in the present, not quite in the past. Yvonne was somewhat freaked out about having to try different staging, and the more she and Hal went over it, the more worried she became. She started to sing lyrics wrong and, at one point, she just went totally blank. She couldn't remember anything. A five-minute break was called, and she pulled herself together. Dorothy, who had become something of a confidante, was very worried about Yvonne, who, she felt, was more fragile than people realized. At the end of the afternoon, as Dorothy left to go back to the hotel, she took me aside and said that I should call her if I thought Yvonne needed a pal.

Gingerly Hal put Yvonne through her paces on the stage. The new staging went like this: She begins the song sitting on the platform, which is already in place instead of traveling down with her on it. Partygoers, mostly men, surround her. She starts almost conversationally, aiming it at the people around her, but not looking at them. Then on the line "I met a big financier, and I'm here" she stands up and comes slightly downstage. She wanders around a bit, as the partygoers, many of whom have been sitting, rise and follow her downstage, their attention still fixed on her. The lights then fade slowly on them, and they begin to wander into the shadows. By the time she gets to "I've been through Reno, I've been through Beverly Hills," it has practically become a soliloquy to the audience. By the end of the song, she will be standing alone, isolated in three follow spots, from the front and both sides. Hal knew he would be giving the song emotional depth by shaping it into a real solo moment for the character of Carlotta, who could now make a direct connection with the audience. He was excited; Yvonne was nervous. Hal insisted on trying out the new staging that night.

Michael gathered the Montage group, whose performances had become quite peculiar, and he told them: "I saw the show last night, and I did not like it one bit. I will try to be nice in the way I say this, but I may not be able to." He then laced into them all—Fifi for her constantly fluttering hands, Charles and Marcie for never being able to sing on key, and Ethel for all the shtick she'd added, including a

ferocious stomping ending. I sensed that as so much attention was being paid to others over the past couple of weeks, these actors had begun to feel neglected. They were terrified of Michael, and slightly resentful of his harshness, but they listened carefully and promised to make the corrections. As Ethel was leaving the stage, she remarked to me in a strangely offhand way that her son had called to say that his father, George Olsen, had died. "My ex passed away," she said and kept walking.

There was an orchestra call before the performance for "Lucy and Jessie." The orchestration was jazzy and very cool. Everyone liked it. The dancers came out onstage to listen, and even they smiled. There were a few errors found in the orchestral parts—this one had been done in record time—and they were quickly corrected by Mathilde or Jonathan. Because the adjustments made to "The Right Girl" had sounded unsteady earlier in the week, that orchestration was played as well for safety's sake.

With nerves at fever pitch, the performance at night was flawless, and brilliant. The new staging of "I'm Still Here" was a great improvement, and the audience appreciated it more than ever. There were bravos and cheers in the middle of "Lucy and Jessie" and a roar at the end. Everything played well, and at the curtain call Alexis hugged Yvonne and said, "Well, we both got through!" She had long kept her distance from Yvonne, and this was a nice moment of rapprochement.

Friday, March 19

Steve continued to tinker, mostly with the lyrics. Today's changes were for "Waiting for the Girls Upstairs." He focused on the middle section, first making a cut and then changing the style of a lyric. The cut was four lines about remembering the old stage doorman, Max, and it was clean; nothing was lost. The real change came in a section sung by Ben and Buddy. Originally written to be sung by Buddy alone, every other line had been assigned to Ben when he was added to the song:

> Race off the stage.
> "I gotta phone!"
> "Houselights!"
> "Who wants to get a bite?"
> Rip off the wigs.

"Come on, will ya?"
"Strike it!"
"Jesus, I look a fright."
Run up the stairs.
"Who knows the call?"
"Dumbbell!"
"See you tomorrow night!"

It had been staged with them running back and forth and up the steps, as if reenacting the moments they were describing. That made the lyrics hard to understand. So Steve simplified it and gave each guy three lines, with the final three sung together:

Girls on the run
And scenery flying,
Doors slamming left and right.
Girls in their un-
Dies, blushing but trying
Not to duck out of sight.
Girls by the hun-
Dreds waving and crying,
"See you tomorrow night!"

Once again, Sondheim was solving a problem in an inventive way. While the norm is to turn description into action, here the problem was solved by doing precisely the reverse. The action had gotten in the way of clarity, and in changing the lines of lyric into description of what happened, the focus of the song was helped. The puzzle man also created a perfect ABC/ABC/ABC rhyme scheme. Of course, the actors were in a mild panic, having to learn something new and put it in the show that night. Gene was operatic in his concern, but time was wasting. If a change didn't get tried in Boston, it would have to wait through the technical days in New York before being performed in front of an audience.

These weren't the only lyrics that Steve was sharpening. He clarified several of the images in "I'm Still Here" and, in one instance, fixed a lyric that was hard to sing, two words together each beginning with "thr—," into something more singable, and then into something just plain better. Originally:

> I got through three commercials
> And I'm here.

Then to:

> I got through five commercials
> And I'm here.

And finally:

> I'm almost through my memoirs,
> And I'm here.

He also made small cuts in "Love Will See Us Through" and "You're Gonna Love Tomorrow." Maybe this is how the rumors got started about these being cut entirely, but only internal edits were made. Still, the Young Four suspected the worst and were visibly on edge.

It was Michael's dream for the new Prologue to go in tonight, but that wasn't going to happen. It was coming together nicely, and everyone was beginning to recognize that it would be a big help in starting the show on the right foot—but it was too good to rush. Still, Michael was determined to see it in front of an audience before New York, and Saturday evening would be the last performance in Boston.

I was dispatched to buy more white gloves. The idea had caught on, but the dancers, who already had quick changes into and out of their red tailcoats, were worried. They didn't want to have to think of one more thing. And, as Alexis pointed out as she and I were leaving the theater together, "Do they realize what claps sound like with gloves?" She had a good point: the dance section of "Lucy and Jessie" involved lots of hand-clapping. It didn't look as if anyone had thought of that. Two dancers were also being added to the number—Victoria Mallory and Jayne Turner—in order to make the stage seem completely full. Gloves *were* worn for "Lucy and Jessie," and, *yes*, the claps sounded muffled. By "Live, Laugh, Love" the gloves were gone, never to be seen again.

The four principals were still wearing their street clothes for the Follies. Dorothy, ever the team player, who had spent so much time bucking everyone else up, had finally had it and went to Hal to com-

plain. "As a girl I just want to feel pretty once in the evening. I don't want to sing my song in that frumpy dress, especially with staging that was conceived for my slinky dress. Please don't make me do it anymore." Most everyone on the production kept silent, because it seemed so blatantly clear that having the stars of a musical wear dull clothes for their big production numbers was insane, whatever the conceptual justification. Whether it was Dorothy who won the day, or whether it was just plain good sense, they went back into their Follies costumes. The relief backstage was palpable.

When the curtain rose for "Lucy and Jessie," the silver fountain drops were missing. It turned out they had been taken down and were leaning up against the back wall, waiting to be loaded into the first truck of scenery headed to New York. The load-in at the Winter Garden was scheduled to begin at three P.M. on Sunday, and the idea was to fill a first truck on Friday night with every extraneous costume, prop, and piece of scenery that could be done without for the final two performances on Saturday. That truck could be ready for unloading as soon as the New York call began. Obviously, most of the scenery, lights, and costumes couldn't be loaded until after the final performance, but this was getting a leg up on the load-out. The audience didn't know any better.

Carl Fisher and his wife, Joan, came up from New York, bringing with them some new waiters' costumes for the improved Prologue. Carl had been holding down the fort at the Prince office in New York. He said the advance sale in New York had started with a bang but was now reduced to a whimper. "Maybe," he suggested, "we've exhausted the Boston word of mouth." He reiterated that the Boston gross in the final week would not quite reach the $100,000 goal Hal had hoped to achieve. He also explained the story about the large billboard at the Winter Garden, the one that Hal still didn't want to rent but which Ruthie and others felt would be great. Hal was still balking at the initial cost of $3,000 and the $250 per month maintenance. What Ruthie and the others knew, of course, was that a show in the Winter Garden without the billboard looks like a flop that knows it won't be staying long. Hal realized he was stuck. He had to use it, so a design and plans for installation were proceeding.

The performance was sluggish, and afterward there was a one-hour overtime rehearsal for the Prologue. John Berkman was late, so Steve played the piano, doing the best he could since he didn't know how his

songs had been arranged for the choreography. Justine Johnston, Equity deputy, was the first one out of her costume and down for rehearsal, determined to keep a close watch on the clock. One hour of overtime was going to mean sixty minutes and no more.

Saturday, March 20

The last day in Boston. Hal had been working with Jim on Sally's "mad" scene. A final version was rehearsed at eleven A.M. with great precision, and everyone felt a problematic moment had probably been solved once and for all. Hal had a few brief notes, then Michael took the stage for some further cleanup work on the Prologue. The full company was present, whether they were in the Prologue or not. As the performance time drew closer and the crew heads arrived, some costumes and props became available for the rehearsal; but there wasn't a lot of time, and everyone had to get ready for the matinee.

The matinee was rough—Fifi got her shoe caught in one of the steps coming down for "Beautiful Girls" and nearly fell over, and Gene botched the new lyrics in "The Girls Upstairs," although John McMartin had them down cold. Lighting designer Jules Fisher, who was dating Graciela Daniele, stood for the performance and loved every minute of it.

The orchestra was called at six to play through the new Prologue. The company was called for 6:10—precisely an hour and a half after the curtain fell for the matinee, because Equity rules decree there be at least that much time between calls. For the first ten minutes, Hal Hastings talked the orchestra through the music, Mathilde and Jonathan standing by to answer any questions. Then the company came wandering on, including the onstage band, who had a more prominent position in the new version. After hushing everyone, Hal gave the downbeat. At first the music was somber and serious, and the cast looked worried. Then as "That Old Piano Roll" and "Broadway Baby" kicked in, the mood changed dramatically. Suddenly it sounded like fun. When it was over, Michael asked everyone to get in position so it could be run with the staging and orchestra. This time through, something very special happened: it was majestic, it was atmospheric . . . it was beautiful. Everyone applauded. Michael had been working on this for the whole Boston run, and now that it was put together, it felt very good indeed. Bob Avian congratulated Michael, who was smiling

immodestly. "Yes, I did that," he said. Dorothy threw her arms around Steve and gushed, "It's like our baby is walking." It gave a great boost to the end of the Boston run. The performance was wild, and everyone finished on a high.

When it was over, the stagehands started breaking everything down and loading the trucks. I went out for dinner with Dick Jones and my grandmother, who had come up from Plymouth to see the show. As I walked back to the theater at half past midnight, nine trucks ("Clark Transfer—Getting the Show on the Road") were lined up along Tremont Street. Three more were parked, ready to be backed, one at a time, into Allen's Alley, to be filled as quickly, and as noisily, as possible. Clanging, yelling, pushing, banging—pieces of the set, mostly made out of metal anyway, were being loaded in as fast as they were disassembled. Lighting equipment, wardrobe trunks, prop trunks, music trunks, stage managers' desks—everything *Follies* was being rolled out of the Colonial and onto a truck. The stagehands and haulers had done this before, and they lived for the excitement—and golden overtime— of a load-out. It was after midnight of a Saturday night, and it certainly sounded like a madhouse. Fritz Holt was standing guard over everything, and all the department heads were looking after their own. Someone had plotted what was to go in which truck and in what order, so both load-out and load-in would go smoothly. There were, after all, only four days before everything had to be fully reassembled and ready for the first preview performance in another city.

Fritz casually mentioned that at ten o'clock on Sunday morning there would be auditions at the Alvin Theater in New York for a replacement for Ed Steffe.

I went back into the theater to get a final look at it. Organized chaos. The theater no longer looked like ours; already the set was more than half gone, pipes were being lowered from the flies, lights were being unbolted, pieces of gray scenery were being detached and rolled up. And there were people everywhere on the stage. In the darkened auditorium there was only Jack Mann, coiling up his cables and packing away his sound equipment. I found house manager Alex Mohr, who had promised me one of the posters from the display cases in the outer lobby. His word was good; we went out into the dark lobby, where he took a key, opened one, and gave me a window card. It was actually just a sheet of paper stapled to a blank cardboard back, but it had "Colonial Theatre" printed across the bottom.

Follies was going home, and it was leaving in far better shape than it had arrived. The Boston run was successful, but when a show moves from out of town to Broadway, it can seem as if it's traveling between two totally unrelated galaxies. We had seen both triumphs and disappointments in Boston, but no regrets. Playing out of town was the best thing *Follies* could have done. Now it was on to the Great White Way.

11

"What Will Tomorrow Bring?"

BACK TO NEW YORK AND BROADWAY PREVIEWS,
MARCH 21–APRIL 3

unday was travel day. The load-out at the theater continued into the small hours of the morning, and by midday Sunday not a trace of *Follies* remained at the Colonial; the entire physical production was in trucks somewhere between Boston and New York. The challenge was to reassemble the show in New York efficiently, and for the most part the last items loaded out were the first items loaded in. Time was tight, with the first preview scheduled for Thursday. And in New York, unlike Boston, there was no Allen's Alley where trucks could be parked; the Winter Garden extended from Broadway to Seventh Avenue, with the loading dock on Seventh Avenue. The *Follies* trucks could line up in the block between Fiftieth and Fifty-first Streets, but it was a busy Manhattan thoroughfare, even on a Sunday. Somehow, though, it all went as planned: hanging pieces in first, including drops and lighting rigs; then the raked deck, including all the winches and cables to move the units; then the angled floors; and finally the seven steel units on the sides and the downstage towers. Trunks with costumes were brought upstairs to the wardrobe room, which looked out onto Fiftieth Street. Prop trunks went to the basement, as did all the music. There were two small set pieces that hadn't been used in Boston; they were delivered from Feller's and were laid out gingerly over seats in the auditorium. Although Broadway stagehands tend to be thought of as guys who spend a lot of time hanging around, watch them during a load-in. There is no better indication of

Home at last—the marquee of the Winter Garden Theater, New York.

just how skillful they are than to see them deal with the logistics of loading a big show into what amounts to a surprisingly small space.

The actors traveled back to New York in much the same way they had gone to Boston, most of them on buses, though the principal actors and creative staff flew. Some drove, and I volunteered to rent a car to drive Yvonne. Along the way, I showed her some New England sights, including the O'Neill Center in Waterford, Connecticut. Not quite a B movie, not quite a Robert Anderson play, the two of us walking on the Connecticut beach on a cold March day, she wrapped in her white fur, me in a plain winter jacket, would have made a curious sight for any of the people I knew at the O'Neill. We ran into no one.

When we got to New York, I couldn't wait to go down and see the theater, so before returning the rental car, I drove down to have a look. The main entrance of the Winter Garden is on Broadway, but there is a second marquee on the Seventh Avenue side. The enormous bill-

board, about which there had been so much discussion, was on the Broadway side, and still empty, although there was evidence of work being done to prepare it for painting. But the marquee was lit up, and it said *Follies*. The entire poster was reproduced on the left side, against a white background, but on the right was the lettering of the title only, separated from the artwork and with its vanishing point visible, so it looked as if it was zooming out at you. Underneath it said "A New Musical." I assumed the idea was to punch up the title itself, but it was slightly jarring seeing the title all by itself. Otherwise, things were quiet; all the commotion was on Seventh Avenue, where the trucks were spilling out their contents, briefly onto the sidewalk and then in through the theater's large loading doors. It was as noisy as the Boston load-out had been the night before.

The company wasn't wanted at the theater until Tuesday—till then they'd be back at the American Theater Lab—but I decided to stop in on Monday to get a look inside. At ten A.M. only the farthest upstage hanging pieces were in view; the rest of the drops and hanging scenery had already been raised up and out of the way. The deck was in pieces all over the stage, slowly being assembled like a puzzle. Some of the set looked beaten up by the move, but I was reassured that touch-up work would make it all look like new. The theater, which had been dark since the abrupt closing of *Georgy*, a musical version of the popular film *Georgy Girl*, in the spring of 1970, was being cleaned and spruced up. Originally built in 1885 by William K. Vanderbilt as the American Horse Exchange, the Winter Garden had been renovated many times over the years, at first turning a building meant for the display and sale of animals into a bona fide theater. It was wider and lower than most Broadway theaters. The Shubert brothers leased it for revues in 1911, creating a garden motif for the interior design. The great theater architect Herbert Krapp spearheaded a major renovation in 1923, "in the more traditional Adamesque style," and nothing, other than routine maintenance, had been done to the theater since then. Some alterations to the orchestra pit had been made for *Follies*, however, and the show was asked to share the costs with the landlords. Chandeliers were lowered for cleaning, painters were doing touch-ups on walls and molding, seats were being vacuumed and railings polished. One cleaning woman said she hoped the show would run a long time since, frankly, she needed the work. She was worried, though; she said she'd read somewhere that the first act didn't work.

Boris had designed the show specifically for the Winter Garden, and had taken its width into consideration from the beginning. The two set elements that hadn't made their way to Boston were crumbling proscenium columns, strewn with rubble at the base. The proscenium arch of the Winter Garden is one sweeping frame without caps on top of the verticals. Boris's set pieces created false caps, which defined the opening in a more traditional way. These units were attached to the theater's actual proscenium; they helped blur the reality of the set, so you weren't sure where the still-intact Winter Garden left off and the crumbling Weismann Theater began. They also provided a preview of the set for the audience, since they remained visible when the house curtain was lowered.

Fritz Holt was once again in charge. Boris and Lisa were in the auditorium watching, noting things that needed to be attended to and available to answer technical questions as they arose. Tharon Musser and Spencer Mosse were there as well, doing what they could with the lights until they were given their time to focus. Jack Mann was rummaging around, setting up his sound equipment.

The rehearsals, back downtown, were mostly about maintenance and filling time while waiting to get into the theater. Obviously, everyone was excited about being back in town, and everyone had felt a boost from the success of the new Prologue. Michael still had a few details to clean up, but now that the company had become used to the actuality of the set, the possibility of getting anything done on the flat floor of the rehearsal room where it had all begun was remote. Hal ran a few of the notorious trouble spots, but the day was decidedly taken at ease. Mary Bryant had designs on the leading ladies, as several publications, including the *New York Times*, wanted to do triple profiles of Alexis, Dorothy, and Yvonne.

By Tuesday morning the set was basically back together. Crew members were everywhere, welding pieces of metal, focusing lights, pushing and prodding planks. The piano was up on its platform for the onstage band. I climbed up to the theater's small balcony, which only had seven rows, and took a look at the set. The two proscenium pieces had been installed, and the downstage towers, which had been obscured by the proscenium in Boston, were now visible. For the first time, the design made complete sense. Boris had taken every aspect of this theater—the good parts and the bad—into consideration. He had designed the set in Cinemascope. The skeletal nature of the side units

and the towers offset the gray floors of the central stage platforms. The light bridges were more visible, both on top and on the sides, which simply added to the overall sense of theatricality.

The company was called to the theater in the early afternoon. The plan was first to get acquainted with the new surroundings and then to get back onstage. Fritz and George and John had been preparing for everyone's arrival, having made the dressing-room assignments. Unlike at the Colonial, there were no dressing rooms on stage level; they were all up at least one set of stairs. That was the lay of the land, and there was nothing to be done about it; but the rooms assigned to Alexis, Dorothy, and Yvonne had been decorated to suit their individual tastes, a clever way of welcoming stars to what are, in truth, tiny, dark, and rather unappealing rooms. There were fewer flights of stairs than at the Colonial but also fewer dressing rooms. There was still a stage managers' office on one of the higher floors where the sturdy red IBM typewriter was properly installed.

Another problem was traffic. Dressing rooms at the Colonial were all off stage left; at the Winter Garden they were all off stage right. That meant that every entrance had to be rethought, since the amount of time needed to get from dressing room to stage would be different. This had, of course, all been discussed, but there were divas in our midst. And the reality is that despite Broadway's aura of glamour, there is nothing remotely glamorous about the backstage of a Broadway theater. The stages are small, and the support facilities are squeezed into any available space, usually upstairs or down in the basement. But today the company had bigger things on its mind, so no one was about to make trouble over space or dressing-room assignments. What they were really concerned with was facing that first New York audience in two days.

After finding their dressing rooms and being shown where the pass doors were to get out into the house, the company assembled in the first few rows. Steve and Jim were sitting farther back, talking with each other and with Boris and a few others who were straggling in. Hal leaned up against the orchestra rail and gave a brief welcoming speech. "Well, we're here," he began. He was anxious to do a run-through, obviously without costumes and lighting and orchestra, but he also knew better than to rush the technical preparations. Looking around, he smiled and said, "Clearly, they need every available moment." Michael ran a couple of things—first "Loveland," changing a few of

the steps, and then "Love Will See Us Through," stopping to work with Harvey Evans and Marti Rolph. Steve had cut a part of the verse late in Boston, but otherwise the song hadn't been touched in weeks. It was strange for that song to be rehearsed at this point; it seemed as if something was up, but no one could tell exactly what. Michael was focused more on the performances than on the staging itself. Then he ran through the new Prologue, just to make certain Saturday night in Boston hadn't been a fluke.

At 3:45, after both Hal and Michael had finished with their small rehearsals, Hal called for a run-through. He wanted everyone to get the feel of the theater, which was very different from the Colonial. Unlike during the tech period in Boston, there was now a general sense of confidence. Ethel, as always, was a pro, and paced her new route from the dressing room to the stage. She was loving it—ecstatic to be back in the Winter Garden, where she had made her Broadway debut in *The Passing Show of 1922*. And Fifi seemed resigned to her place in the show. She had figured out that *Follies* wasn't about Solange LaFitte. She wasn't going to make a fuss about her song; she wasn't going to make a fuss about anyone else's role; and she had also got the message loud and clear that Ethel wasn't interested in being her buddy. But she hadn't been totally overlooked: toward the end of the Boston run, she was profiled in the *Boston Record American*, where she finally found a willing audience for her stories about her "famous feud with Earl Carroll" and her "tantrum that wrecked a Cleveland dressing room" and her "bath in the public fountain in the center of Indianapolis." For the press she was full of spirit: "Now I've finally made it. I don't want to go back to my youth. I was always worn out then. Youth can really do a woman in! Oh, la la!"

The run-through was exciting, and there was something special about finally seeing *Follies* on the stage for which it was intended. The company felt good about it, and as soon as it was over, the stage was turned back to Fritz and the crews. Rehearsals now were moved to the Broadway Arts Studios, uptown on Broadway, above a car dealership.

Michael went on polishing numbers, some of which needed no polish, but he was a perfectionist and wanted to fine-tune every moment. "Buddy's Blues" was this afternoon's victim, with Buddy and his two Follies girls, who finally accepted the number and performed it well. "There's a step that will get you a hand when you three cross the stage together—let's find it," Michael said. Gene suggested a certain dance

figure, which Michael graciously accepted. "Okay, then, let's see what happens if you strut, corny as that may sound." It worked, and the number was better. He also mentioned a little technical addition to the number that was scheduled to be tried as soon as the stage was available. Then he took the women through the mirror number, and gave supportive notes: "Start off looking absolutely glamorous. But remember that you are chorus girls who are having fun."

By Wednesday, all departments had gotten themselves organized and reasonably ready for performance, but this was the day for everything to be a little off. The afternoon run-through added costumes and orchestra. Sound wasn't finished, nor was the lighting ready. There was excitement, yes, and anticipation, but there were also raw nerves. Steve announced that this was one day that he always hates, because what seemed so together three days earlier always falls apart in the interim and needs to be put back together; at best it's always ragged. Little mistakes were made: Ethel Shutta took a fall but picked herself up and continued; Justine Johnston dropped her cane, which rolled off the stage; and some of the costumes were off being repaired. The orchestra seemed very loud, especially during the moments of underscore. Hal wandered down to the rail, yelling that the music was too loud. Sheila Smith, who had been with *Mame* at the same theater for years, muttered quietly that the orchestra was always too loud in the Winter Garden.

After a dinner break, during which the crews kept working, there was a full dress rehearsal at the normal evening performance time. There was no audience, but many members of the greater *Follies* family were on hand. Judy, the people from Hal's office, Mary Bryant and her staff, many of the design assistants, and the usual friends at court. Martha Swope and her assistants wandered the first few rows shooting the show, and Van Williams, another theater photographer, was moving around the theater as well, taking shots from different vantage points. Earlier, Mary Bryant asked me to come to the back of the theater because she wanted a photograph of Hal and me together "for the files."

The show looked and felt great. The lighting had come a long way from the day before, and what was now onstage was the show that had closed in Boston. It was home. Not only did the set look as if it belonged in the space but the lighting was more precise and atmo-

spheric. The sound was complete, although there was talk about rere-cording some of the sweetening vocal tapes to suit the specific acoustics of the theater. Since the audience was never to know the tape was playing, it was important that it sound exactly like it was coming from the mouths of the people onstage. After the curtain came in, Hal called for it to be raised, then went down to the orchestra rail, thanked everyone, and told them all to go home and get a good rest. There would be a rehearsal in the afternoon tomorrow, then the first New York preview at night. He felt they were ready and was very upbeat.

On Thursday afternoon, once the cast had assembled, Hal an-nounced that the intermission would be in a different place that night. The question of the intermission—where it should go, and whether there should be one at all—had been dormant since the beginning of the Boston run, where, after a couple of previews without one, the show had played consistently with a break following "Too Many Mornings." Someone had now changed his mind—no one knew who—and Hal announced that the act would end several minutes ear-lier after "Who's That Woman?" thus saving both "I'm Still Here" and "Too Many Mornings" for the second act. This came as something of a shock to everyone, but as always, Hal was firm in his control and fierce in his determination. The first act would now close with the end-ing of "Who's That Woman?" and the second act would begin back into the middle of the song, so the ending would be repeated. Then things would proceed as before, with Weismann saying, "Are there any hungry actors in the house?" after the applause, followed by Stella's line, "Wasn't that a blast?" which often elicited a second hand. "Who's That Woman?" had consistently stopped the show, so ending the act on it would clearly create a rousing finale to act one. Since the time sequence of the entire show was essentially continuous, it didn't matter where the break came, and this way would make it even more obvious that the second act continued directly from the first. Michael found an appropriate spot in the number to begin again, and then, in consulta-tion with the two Hals and Steve, ascertained where the orchestra should start and when the curtain would rise.

Then Hal spoke again. "We don't have time for a lot of little things, although there were a lot of things that distressed me during last

night's run-through. We'll work on them today, tomorrow, and Monday, and the rest of next week we'll work almost exclusively on music." He then gave specific notes, some of which he admitted were things he just hadn't noticed in Boston. He told Fifi that she was "doing something horrible—wagging your finger as you cross on 'Beautiful Girls.' " "But I've been doing that for four weeks!" she said. He saw Ethel Shutta chatting with Mary McCarty during the number, something she had also been doing for weeks. He thought Ethel's line readings in her first scene were growing dull. Her joke wasn't landing: "It's always sad to lose a husband. I lost five." She vowed to do it better. He said that Heidi Schiller (Justine Johnston) would be seated onstage and simply revealed rather than make her entrance, which seemed to be getting longer and longer with each performance.

Michael was next. He was upbeat and cheerful. "You all played with a hell of a lot of energy, and that's great. The Prologue was good, but it has to be played a little faster." He complimented the women on the mirror number, reminding them always to keep smiling, that everyone is watching their faces, which must show enthusiasm and spirit. He wanted to fix several things in the "chaos," making certain everyone was aware of entrances and exits—especially the exits, as they had to be quick, since the scene that followed was very quiet. He wanted Young Sally and Young Phyllis to be in their Prologue costumes—identical feathered and beaded chorus outfits, one black and one white—which they would keep on for the final scene. Young Buddy and Young Ben would be in their casual street clothes, but placing the women in Follies clothing put them squarely in the world of the past. He had a few other fine-tuning thoughts: he asked for the music for "Loveland" to come in three beats later because it was so loud, and he wanted only two bars of vamp before "Beautiful Girls." He cut the musical "button" from "Bolero d'Amour" so that it would continue into the next scene without a stop.

As in Boston before the first paying audience, all the tech paraphernalia had to be cleared from the auditorium. There was less of it, but when the house lights were brought up full in preparation for the crowd, things were reminiscent of a month earlier. The ushers were loading Playbills in stacks at the rear of the aisles. Outside the theater, there was some new activity: sign painters were now hanging from the top of the big billboard, painting the word "FOLLIES," with headdress, in the middle of the white expanse.

There was clearly a buzz in the house as the audience entered. They looked to be an eclectic mix of musical-theater buffs, *Follies* fanatics who must have been in Boston at some point over the past few weeks, and just plain theatergoers, although the latter group was clearly outnumbered by the former two. Whether they had seen the show in Boston, or just heard about it from someone else, this audience was crackling with excitement. The buzz continued as the house lights dimmed and the drumroll began. "Bravo" was yelled along with applause as Yvonne and Alexis made their entrances; the others just got applause. Each woman received a hand as she appeared at the top of the stairs for "Beautiful Girls." That never happened in Boston. The audience was attentive from beginning to end. They laughed at the humor and clapped wildly at the end of the songs. When Ethel brought down the house with "Broadway Baby," Hal, standing with the entire creative staff at the rear of the theater, turned and said, "You know, *70, Girls, 70* is all about getting out there and strutting your stuff, but there is really only one old person today capable of doing that—and we have her." There were big laughs on some of the more campy lines, like Alexis's "Let's dish" to Dorothy, and Yvonne's "I haven't seen your picture in the papers in a while" to John. At the end, there was a long and loud response for each principal during the curtain call. Everyone was relieved and excited. It looked as if New York would take to the show. We had made it this far, but the creative staff still wanted to tinker. And there was only one week left until the critics arrived.

I loved what the show felt like in the Winter Garden. It fit the space like a glove; somehow the scale of the theater, the production, the actors, and the text all meshed into one. I couldn't imagine it anywhere else, and had almost forgotten what it looked like at the Colonial.

When the company assembled in the house for Friday-afternoon notes, Hal told everyone, "Well, I guess they liked us." There was a distinguished, silver-haired man standing nearby, diminutive in stature but elegant in style. "Ladies and gentlemen, I'd like you to meet Arnold Moss. As of tomorrow night, he will be assuming the role of Dimitri Weismann." The announcement came with no more preparation than that, but it was long felt that something like this was in the

works. Moss had auditioned on Sunday, and it had taken the week to make a deal with his agent. Ed Steffe was staying on with the company and had agreed to remain as the standby. He was present, and was extremely gentlemanly about the whole situation. It was then Moss's turn to address the company, and he said that he had watched the show the night before and knew that it was something quite extraordinary. He said he was honored to be part of the company and would do his best to get up to speed as quickly as possible. It was hard to fault management's decision, and the company just accepted the news. It was too close to the opening for anyone to feel that there would be another firing, even if this one brought the total to three: Donald Weismuller, Dortha Duckworth, and Edwin Steffe.

Hal proceeded to give a slew of little notes, tossing each page into the orchestra pit when he was finished. Small line changes continued— Ben's joke line to Carlotta about the pronunciation of West German Chancellor Willy Brandt's name was cut—and there was plenty of tinkering with staging moments. Steve had a few musical notes that Hal Hastings took on. They were, as always, about staying with what was written and not taking liberties.

I had been maintaining an up-to-date script all through Boston and I had used it to make copies of pages as needed, but Arnold Moss's arrival caught me off-guard, and I hadn't heeded the warning I had been given that there would be auditions for a new Weismann. I hadn't had time to prepare a copy for him. I was asked to hand over my copy, which I did, reluctantly. He learned his lines quickly, however, and was able to return my script to me within a couple of days. Some requests for the script were beginning to come in from the press, so I needed to have a couple of extra copies on hand. To do that, I went to the Prince office in Rockefeller Center and fed the pages, one at a time, through the Xerox machine. There was always some good gossip to get from the people who were office-bound, but mostly they wanted to hear from me about what was going on in the theater.

The new placement of the intermission was deemed a partial success. Hal said it "helped the book in every possible way." But starting the second act in the middle of a song seemed confusing. Turning the clock back in real stage time was one time twist too many; some audience members thought it was just a mistake. So a new decision was made: tonight the second act would simply begin with the final tableau of the song—exactly where the curtain had fallen at the end of act one.

If anyone was alert enough to notice, the song ended in a spread-out version of the initial pose in which the six present-day women stood in three pairs. There were now six pairs, with each woman opposing her own ghost figure. It was the culmination of some brilliant staging—the stage now filled with twice as many bodies, half of them in the present and half in the past. That was the image the audience would now experience both at the end of the first act, and at the start of the second. And so it was at Friday night's performance.

Preview number two, on Friday, went well, though minus the euphoria of Thursday night. Lines of dialogue that had gotten big reactions on Thursday were received with silence. There were still cheers, to be sure, but the overall reaction had clearly come down a notch. Some in the company felt this was a more realistic idea of how the show would play. The cast was still giving its all, and there was plenty to be confident about, but New York is New York. Carl Fisher acknowledged that there were fewer complimentary tickets at each subsequent preview, so reactions would be more those of normal ticket-buying audiences. Some celebrities were coming by to see the show as well. After Yul Brynner saw it, he became a vocal advocate, calling *Follies* the best musical he had ever seen. Such declarations were encouraging.

By Saturday morning, the thinking about the intermission had changed yet again. New decision: the second act would still begin where the first act had left off, but the ghost figures would no longer be onstage. That would leave the present-day characters spread out in their positions at the end of the song, but their memories would have vanished. I thought that was a really interesting idea, and that it played into the sense of memories coming and going in an instant. It had been pointed out that maintaining the same image meant that the chorus women who danced the number as ghost figures had to stay in their mirror-chip tutus during intermission. They weren't thrilled at that idea, and obviously they had a spokeswoman who made their concerns evident. Michael told the company: "At the request of Graciela, she and her friends will not be onstage at the beginning of act two." Because the second act was starting at the end of the number, it was felt that there should be some entr'acte music. Hal Hastings quickly arranged for the second half of the Prologue to be played, starting with the up-tempo "That Old Piano Roll" and continuing through "Who's That Woman?" (the orchestra could simply turn to the front of their books). That is how the show was played at the Saturday matinee. On

the final note of "Who's That Woman?" the curtain rose. The ghosts had vanished. It worked. Past and present, memory and reality, old and young—they were being messed around with yet again.

Michael wanted the onstage band to segue back into their party music from "Who's That Woman?" at the top of act two. The problem was that they hadn't been used in the song, and therefore it wasn't in their repertoire, so they were a little grumpy; they really didn't want to learn anything new at this late juncture, but they tended to improvise anyway, so they were able to get a lead sheet and work up a passable arrangement.

The saga of the intermission wasn't yet over. By midday Saturday, another new/old idea was floated: perform the show without intermission. Steve was opposed, but Hal wanted to give it a try. So for the fourth time in as many performances, the show was played differently. Running time was slightly over two hours, and on Saturday night, which was also Arnold Moss's first appearance, it was performed as one act. Hal loved it, and felt it was right for the arc of the show. Michael was noncommittal. Steve succumbed to Hal's enthusiasm as did everyone in the company, whether they cherished losing the time to take a breather or not. "Well," said Hal, "life is full of surprises." Each of the previews had played with a different act break, all of which were different from any of the configurations in Boston. From Saturday night forward, through all the New York performances and the brief tour that followed, *Follies* was played without an intermission. The people who were the most bothered were those who ran the concession stands, who were thus robbed of their prime sales opportunity.

Sunday was a day off, and it was the night of the Tony Awards. *Company*, which was up for fifteen Tonys, won seven: Best Musical, Best Lyrics, Best Music, Best Book, Best Director of a Musical, Best Producer, Best Scenic Design. Sadly, *Company* took none of the prizes in the performing categories, for which five cast members had been nominated: Best Lead Actor (Larry Kert, who was nominated in an interesting rules twist, since he hadn't opened the show), Best Lead Actress (Elaine Stritch and Susan Browning), Best Featured Actress (Barbara Barrie and Pamela Myers), and Best Featured Actor (Charles Kimbrough). And Michael Bennett, in his fifth consecutive nomination for Best Choreography, lost out to Donald Saddler's toe-tapping

extravaganza *No, No, Nanette*. Steve Sondheim had never won before. In accepting his first Tony, as composer, he acknowledged Jonathan Tunick's orchestrations as "the most brilliant ever made for the musical theater." He thanked Hal Hastings and then said, "I've never thought very highly of awards, but I must say, it's awfully nice to receive one." Coming right back to collect another Tony for his lyrics, he said, "It's even nicer to win two." It was Hal's second as director and fifth as producer. For Boris, it was win number three, and in his speech he said it was "the most exciting assignment I ever had . . . to do something for this magic city." At the end of the evening, when the award for Best Musical was handed out, Hal brought Ruthie up with him and asked her to do the speaking. Many at the award ceremony had already seen *Follies* and probably assumed they'd be seeing the same gang again at next year's ceremony. The evening must have been especially disappointing for Michael. His nominations began with *A Joyful Noise* in 1967 and continued every year: *Henry, Sweet Henry* in 1968, *Promises, Promises* in 1969, *Coco* in 1970, and then *Company* in 1971.

Monday's rehearsals began with a lot of Tony congratulations, after which Michael cut the entire verse from "Love Will See Us Through." Harvey Evans and Marti Rolph were devastated: this was their one song, and now half of it was gone. Michael also had the Old Four remain onstage during both Young Four numbers, standing to the side in their street clothing, just watching as their younger selves performed. It was yet another attempt to make certain the audience got the connection; it was also a neat flip of the moments in the Prologue when the ghost figures stood by and watched as their present-day counterparts made their entrances. Yet it seemed odd—somehow, after the song "Loveland," we had been taken back to somewhere else; and to have the modern characters stay around and watch hadn't worked in Boston, and it wasn't going to work now. It seemed unnecessary. My conclusion was that some audiences were simply never going to make the connection, and everyone would have to accept that fact. I didn't know where the new idea had come from, but it was becoming apparent that Hal and Michael were at odds once again. According to Hal, Michael wanted both of the Young numbers cut, as well as "The Road You Didn't Take." Steve was siding with Hal.

Generic photographs had been in the lobby display cases, but were being removed in preparation for mounting new shots taken at the run-through on Wednesday. When the new photographs went up, still black-and-whites, some of the cast members became grumpy at the choices made. There was one large photo of Justine Johnston and Victoria Mallory singing "One More Kiss." No one quite understood why. It was, however, a good photograph of a modern character and a ghost character together, which is probably why it was chosen.

A new scenic element for "Buddy's Blues" arrived on Monday: a flying harness. The idea was that as Gene Nelson yelled "Hello!" over the nervous vamp of the number, he would pop his head through the curtain at the top, and then slide down through the center slit to the stage level, accompanied by a slide in the music. Once there, he would sing the verse with only his head showing. When he came through the curtain, he would be driving his little toy car and the audience would see for the first time that he was dressed in an electric-blue jacket and loud plaid pants. He was the first of the four principals to do a song in the Follies section, in Loveland, and I guess someone thought it would be a good idea to make a splash about being in a different reality. The harness was rigged, Gene was strapped in, and he was hoisted up to fifteen feet or so above the stage floor. Once up there, he grabbed on to the curtain for dear life, unsure of how to balance himself in the harness. Then he laughed and hollered that it was a mighty odd feeling. They lowered him to stage level and somehow he got down without a mishap. After a few tries he got the hang of it. Getting the costume rigged with the harness and the toy car hanging from his shoulders took some coordination. After some clumsy attempts to strap on the car after he was back down at stage level, it seemed easier to simply have him fly up with the car attached. That way, once he arrived at stage level, "all" he would have to do was remove the harness and put on his jacket—while singing the verse to the song. There wasn't any leeway in the music, so everything had to be timed perfectly. After a few dry runs, the whole sequence was worked through with the two girls. It was silly, but it was very vaudeville and completely appropriate. Michael, still tinkering with the very end of the number, changed some of the movements and asked if it was okay for both girls to sing along on the final chorus. Those changes were made, and the staging went in that night, harness and all.

Hal took the rest of the company out into the lobby for notes. He was in a sentimental mood and first spoke about the Tony Awards and how thrilling it was to have a show that he cared about so deeply acknowledged by the theater community. He complimented Ruthie for her deft handling of her speech accepting the award for Best Musical, and the company gave her a nice hand. She had never really connected with the company, choosing to remain with Hal or as a go-between with Fritz and the technical side of the production.

Plans were proceeding for the recording of the cast album on the Sunday following the opening. While the people from Capitol Records seemed enthusiastic, it was still up in the air whether they would agree to a two-LP set. Hal was working behind the scenes to persuade them to go for two records, and he indicated to the company that he thought he was making progress. Larry Cohen had been asked to write the liner notes. I, of course, was thrilled: since he and I hung out a lot, I had a preview of what he was writing, and he was using "my" typewriter up in the stage managers' office. (His notes turned out to be superb; they even got a mention in the review of the album in the *New York Times*.) Alas, late Monday afternoon final word came from Capitol that they would not go for two records, which put everyone in a foul mood, including, of course, Dick Jones. He now had to propose cuts throughout the score in consultation with Steve. I was handed the task of creating lyric sheets that accurately reflected all the changes and cuts. The music department would be making its own "maps" of what would be recorded for the orchestra, and that would keep Mathilde and her crew busy.

Monday's performance was down, with some of the bad old habits cropping up again. Yvonne messed up a bunch of lyrics, which caused Hal and Michael, standing in different places in the rear of the theater, to turn their backs to the stage at exactly the same moment. Gene seemed to walk through his performance but acquitted himself perfectly with his new "Buddy's Blues" gymnastics. The audience loved it. Arnold Moss was settling in. This, his second performance, was more confident and relaxed. He gave off the air of someone in charge. Finally we had a real Weismann. Ethel got a rousing reaction for "Broadway Baby," but after the show she shrugged and said, "You

know, I just let compliments go in one ear and out the other." One of the fan drops in the Follies sequence got stuck—something that had never happened before.

Later that night, Gene's wife, Marilyn, phoned Hal at home. She had an emergency and was having trouble reaching Gene: their eight-year-old son had been hit by a truck on the way home from school and was in a coma in a Los Angeles hospital. Hal went to the hotel where Gene was staying (he had turned off the phone), broke the news, and brought him over to the Prince house so he could more easily connect with the West Coast. Obviously Hal wanted to help in any way he could, but he also had a duty to the production at hand. How would the opening of the show be affected if Gene had to rush back to Los Angeles? The child was being cared for by the same doctor who had treated Patricia Neal when she had her stroke, so at least he was getting the best care possible. His present situation could alter dramatically at any moment, or it could drag on unchanged for a long time. If Gene had to fly back to Los Angeles, either the opening might have to be postponed or the show would open with an understudy in one of the lead roles.

This was a professional crisis for Hal the producer. Ever since the middle of the Boston run, Hal the director had been far more in evidence, but here was a situation that needed a producer's expertise. Producers are loath to postpone—no matter how dire the personal crisis, word always goes out that the show is in trouble. Hal had invited the critics to begin coming toward the end of the week, so that they had a choice of several performances they could attend. This was a policy he had initiated a few years earlier, suspecting that it helped the actors by not putting all the pressure on one opening-night performance. Cleverly, he also always invited the important critics to the opening performance as well, should they want to come merely as guests. But with this new dilemma, one possibility was to be completely open with the critics, tell them exactly what was happening, and invite them to a performance earlier in the week. Then at least they could see the complete cast, and if Gene had to fly out over the weekend, the reviews would reflect the official opening cast. That was the direction his thoughts were leaning, but by Monday night, things were still uncertain. For the moment, the status quo would be maintained. At one point Gene turned to Hal and said, "I have always made the wrong decisions in my life, and one of the first right decisions I have ever made was to do this show."

Obviously, the stage managers would have to be alerted to the situation. Gene's understudy, Dick Latessa, would have to be rehearsed, since there was now the very real possibility that he would go on. Dick arrived early on Tuesday and was put through the blocking by Fritz. Nothing was said to the company when they arrived for rehearsal. The overnight news from the hospital was hopeful. Hal, however, wanted to be prepared, so he ordered a full-page insert for the Playbill, including a large photograph of Dick Latessa and, instead of the usual bio, the following note:

Dear Theatre-goer,
   Due to illness, Gene Nelson will not be seen in the role of Buddy. Dick Latessa will be playing that role at this performance. You may remember him from *The Fantasticks* or *Golden Apple* or *The Education of Hyman Kaplan*. If you are a television fan you may well have seen him on *The Bold Ones, Ironside, Mission: Impossible*, or *Get Smart*. We hope you will enjoy his performance; in fact, we are sure you will.
                                        Cordially, Harold Prince

It was an elegant way to deal with the bleak reality of opening a show without one of the stars.

Cleanup continued: Michael reinstated the verse to "Love Will See Us Through," which he had cut the day before, and removed the Old Four from their watching position. He added a bump before the final chord for the girls' jump into the guys' arms. Harvey and Marti were relieved; cutting the verse had been especially hard for Marti. She had made the decision to move to New York to do this show, leaving her husband behind in California, and while she was very good in her role, it was clear that the Young Four were not getting as well noticed as other members of the cast. She had already been questioning her decision, and when the verse was cut, that seemed like the final straw. At least having the verse to the song back gave both her and Harvey a measure of dignity. Harvey, trouper that he was, kept a stoic posture during this whole episode. I had mentioned that I didn't understand why it had been cut, so after it was reinstated he came up to me and thanked me for any influence I may have had in getting the verse reinstated. Needless to say, I had had none.

Hal cleaned up some of the very end of the chaos. Then Michael

restaged the curtain calls, which hadn't been touched since the quick bows thrown together in Boston. He made them short, starting with the memory figures, which were followed by the present-day characters. Many of the memory principals had to make quick changes out of their red Follies costumes into their black-and-whites, but there wasn't enough time for the entire chorus to make the change. Some weren't included in the downstage bows at all. All five stars came from way upstage center right down front, in order, ending with Alexis who was consistently getting the biggest hand. It didn't look like *Follies* would ever get a set of bows equal to the theatrical ingenuity of *Company*'s.

By the end of the afternoon, Hal made the decision to invite the critics in beginning on Wednesday night, since Gene could be expected to stay at least through Thursday. He wasn't sure he would make this public, but when word came back to Mary Bryant that Clive Barnes, the chief drama critic of the *New York Times*, could only come to the matinee, Hal decided he would inform the entire company after the performance on Tuesday night.

There was another issue developing, so quietly that few were aware of it—or they had conveniently forgotten it. It was Alexis's new dress for "Lucy and Jessie," and she certainly hadn't forgotten about it. The dress had arrived at the theater for its final fitting, and when Alexis emerged from wardrobe wearing it and walked onto the stage, she looked a very happy camper indeed. I don't know what conversations or collaborations had gone into it, but finally Flossie got it right. This one was a bright fire-engine red with a flattering square neckline with loose ruffles around the back. It had mid-length sleeves with ruffles from the elbows and large beaded stripes making an "X" across the front. Three layers of long fringe started at the hip line above the left leg, each a slightly different shade of red, and hung from the waist down to her right knee, angling slightly upward. After showing the dress all around, Alexis went through the staging of "Lucy and Jessie," to everyone's delight. This was clearly the dress she should have had from the start—sexy, flattering, surprising, and utterly suitable to the energetic choreography that Michael had created. And, of course, it was even redder—was it possible?—than her party outfit. The arrival of the new dress also had one unexpected effect. Suddenly, but subtly, it seemed as if the show had become Alexis's. And it had. For the frumpy Sally to discard her pink party dress and step into a floor-length clingy beaded gown and sing a torch song was dramatically

stunning, to be sure. But for the cold, regal woman who spit out acid remarks all night long to emerge in red fringe, revealing a terrific pair of legs, and dance up a storm—well, that was revelatory. And it had turned out that Alexis was also a really good actress, well able to get laughs, be hard-edged when called upon (as in "Could I Leave You?"), and then be able to revel in the fun of "Lucy and Jessie." Dorothy Collins was more than good, and everyone agreed that "Losing My Mind" was the emotional highlight of the evening, but when it came to pure showbiz, it was the sexy movie lady in the red dresses who won the day—and stole the show. From Tuesday night's performance on, "Lucy and Jessie" was just that much more glittery.

Tuesday's performance, completely sold out, went extremely well. Gene gave a fine performance, and at the end there were more than the usual bravos, and most of the audience was on its feet. As soon as the final curtain came down, Hal walked out onstage and addressed the company. By now word had filtered through the company about Gene's son, so they were expecting some kind of announcement. He explained the situation and told them: "Some of the most important critics are coming to tomorrow's matinee and evening, and to the performances on Friday and Saturday and Sunday. So we are really having six openings over the next six performances. I wanted to tell you all this now so you could go home tonight and rest up."

Wednesday was a threshold day for *Follies*. Hal tried to be vague about which critics were coming when, but word began to spread that the *Times* would be at the matinee. Even the most experienced performers can panic when they know the Grand Pooh-Bah is coming, and experience had already shown that some of the performers, Yvonne and Gene heading the list, could be inconsistent, even sloppy, under pressure. And despite the good word of mouth and the interest shown by the press, a positive review in the *Times* was still the undeniable key to box office success. Without it, a show could conceivably survive, but with a ringing endorsement from New York's newspaper of record, a show had all-but-assured hit status. The sense was that *Follies* really needed the *Times*. But there was a problem: Clive Barnes hadn't liked *Company*. On the other hand, in Boston, the critics who hadn't liked *Company* loved *Follies*, and vice versa. And Barnes hadn't been the only New York critic who didn't like *Company*. It had won critics' prizes, and walked off with seven all-important Tony Awards. No one knew whether Barnes had felt like an odd man out,

but some of the more astute members of the *Follies* crew had sensed trouble. There had been that crack about James Goldman in his review of *Abelard and Heloise*, and since then, in an essay, Barnes had made a general comment against the whole notion of nostalgia. All *Follies* could do was hope for the best.

Clive Barnes arrived shortly before the matinee began. I had never seen the man before, and he certainly didn't look like what I'd imagined New York's most powerful critic to look like. Short, somewhat overweight, sloppily dressed, with long and untidy-looking hair, he held his head slightly cocked to one side. Once he sat down, he buried his head in his program. He had been informed of the situation with Gene's son, and looked to see if there were any inserts in the Playbill. He didn't look particularly happy to be there; throughout the performance, he didn't pay attention to much that was happening onstage, nor did he take any notes. I sat in one of the side boxes, charting his every move and expression. I noted a slight smile when Ethel Shutta made her way down the rubble steps in "Beautiful Girls"; a more focused look at the stage at the end of "Who's That Woman?"; a bigger smile during one of Dorothy's scenes. He fanned himself with his program during "I'm Still Here" and his attention seemed to wander during many of the book scenes. I observed big yawns during "Too Many Mornings," "In Buddy's Eyes," and several during "Losing My Mind." There was no discernible difference in his expression when "Loveland" began, but he appeared attentive again during "Lucy and Jessie" through "Live, Laugh, Love" and into the chaos. As soon as the curtain fell, he was up and out of the theater. Larry Cohen, who was standing at the back and saw him leave, reported that he didn't look very happy. Later I was told Mary Bryant phoned his office to inquire if he wanted to use any of the seats set aside for him at other previews and the opening. The response was to release all seats except the opening, that he wasn't sure but might want to attend. Barnes then got on the phone himself to ask how Gene's son was doing, and asked who would go on if he had to leave. He then asked, "Aren't a lot of the dances that Gene does his own? I mean, they aren't dances that Michael Bennett choreographed, are they?" Mary couldn't figure out whether this indicated a bias against Michael, a nod in favor of Gene Nelson, or what. It was a mighty odd comment. As it turned out, Barnes did come back for the opening night performance, but arrived late.

The performance itself had been a bit ragged, with some bad habits

reappearing due, no doubt, to nerves. Yvonne dropped whole lines—
"I've stood on bread lines . . . ," and "Top billing Monday . . ." It's hard
to say what kind of audience a critic should see a show with. There
were groups at all the previews (theater parties are the backbone of the
Broadway advance-sale business), and many of the groups are benefits.
A large enough benefit audience can make for a dull crowd—one that
includes too many people attending purely out of obligation to a charity or a fraternal organization. Both of Wednesday's performances
were full of such groups, and they weren't all that responsive. Other
critics, including those from *Time* and *Newsweek*, came to the Wednesday evening performance, which was marginally better than the afternoon's, although now Yvonne did the song perfectly and messed up
whole stretches of dialogue. Mary Bryant walked out of the theater in
the middle of one of her botched scenes shaking her head and muttering, "I don't believe that."

The leads settled into what would become their individual matinee-
day routines between shows. Alexis took a nap, Dorothy stayed quietly
in her room, Yvonne went to Gallagher's and ate steak. Now that
Barnes had come, and knowing that we would all have to wait five days
to learn what he thought, everyone was feeling helpless and uncertain.
Flossie Klotz, waiting patiently for a man's costume that was late arriving from Eaves, said to me, "Don't go into show business. You surely
have other ways of making a living, and this business really isn't worth
it." Dorothy had a blowup with Alexis, who she felt was being bossy
during one of Hal's note sessions. Near half-hour, Sheila Smith was
going up and down the halls checking to see if the women she understudied had made it back. Although there was a sign-in sheet by the
stage door that every member of the cast was supposed to initial upon
entry, many was the time that someone forgot. Then the stage managers would have to call on the intercom. Sheila obviously felt the
old-fashioned method of peering into doors was the best, and most
fail-safe, way. The one good piece of news was that Gene's son's condition had stabilized, and it looked as if Gene wouldn't be leaving.

In addition to two critics' performances, on Wednesday, after the
evening performance, there was a joint photo shoot for *Time* and
Newsweek, both of which were planning to do big stories. Gathering
the company on the stage following a performance with full costumes
and lighting is an expensive undertaking, necessitating overtime for
virtually everyone, and the magazines were picking up the tab because

they needed their own posed color shots. They couldn't have held the shoot during the day, because Hal and Michael guarded their daytime rehearsal time jealously and weren't willing to give over valuable work time for publicity. And the magazines wouldn't accept the color shots that had already been taken by the show's official photographers, Martha Swope and Van Williams, or by any of the other publications that had dispatched their own photographers. In addition, now that Alexis's Follies dress had arrived, this was the first opportunity to do a photo call with the entire company in their final costumes. Martha Swope and Van Williams came again, but since it was the magazines that were paying for the call, Mary Bryant and her staff made it very clear that they got priority. Before the call began, Fritz asked me to stand by the stage door and greet Elaine Stritch who was coming over following her performance in *Company*. When she arrived, I stuck out my hand, introduced myself, and said that Fritz had asked me to greet her. These were her drinking days, and she looked at me and said, "I don't give a fuck who you are." I simply escorted her in through the pass door and out into the house. Never mind.

Whenever a weekly newsmagazine decides to do a story about Broadway, the entire street is thrilled. To have both of the biggies focus on *Follies* was extraordinary. And there was a rumor going around that *Time*'s might be a cover story. For that, they would need a special shot. Their photographer assembled several poses as potential covers. He posed Suzanne Briggs in her large butterfly showgirl costume on one of the higher stage levels, with Alexis and Dorothy seated below in their Follies dresses, and between them Yvonne, in her one and only costume. The *Newsweek* crew designed some poses of their own, one with Alexis standing among the Dresden showgirls from "Loveland," and another with six of the "black-and-white" showgirls grouped around the five principals, all in their party clothes. Many other posed color shots were taken that night, some of which did indeed end up in various publications: Ethel Shutta with a couple of showgirls behind her, Yvonne dancing around, showing her legs. Many of the numbers as well as the entire Loveland sequence were run, in costume but to piano accompaniment (the orchestra was released after the performance), which provided good opportunities for color shots. *Time* went ahead with its story, and it made the cover. But to the consternation of some, they decided to use a solo shot of Alexis in her fringe dress kicking up her heels, with the caption: "That Old Magic Relights Broad-

way." *Newsweek*, it turned out, had also been planning a cover story, although they were keeping very quiet about it. Their planned cover was also a solo shot of Alexis, standing amid the showgirls of "Loveland." In the end, however, they canceled their story entirely. "We didn't do the story for a variety of reasons—far too complicated to explain in a letter," is how Osborn Elliott, editor-in-chief of *Newsweek* and an old friend of my father's, explained in a letter when he sent me a copy of the cover that they had prepared for the story. Many of the *Newsweek* shots taken that night ended up in an article in *Show* magazine that summer, including another version of the shot of Alexis and the showgirls. Even the cover of *Show* had a shot of Alexis, this one with the dancers from "Lucy and Jessie."

Thursday was a true day off for everyone. Gene Nelson's son continued to improve, and it looked as if he was out of all immediate danger. But Gene had twisted his ankle, and Virginia Sandifur was coming down with a cold. At the theater, some adjustments continued to be made on the technical side, and the stage managers used the day to organize themselves and prepare for the routine of running the show once opening night was out of the way. It had been a busy week for the stage managers.

On Friday and Saturday, Michael and Hal continued to give notes and tinker with lines and steps. Hal Hastings went on polishing the music. Gene and Michael figured out some cuts that could be made in the dance for "The Right Girl" to accommodate his sore ankle. They came up with a shorter version of the number, which played for three weeks until his doctors gave him the okay to do the full dance. Other numbers were drilled for precision. At one point, the ensemble was sitting around on the stage waiting for rehearsal to begin. Michael Bennett said to them all, casually, "Someday I'm going to do a show about dancers, and you're all going to be in it."

Basically, the show was now frozen. There would be no more changes; the show that was now playing would be *Follies* from now on. This was the moment that prompted Ethel Merman's famous comment, "Boys, as of right now I am Miss Birds Eye. I am frozen!" Luckily, the performances on Friday and Saturday went well, and there were critics at all of them. But the big wait was for Sunday, our official opening night on Broadway.

12

"In a Great Big Broadway Show!"

OPENING NIGHT, APRIL 4, 1971

Validation for a Broadway opening is having an Al Hirschfeld drawing in the Arts & Leisure Section of the Sunday *New York Times*—"above the fold." *Follies* had one, and it took up almost the entire top half of the front page. It was annotated "Boston," which meant that Hirschfeld had been up there, although I couldn't say when. He had clearly been inspired by "Beautiful Girls," for several of the leading ladies were depicted lined up on the geometrically shaped playing area. Front and center was Alexis, captured in a posture with an odd twist she made with her body and arms as she crossed downstage. I hadn't noticed it, but it was one of those character quirks that Hirschfeld captured so uniquely. Every time I saw the cross from then on, I thought about the drawing. (Even Alexis was amused.) Standing behind her, up on the platform, were Dorothy and Yvonne, as well as Ethel, Fifi, and Mary McCarty. There were no men anywhere. The other women's poses and bodies were also nicely done—best was Ethel, whose stance, pointed finger, and facial expressions were unmistakably *her.* Hirschfeld included the ghost figures by lining up six females at the rear, corresponding to the six women down front, but with different postures. (There were seven "Nina's," all well disguised in the feathers, fringe, and architectural details.)

A joint profile of Alexis, Dorothy, and Yvonne accompanied the drawing, under the headline, "Three Show-Biz Girls and How They

288

Hirschfeld's drawing from the New York Times: *Fifi D'Orsay, Ethel Shutta, Alexis Smith, Dorothy Collins, Mary McCarty, Yvonne De Carlo.*

Grew." A few characteristic quotes—Alexis: "I haven't pursued a career seriously for ages, and I'm not pursuing one seriously now." Dorothy: "Believe me, it's wonderful being in *Follies*, but that's just the icing on the cake. It's Ron [husband Ron Holgate] who has brought such joy into my life." Yvonne: "I'm too dumb to be nervous about New York."

The company was called for two P.M. This was a Hal Prince tradition, to assemble the company on the afternoon of the opening and walk through the entire show. It gave the actors something to focus on during the day, and brought them into the by now familiar surroundings so they could be as relaxed as possible for opening night. Although many influential critics had already seen the show, an opening was an opening; tonight was still a big deal. There would be a lot of press attention. There would be celebrities and family and friends. The better things went, the better the chances for a long and happy run.

Of course, before the cast could get to the stage they had to make their way through the heaps of flowers and gifts strewn all over backstage, up the stairs, in the hallways, and in everyone's room. Deliveries continued all afternoon. Gifts were passed around among the members of the company. Steve gave each of the principal actresses one of their costume sketches, framed, and to Jim he gave the original Hirschfeld drawing. Jim had sterling-silver stars engraved with "FOLLIES" for the principals; for the rest of the company, myself included, he had the cover of the New York Playbill made into a plaque. My note read: "Dear Ted, With gratitude for a lot of coffee and a lot of good will." Yvonne gave champagne; Dorothy wrote lovely notes to everyone (to me: "For all the teas—root beers—sandwiches—and my beautiful 'revised' script, my thanks—and my love—Always, Dorothy"). Alexis gave Brooks Atkinson's book *Broadway* to her fellow performers. Hal had copies of the Hirschfeld drawing made. Ruthie gave everyone a large glass mug with "FOLLIES" etched in the front. To me she wrote: "To Ted from Ruth with thanks for being a great 'go for' (as I was once)." Sheila Smith gave each of the women a bottle of champagne with a hanging tag dated the same year as the reunion banner they wore during "Beautiful Girls." She also made cards with small round mirror chips glued to them, onto which she had etched, for each person individually, the name of the show, the date, and the person's name—all in reverse ("Just a little remembrance of *Follies* and the 'Mirror' number"). Ethel Barrymore Colt gave me a medallion of St. Genesius ("Patron Saint of actors. Let him guide you well"). By rough estimate, Dorothy got the largest number of flower arrangements. Fifi said she would be taking all her flowers to a sick woman staying in her hotel. Ethel Shutta was pained by each successive arrangement of flowers, appalled at how much they must have cost.

When I was at the office on Friday, Annette had asked me if I could take something and not open it until Sunday. Then she handed me a box about the size of a shirt, but heavier, wrapped in silver foil. It was Hal's opening night gift to me; it was one of the photographs that Martha Swope had taken of Hal and me standing at the back of the theater earlier in the week, in an 8" × 10" Cartier silver frame engraved: "FOLLIES—April 4, 1971." His card said simply: "Thanks, Ted! Yours, Hal." I was floored. And moved. To this day, that frame

One of the photographs taken by Martha Swope
for my opening night present from Hal.

has stayed with me, though I'll confess that I've never displayed it with the original photograph.

Once the company assembled, Hal gave a few final touch-up notes, and then started at the top of the show, easing through the book scenes and marking through most of the numbers. He was subdued, but generally upbeat. There was a new person in evidence today: *The New Yorker*'s infamous reporter Lillian Ross, who was hanging on Hal's every word for a profile (which, incidentally, never ran). She had a small child in tow and was furiously taking down everything anyone said.

I was asked, for what turned out to be the last time, to go out and get coffee. Suddenly I felt nostalgic—it was starting to sink in that my experience with *Follies* was about to come to an end. I was still typing and collating lyric sheets for the cast album, a task that would keep me busy through the week, but with that my duties would be over. Fur-

thermore, having spent three months away from school, I had promised to return for the last month, mainly to participate in the theater department's spring one-act plays.

Rehearsal ended at four P.M. Hal excused everyone and reminded them that half-hour was 5:45, since the opening night curtain was scheduled for 6:15. I went home, changed into a tuxedo, and corralled my comrade for the evening, a classmate named Drew Ketterer. (I had been offered two good seats in the center of the balcony for the opening, and had been invited to the party as well.) Drew was my best friend at Connecticut College, yet we two couldn't have been more different. The sum total of his show-business interest was a Victor Herbert song, "Every Day Is Ladies' Day with Me," and I suspected that had more to do with the sentiment of the lyric than with any abiding interest in light opera. He had never seen a Broadway show before, much less attended an opening night. I thought this would be a good introduction into my world for a friend who had already declared government as his major. (No, it didn't change his career path; Drew later became attorney general for the State of Maine.)

By six o'clock, backstage was ready. The callboard was plastered with telegrams. "Congratulations on a great show. I've seen it twice so far and loved it. You are marvelous. Keep socking it to them. Best, John V. Lindsay." From Gene Kelly: "All the luck of the Irish to you, Fred, and everyone connected with 'Follies.' I don't have enough money to send all my friends separate wires, but start with Prince, Sondheim, Nelson etc. and work your way through the cast." Individual members of the company sent telegrams to the full company as well: "Each and every one of you are the jumping end. How proud I am to be with you. Love, Gene." "Enjoy our farewell opening. Love, Alexis." "Good luck to a wonderful company. John McMartin." "There is no way to make our show more beautiful than you have made it. It is a dream come true and I cannot convey to you how much that means. Jim Goldman."

Out front, the audience was gathering. This was a black-tie event, and a dressy one at that. All the people who had been working on the show in blue jeans and sensible clothing were now decked out in their finest. The unwritten rule seemed to be to come in black or white. Most of the men wore black tuxes, but Michael Bennett's was white. Most women were in black formal gowns; Ruthie and Flossie were both in white. Time had clearly been spent in hair parlors and at the makeup table; even Mathilde Pincus and her sister and mother were dolled up

and looking glamorous. Police had cordoned off an area in front of the Winter Garden's entrance on Broadway, with space for limousines to pull up, in full view of the paparazzi and the newspaper photographers behind the barricades. The autograph hounds were out in full force. Any well-dressed figure they didn't recognize they would ask, "You in show business?" Celebrities began to arrive—Danny Kaye, Lauren Bacall, Ethel Merman, Mayor John Lindsay, Betty Comden, Adolph Green, Ruby Keeler, Patsy Kelly. Those who wanted to see their pictures in the papers lingered beneath the marquee. Inside the lobby, the decibel level was higher than it had been at any of the previews. No one was in a hurry to sit. The place felt like a big, elegant party.

There was one commotion, however. A hairdresser from *Company* had arrived, visibly stoned. As he went down the stairs toward the men's room, Ruthie blew up: "I want that man fired. I want him fired." Company manager John Caruso went after him and asked him to leave the theater, which he did; but then he returned a moment or two later. Once again he was asked to leave, at which point Ruthie spoke up again. Hal was standing with Lillian Ross, and when he saw what was going on, he stepped in. "No, I will not have that man fired," he insisted. Flossie, who had observed it all, told him that Ruthie had already ordered him fired. "I don't care what Ruthie said, I will not have that man fired." Ross was eagerly making notes. Hal went over to the man, spoke quietly to him, and then came back to the gang. "I've spoken to him and he's going to go home." Indeed, out he went, and into a cab.

Getting the performance started anywhere near the scheduled time was difficult; three times the house lights were dimmed to try to get everyone into their seats. Finally, fifteen minutes late, the house lights dimmed out completely, the audience applauded, the drumroll began, and the opening night performance began.

The cast was clearly nervous. Michael Bartlett, who had finally gotten his lyrics down cold, started inventing once again—". . . nothing receptacle . . ." Dorothy seemed a little tentative, which was new. Gene was doing the shortened version of "The Right Girl," and Virginia Sandifur, who was feeling ill, sounded a little raspy. Yvonne completely blanked in her scene with John McMartin, so he had to feed her lines back to her as questions. When she got offstage she just laughed it off. But none of it mattered: the audience hooted and hollered all night long. They cheered, they laughed, they yelled "bravo" after the

"Loveland" in full regalia.

mirror number . . . and at the end they stood up en masse. The cheers just got bigger and bigger as each successive performer came out for a curtain call.

And as soon as the final curtain fell, the stage was swamped with well-wishers, photographers, friends, and production people hugging, kissing, slapping each other on the back, and generally carrying on. Danny Kaye went over to Dorothy and said, "Look at you. A little while ago you were selling Lucky Strikes and now before you know it you'll be showing your tits onstage!" Yvonne clung to me for a while, until some of her California friends came and whisked her away. The company was still onstage and in costume, trying without much success to make their way back to their dressing rooms to change for the party. Mary Rodgers found Steve and said, "I should never go out of town again. I didn't like this show in Boston but I love it now." Backstage was total mayhem—there were five times as many people milling about as there would ever be after any other performance. Lines of people trying to get up the stairs would brush by lines trying to get

down. Showgirls with towels draped around their middle were trying to make their way up to their dressing rooms. It was chaotic, but spirits were soaring.

The opening night party was held at the Rainbow Room—thrown, as the invitation read, by "Tommy Valando, Capitol Records, Inc. and Williamson Music, Inc."—the two music publishing companies that represented the score in addition to the record company making the album.

Broadway opening night parties are multilayered events. The people who have worked tirelessly to get the show on want to party with their friends and colleagues. Celebrities who need to see and be seen are there in force, often trailed by photographers, both professional and amateur. And yet that cloud of uncertainty hangs over the festivities, as everyone knows that at a certain point in the evening, the press department will have received advance copies of the morning reviews.

The Rainbow Room was a spectacular place for the party. Being whooshed up to the sixty-fifth floor of the main building of the Rockefeller Center complex in an art deco elevator is an impressive way to begin. Stepping into the Rainbow Room itself is even better: it is a large room with a bandstand against the west wall, tables surrounding a round dance floor at its heart, and stunning views of the city from windows on three sides, looking south to the Empire State Building, east to Long Island, and north to Central Park. It certainly captured the feel of a glamorous age gone by. The people traffic continued all night. Lisa and Boris Aronson were in the elevator with me, hoping they wouldn't be the first to arrive. Ethel Shutta made a point of introducing me to her son and daughter-in-law. Fifi asked if I would escort her over to Judy Prince, whom, she said, she had never met. Husbands and wives of members of the company, many of whom had been invisible over the past three months, were taken around from table to table for introductions. I remember at one point Elaine Stritch turned to Ethel Merman and said, "Isn't it too bad that Alexis Smith has gotten so fat and ugly," to which Merman replied, "Christ, she looks like a microphone!" The band was playing—songs, it seemed, by everyone but Stephen Sondheim. Danny Kaye took Gene Nelson out onto the dance floor. Lauren Bacall hung on to Sondheim, off at a table to the

side. There was a lot of table-hopping, hugging, drinking, greeting. I thanked Hal for his extraordinary gift to me. "It's a memory for us both to remember," he said.

After an hour or so, I wandered out to where the press people were hanging out to see if they had any news. There was a group clustered around the phone booth. Mary Bryant was on the phone with Ingram Ash, who was at his office, where he could watch all three television news programs, retrieve reviews from the wire services, and take phone calls from the newspapers. He spoke to Mary, who gave the news to Hal. "UPI is good . . . AP is mixed," she said. "The television reviews are uniformly good." The *Daily News* was a rave, and it looked as if the *New York Post* was good. She listened a little longer, then signed off, after which she asked to speak with Hal alone. Even the now omnipresent Lillian Ross stayed behind. No one knew exactly what they were talking about, but we had a hunch.

The party continued merrily. After a while, Hal came back into the main room, went over to the microphone, and asked the band to stop playing. He asked for everyone's attention, as he had done in Boston, although that had been in a far smaller room with far fewer people around. Now it was for real. Once everyone had quieted down, he began: "The last time I was in this room was for a show for which I was only the producer. That show was *Fiddler on the Roof,* I had seen the lines at the box office and I knew that it would be fine. The reviews, lo these seven years ago, were mixed. That was then. Tonight, however, I care even more since this show is *ours.*" A big round of applause and cheers. "It is ours—the fifty-four of you in the cast, and all of you who have been working on the show. This time I do care. So . . ." and he took a pause. "The weekly magazine reviews are swell. The television and broadcast reviews are swell. The *News* and the *Post* are terrific, but the *Times* is not terrific. He found the show shallow, although he had nice things to say about all the people involved. It is, however, much better than his review of *Company.*" The guests didn't quite know what to make of this. It surely wasn't good news, but no one could tell how bad it was. Hal went on: "But I just want to tell you all that I am sick of this man, and I can assure you that this review will not go uncommented on. I think I will declare war on this man, and I know there will be a lot of support with me to see that this man is done away with! Let's send him back to England!" Up rose cheers and loud bursts of applause. This was risky—no one in the theater community particu-

larly liked Clive Barnes, but then they seldom like the person holding his position. Still, twice in a row he seemed to have completely missed the point of a Hal Prince show that had excited so many others, and Prince wouldn't take that lying down. The news that everyone had been waiting for was bad, but the bad news had been delivered in an inspirational and upbeat way. Hal was defiant; he was in charge. The party could continue in a jolly fashion, and it did.

Hal's unprecedented moment at the Rainbow Room did not go unnoticed. Earl Wilson wrote about the incident the next morning, under the title "Producer Bites Critic." And in its weekly edition, *Variety* wrote:

> The Sardi's set and Shubert Alley are doing a big pro and con about Harold Prince's 10-minute diatribe against Clive Barnes. . . . There is a good deal of sympathy for Prince's emotional outburst, though others recalled that David Merrick's several blasts against Barnes did not prove to the producer's advantage.

The show had been handed the verdict everyone feared: the *New York Times* didn't like it. If Barnes did in fact like it more than he'd liked *Company*, he didn't like it *much* more. The first paragraph was indicative of his tone, and of his dilemma:

> The musical "Follies" is the kind of musical that should have its original cast album out on 78's. It carries nostalgia to where sentiment finally engulfs it in its sickly maw. And yet—in part— it is stylish, innovative, it has some of the best lyrics I have ever encountered, and above all it is a serious attempt to deal with the musical form.

His negatives grossly outweighed his positives. In reference to the four lead characters, he wrote that "their marriages are not working out. (They rarely do in Sondheim musicals.)" He continued:

> The book is well enough written. . . . The writing is far better than the shallow, narrow story, raising expectations that are never fulfilled. . . . Sondheim . . . is a Hart in search of a Rodgers, or even a Boito in search of a Verdi. . . . His words are

a joy to listen to, even when his music sends shivers of indifference up your spine.

Some positives:

> I think I enjoyed it more than the Sondheim/Prince last torn marriage manual "Company." . . . It is a carefully chosen cast that works very hard. . . . My personal favorite was Alexis Smith [who] looks wonderful—and she has a mixture of ice and vitality that is tantalizingly amusing. . . . The lyrics are as fresh as a daisy. I know of no better lyricist. . . . His words are a joy to listen to.

Hal, as producer, had one important task to accomplish as quickly and effectively as possible: demonstrate to the readers of the *New York Times* that their man was wrong. He did this by taking out a large and expensive ad in the Arts & Leisure Section. Spread over all of page two and half of page three were thirty quotes from a variety of extraordinary reviews. He dealt with the situation at the *Times* in as humorous a fashion as he could: the final quote was from Clive Barnes: "I think I liked it better than 'Company,' " which was followed by an asterisk referencing *Company*'s double win as Best Musical by both the Tony Awards and the New York Drama Critics' Circle.

There was another irony. Despite the large rave-filled ad, the Arts & Leisure Section led off with a review by the *Times*'s other theater critic at the time, Walter Kerr, who was even more scathing than Clive Barnes. The headline: "Yes, Yes, Alexis! No, No, 'Follies'!"

> "Follies" is intermissionless and exhausting, an extravaganza that becomes so tedious . . . because its extravaganzas have nothing to do with its pebble of a plot; and the plot, which could be wrapped up in approximately two songs, dawdles through 22 before it declares itself done. . . . Ingenuity without inspiration can quickly become wearing, and we are not too long in our seats before we realize that no one has had an idea for the evening capable of sustaining its weight in silvered feathers.

On and on he went, excoriating almost every aspect of the show. And yet, on the very next page, were enough stellar quotes (not two-

word blurbs, but extended quotes) to convince any reasonable theater-goer that this was a show worth seeing:

"Follies" is a pastiche so brilliant as to be breathtaking at times. Indeed, it struck me as unlikely that the tools and resources of the Broadway musical theater had ever been used to more cunning effect than in this richly imaginative work. (Douglas Watt, *New York Daily News*)

The frontier of the American musical theater is wherever Harold Prince and Stephen Sondheim are. With "Follies" . . . they have put together an act of dramatic creation even more daring than making a Proustian film. Sondheim's entire score is an incredible display of musical virtuosity and expertise. (T. E. Kalem, *Time*)

"Follies" is a brilliant show, wonderfully entertaining, extraordinarily intelligent, and having both a stunning direct appeal and a rare complexity of feeling and structure. (Jack Kroll, *Newsweek*)

I confess to you that I am in love with "Follies." I found it spectacular. This for me was the most relevant, entertaining creation I've seen on Broadway in a long time. I've seen it 3 times in 4 nights. (John Schubeck, ABC-TV)

And so on . . . And farther back in the same section was a full-page ad taken by Capitol Records. Set in the middle of an otherwise empty page were the following lines set in the same typeface used in the show logo: "The Winter Garden Theater is dark today. The cast of *Follies* is away recording for Capitol."

All of this is not to say that the *Times* stood alone in disliking the show. In fact, the reaction to the show in New York was an even more pronounced version of what had happened in Boston, where critics were either on one end of the spectrum or the other:

It is like trying to make the Eiffel Tower stand on its head, or building the pyramids from the apex up. . . . Some fragments

can be salvaged from the debacle . . . nostalgically cloying, [and] smoggily pretentious . . . (John Simon, *New York* magazine)

It is the sort of show that would be easier to miss entirely. The musical numbers are so ordinary, however, that what starts out promisingly never gathers more than mild movement and presently grinds to a standstill. Sondheim's music is relentlessly monotonous and his lyrics are so labored that the numbers become interminable. The show bristles with inept direction. Harold Prince and Michael Bennett can both go stand in a corner. (Hobe Morrison, *Herald News of Passaic*)

The weakest element of a Harold Prince musical is usually the book and this one is intolerable. (Julius Novick, *Village Voice*)

Taken as a whole, the collection of reviews *Follies* received was as rangy as possible. The hope is always for the intelligent reviewers to be linked with the influential publications. Unfortunately for *Follies*, the more influential the medium, the less adventurous the critic seemed to be. Many critics were more than willing to minimize the weaknesses in favor of celebrating the strengths, but often those brave souls were not situated in papers with wide circulations. And as with Boston, some wrote perceptive and probing analyses of a show they recognized as complex. A few examples:

"Follies" is a fresh, new musical; it is not a great musical. It may, however, be an epoch-making musical. It succeeds in collapsing and expanding time like an accordion, in juxtaposing the past and present in such a way that each comments on and gently mocks the other. That's new and may influence musical comedy concepts to come. (Howard Lord, *Long Island Catholic*)

"Follies" is most trenchant when the pathos of performance is allowed to come through the elaborate contrivance of plot and spectacle. Prince and Bennett have treated the musical numbers with loving dedication and style. But neither they nor Sondheim are thinkers, and if "Follies" can be faulted it is on the grounds of its limited emotional and intellectual range. It is a bold musical which uncovers ideas it is unwilling (or unable) to pursue. It

outlines the process of delusion and also argues for more authentic priorities for the imagination. I'll bravo for that. (John Lahr, *Village Voice*)

For all its rainbow razzle-dazzle, "Follies" is a plaintive anthem to loss: the loss of youth, of love, of the delusions of the past. A disturbing seriousness underlies the glitter of this hard, sad, marvelous musical—a discomforting view of life: we act as best we can, and sometimes the consequences of our past mistakes are hidden for years; self-knowledge comes late and the lack of it can produce frightening results. Strange, sober matter for a musical. By anatomizing the wrong turns we take in life, the dusty answers time brings to our fantasies, "Follies" forces us to preside over the death of dreaming. It is a courageous, not a comforting show. (Arthur Friedman, *Phoenix*)

The show continued to generate an amazing amount of publicity. The cover story in *Time* appeared in the May 3rd issue. In addition to a lengthy feature on the show, it also included a mini-feature, "Sondheim on Songwriting," in which he responded to several specific subjects—for example, "On Rhyming: Clever rhyming is easy . . . Hammerstein said that the really difficult word to rhyme is a word like day, because the possibilities are so enormous" and "On Lorenz Hart: I find him sloppy all the time," "On Lyrics and Poetry: Poetry exists in its conciseness . . . lyrics exist in time." Louis Botto's article on Hal appeared in the May 18th issue of *Look*, with several wonderful color photos, including a two-pager of Hal sitting on the steps of the Colonial Theatre surrounded by the showgirls in their most elaborate costumes. *Show* magazine ran its cover story in July, and a new Avedon photograph of Alexis and some of the showgirls appeared in *Life*. In February of 1972, *Forbes* ran a cover story on Hal; the magazine's cover showed Hal's face imposed on the *Follies* poster, with his expression the same as the face on the poster. *Theatre Crafts* did an article on the costumes in its May/June issue; *Stereo Review* featured Steve in July; and *After Dark* sent Craig Zadan to interview Steve for its June issue.

Also in June, David Frost devoted the entirety of his ninety-minute TV talk show to *Follies*. This was rare, and in addition to the five principals, Frost invited Steve, Hal, and Jim Goldman. The program provided some amusing moments, including John McMartin's witty and

understated comments about how he got into the show: "I went out to California last year because I wanted to work in films, and when I arrived, the various studios went bankrupt. So I spent most of the year practicing driving to the airport. Then in December I got the call to come back east to audition for three shows. I got on the plane, I auditioned, they wanted me, and here I am." Yvonne spoke about having auditioned for the role of Phyllis, and of receiving a very sweet note from Hal saying that it wasn't going to work out, and then getting a call from her agent about "another part in there that would be very suitable." She then sang "I'm Still Here"—and, no surprise, she went up on the lyrics. Then, to give some sense of how Yvonne's Carlotta (and the show in general) evolved, Steve played "Can That Boy Fox Trot!" Alexis giggled when clips from her movies were shown, and both she and Gene spoke convincingly of the excitement of coming east for this particular adventure. Dorothy just kept saying how thrilling the experience was for her and how much admiration she had for everyone connected with the show. Hal and Jim were asked to describe the complex genesis of the show. All in all, it was fun, lively television—and the kind of publicity that everyone on Broadway craves.

The *New York Times* ultimately acknowledged that the show was controversial. *Follies* had a champion in culture editor Seymour Peck, who continued to encourage various articles, both pro and con. Three weeks after the opening, a rave review by Martin Gottfried titled "Flipping over 'Follies'" ran on the first page of the Sunday Arts & Leisure Section. He said: "I am convinced *Follies* is monumental theater . . . if it is not consistently good, it is always great." Having received many letters in response to their double-whammy in-house negative reviews, the paper devoted the entire Drama Mailbag on May 2 to the controversy surrounding the show. Labeled "Feudin', Fussin' and 'Follies,'" it led with an eloquent letter from historian and author Arthur Schlesinger, Jr., in which he complained about New York's newspaper of record having an Englishman wielding so much power over several recent shows that were not to his taste:

> "Follies," with its complex and sardonic commentary on the American Theater and on American mores in general, is a peculiarly American show. Its wit, its pace, its sense of parody, its self-mocking nostalgia, its ironic exploitation of myth—all con-

Dorothy Collins and John McMartin—Sally and Ben—what might have been.

Alexis Smith and Gene Nelson—Phyllis and Buddy.

stitute a marked case of American exceptionalism. One can understand why Barnes, bred in another tradition of musical comedy, was baffled by "Follies" and felt compelled to put it down.

Immediately following, Barnes responded, "Should only homosexuals review homosexual plays? . . . An immigrant to any country must expect one or two ethnic slurs. It is only surprising when they come from the man who occupies the Albert Schweitzer Chair in the Humanities of the City University of New York."

Other letter writers included two actors who came to the show's defense—Jerry Orbach: "Clive Barnes has been wrong a few times in the past, but in the matter of 'Follies' he is criminally mistaken"; and Remak Ramsay: "Barnes completely missed the basically idealistic and optimistic point of the show: namely, that despite whatever difficulties there may be in any deep relationship, we all risk losing our membership in the human race if we fail to make an emotional commitment to somebody." Two other letter writers spoke out against the *Times* men—Tom Cuoto: "While Kerr saw some of the trees, he never managed to see the forest"; and Geraldine Stutz: "That your critics—alone—failed to hail 'Follies' with hosannas is sad and significant for the *Times*. But that they did not even recognize the monumental breakthrough for the musical theater, I find appalling. Where are their eyes and their ears—and their expertise?" They did find one person who sided with their men: Allen Churchill, who wrote, "Hal Prince chanted, 'send him back to England.' 'Follies' is one of the dreariest and least rewarding shows I have seen in a lifetime of theatergoing. It is a fraud perpetrated on the public."

Follies had arrived. It was being talked about and written about, and it was highly visible. The Tony Awards weren't going to come around for another year, but it did get recognized by some lesser panels. As soon as it won the New York Drama Critics' Circle Award later on in the spring, Hal had the words "BEST MUSICAL" painted on the marquee below the title.

The recording of the *Follies* cast album was my final official project as gofer. It took place at Manhattan Center, an odd building on West Thirty-fourth Street between Eighth and Ninth Avenues, built as

an opera house at the turn of the last century by Oscar Hammerstein I. His goal was to produce opera competitively and put the Metropolitan Opera Company out of business. This was in 1903, and his plan failed, although he did scare the Met sufficiently for them to pay him a significant sum of money not to produce opera in New York for a specified period of years. On the seventh floor of his building, Hammerstein built a stately ballroom with a fully equipped stage at one end. The acoustics in the room were quite good, and in the 1960s and seventies it was used by a variety of recording companies to record albums involving large forces—full orchestras, choruses, and so on. It was used for recordings of operas, and Capitol often used it for cast albums. (Capitol's corporate home was its famous round building in Hollywood; all it kept in New York were some offices on Sixth Avenue and a small studio on West Forty-sixth Street, in the same building that housed Eaves Costume Company.) This was still the era when companies boasted unique recording technologies and sound qualities all their own—"Stereo 360" from Columbia Records, "Dynagroove" from RCA Victor. Capitol, however, professed no such proprietary innovations, and when they used Manhattan Center for recording, they simply hired whatever mobile recording equipment a given session called for. Such was the case with the *Follies* cast album.

Every song used in the recording had been subjected to internal cuts, and most musical transitions were cut entirely. Because the entire album had to be recorded in one day, the company's day off (for which cast members were paid one week's salary), the schedule was carefully designed so that no one had to spend extraneous time in the studio. (The orchestra, of course, was there for all four three-hour sessions.) A certain amount of time was carefully allocated to each number, and once that time expired, they had to be "on to the next." Otherwise, the domino effect took place and the day could conceivably end with a song not being recorded. There was, moreover, one song that Dick Jones didn't want to include on the album but which Steve Sondheim most definitely did. The song was "One More Kiss," and the compromise was that if there was time, it would be recorded, even if Jones couldn't promise it would end up on the album. (It did get recorded but didn't make its way onto the album until the CD reissue years later.)

The cast handled things well. Dorothy seemed to be the most comfortable, perhaps because the recording studio was where she was most

at home. Everyone had special lyric sheets that indicated how the truncated versions of each song would go. This was slightly unnerving for some, but for the most part they were troupers.

What wasn't any fun was the technical end. One problem was that a large coatroom just off the elevator lobby served as the control room, and it had no visible connection to the main floor, where the orchestra and singers were located. There was sound communication, but because the engineers couldn't see the performers, the control room might as well have been blocks away. Although recording engineer Andy Wiswell and the Capitol recording staff had what should have been enough time to set up, the session was plagued with technical glitches. For example, I was standing in the makeshift control room during a take of "Waiting for the Girls Upstairs" when suddenly a buzzing sound could be heard on every other beat. It seemed to come from the bass, so the take was stopped, and before it could continue one of the guys had to run out onto the floor, check the connections to the microphone next to the bass, then run back into the control room and try it again to see if that fixed the problem. It hadn't. Suddenly the wires and the microphones were taking up precious time that should have been spent laying down performances. Problems continuously arose throughout the day—some microphones weren't turned on when people began to sing, sometimes the actors were standing too far from the microphones. Jones had no choice but to forge ahead as best he could.

When the album came out, it looked great: the cover was well printed, although they opted for the whole poster on the front; the insert had nice photographs and Larry Cohen's excellent notes. But the technical problems were clear from the first release. There was a lot of unhappiness over the songs being abridged, and the fans were down on the album from the very beginning. In *The Harvard Crimson*, John Viertel, a classmate and friend of Frank Rich's, wrote, "The production of the album has taken the fire out of *Follies*. No care has been taken to allow the riches to surface. The album is a commercial venture in the worst sense of the phrase." He then quoted a line from "Lucy and Jessie": "In Sondheim's own words, 'It is a sorrowful precis, It's very messy.' " It does capture the performances of the original cast, but the technical shortcomings have, to this day, made the original-cast album of *Follies* a disappointment.

Publicity kept coming. Stars attending performances were chronicled in the gossip columns, as were the whereabouts of the leading actors. There were further articles about the performers. Fifi, resolved to doing her bit for what looked like a hit show, gave an interview in which she was quoted as saying, "Hal Prince is going to heaven, whether he likes it or not. Can you eemagine, geeving me a break on Broadway? I'm 67 and I make my Broadway debut!" Dorothy was followed backstage during a performance for a profile in the *Daily News Sunday Magazine:* "Racing around backstage as usual, she shouts 'happy show!' to every performer in the general vicinity. . . ." Alexis avoided the press when she could, but was frank—about herself—when she was corralled into giving interviews. From one: "In Hollywood I always got the roles I didn't want, the ones everyone else turned down. They would start at the top of the list—first Bette Davis, then Ida Lupino, then Ann Sheridan. If they didn't want it, I got it." Even some members of the chorus got press attention. Ursula Maschmeyer, the tallest of the Las Vegas showgirls, lamented that "there are no stage-door Johnnies on Broadway. It's very boring every night, like a walking coat hanger putting on glamorous clothes and trying to look glamorous." Ethel Barrymore Colt gave an interview in which she described being the daughter of Ethel Barrymore, recognized as the first lady of the American Theater: "When I started in theater I was eighteen, straight from the convent, with no dramatic training, and I was a dreadful failure. Then I became a singer—at least no one could say I didn't sing as well as my mother!"

The running of the show became routine. Ethel took to drinking more than she had been and occasionally showed up for performances in questionable shape. But Fritz Holt had only to arch an eyebrow and say, "*Ethel . . .*" and she would clean up her act. Alexis remained somewhat aloof from the company, although maintaining the friendships she had made early on, most noticeably with hairdresser Joe Tubens. Yvonne was out on the town whenever possible; she even managed to get herself into some situation that resulted in a long black limo showing up several Saturday nights in a row with a couple of serious-looking men standing by to escort her out to a certain Long Island night spot where she would sing. Some cast members left during the

run—Fred Kelly was the first, invoking a two-weeks'-notice clause in his contract. (He wrote a gracious letter of resignation in which he detailed the several roles he understudied and got to play, and ending by saying, "Thank you again for the 'pleasure of their company.'") Virginia Sandifur left to "join the national company of *Applause*" (which she didn't stay with for long). Kurt Peterson left for a revival of *On the Town*, and Sheila Smith went on to *Sugar*, the musical version of *Some Like It Hot*, in which she would play Sweet Sue, the leader of the all-girl band. But for the most part, the company remained intact, although by the end of the run in New York many in the cast were missing performances on an almost regular basis.

I went back to college, but stopped by from time to time to visit. Everyone remained cheerful, and people seemed happy to see me. I would drop in on Yvonne, who would greet me just as cheerfully as she always did. At one performance when I was visiting, she changed a line, "He's just a thing. But he's twenty-six," to "He's just a thing. But he's twenty." I flattered myself to think it might have been for me, but it might also have been her unique memory up to its usual tricks. She sent one letter, in which she told me of her boys' arrival for the summer. I sent her a reply. Years later I was touring through Universal City in Los Angeles when I saw her name up on the billboard as the "Star of the Day." I wondered if I ought to seek her out and reintroduce myself; it didn't seem to make any sense.

The show started off strong at the box office, with grosses rising each week through the spring to a high of $107,549 for the week of June 5th. Then it began a slow decline, which prompted *Variety* to observe, when the gross dipped to $79,832 in July, that "*Follies* sagged to a new low and now appears to be a questionable payoff prospect." It continued to run, with grosses fluctuating week to week, hitting a low of $31,854 during the notoriously bad Christmas week. The Tonys helped give it a boost in the spring, when it won a total of seven awards of its ten nominations. It swept the design categories—Boris for sets, Flossie for costumes, and Tharon for lighting. Steve won for Best Score (there was no longer a separate award for lyrics and music). The only performer to win was Alexis, who beat out fellow nominee

Dorothy for Lead Actress. Gene Nelson was nominated for Featured Actor, but no one else was nominated in either featured categories. Hal and Michael won for Best Director, and Michael won his first Tony for choreography. Jim Goldman's book and the show itself were both nominated, but both lost to a musical version of *Two Gentlemen of Verona*. Among other ironies of the Tonys: Phil Silvers and Larry Blyden won Best Actor and Best Supporting Actor for a revival of Steve's *A Funny Thing Happened on the Way to the Forum*, and the writer who took the Tony from Jim Goldman was *Follies* friend and admirer John Guare, whose adaptation of *Two Gentlemen* wasn't even contemplated when *Follies* first went into rehearsal. Upon receiving his Tony he remarked: "I don't know what to say. I'm an investor in *Follies!*"

The grosses never got back to a decent level, and all the creative staff agreed to waive their royalties. Finally, the show could no longer sustain itself. Hal, however, came up with the innovative and positive-sounding plan of closing in New York and moving the entire production west, first for one week at the outdoor St. Louis Municipal Opera, and then to open the brand-new Shubert Theater in Los Angeles. The hope was for it to remain at the western Shubert on an open-ended basis, before taking off on a major tour.

The final New York performance, on July 1, 1972, was number 522. It could only be described as riotous. Throughout the run, the show had amassed enough fans to make the final performance sell out far in advance. They cheered, they screamed, they stopped the show at every possible moment. Kurt Peterson's plan changed, and because he had agreed to go west with the show, he asked if he could do the final New York performance. His replacement agreed, and when the stage manager announced, "At this performance the role of Young Ben will be played by Kurt Peterson," the place went wild because an original cast member had returned. When Stella said, "Wasn't that a blast?" the place went wild. Yes, everyone in that theater agreed: it had been a blast. And now it was over. One fan claimed to have seen it sixty-five times.

Most of the original cast made the trek west and opened in Los Angeles—Ed Steffe was back playing Dimitri Weismann, Terry Saunders had replaced Sheila Smith, Jan Clayton replaced Ethel Barrymore Colt, and Alexandra Borrie took over from Virginia Sandifur as Young Phyllis. A few of the partygoers and choristers had left as well—Dick Latessa, Graciela Daniele, Charles Welch, and Marcie Stringer. Otherwise, it was the original cast intact.

The show failed to catch on in Los Angeles. It closed on October 1, 1972, and with it the proposed national tour was scrapped. There were conversations about a movie version, mostly with Daniel Melnick at MGM, so the costumes were sent to the studio. The plans were dropped—one problem was that Jim Goldman hadn't been included in the conversations—although a couple of years later MGM released a nostalgic film titled *That's Entertainment!* which used old movie stars to introduce clips from musicals made while they were young, often filmed on what was left of old sets and soundstages in Hollywood. Both Hal and Steve suspected it was inspired by the notion of making a film of *Follies.* Hal's original idea was to gather a group of bona fide older film stars—Bette Davis and Joan Crawford had agreed to participate—and create a real party in an old soundstage and film it in cinéma-vérité style. Twentieth Century-Fox also flirted briefly with a movie version. Two screenplays were commissioned.

According to *Variety*, the show closed as a total financial failure, with a cumulative loss of $792,000.

At the Winter Garden, the final scene.

Afterword

"... Still here"

Audiences interested only in nostalgia should not see Follies *now. Let them wait until it is revived in, say, the mid-1980s. Then this imperfect but glittering production will be an item of genuine nostalgia—the show that turned the American musical theater around and pointed it forward.*

STEFAN KANFER, *TIME*, MAY 3, 1971

Stefan Kanfer was right. *Follies* was indeed revived in the mid-1980s, three months past the exact midpoint, in September 1985, not as a production, but as a gala all-star concert with the New York Philharmonic. This time it was received with great enthusiasm, its two performances completely sold out, and to a certain extent it was greeted as "an item of genuine nostalgia." But more important, the show had finally come of age; it was acknowledged by the press as a work of major consequence. "Where were you on the night of September 6?" asked James Kirkwood in the liner notes for the album made of the concert. "There are openings and closings and benefits and testimonials ... then there are 'major events' which come along every decade or so ... well, add to the cherished small quota of 'events' ... *Follies* at Avery Fisher Hall. The thing about these evenings is: they simply erupt into mythic events through a mysterious combination for which no one has the recipe." The concert soon began to be referred to as legendary. Newfound interest in the show was one of the results. A full-scale London West End production was mounted in 1987, and other incarnations followed, both in concert and in full production, around the world: Ireland, Germany, Australia, and various places in the United Kingdom. The United States had been

keeping the show alive with interesting attempts through the years—one production in Birmingham, Alabama, even boasted seven ex–Miss Americas in the cast—and the rave reviews received by a 1998 production at the Paper Mill Playhouse prompted Broadway transfer rumors. A Broadway revival was produced by the Roundabout Theater in spring 2001. In January 2003, a concert performance in Ann Arbor, Michigan, cast Harvey Evans, Kurt Peterson, Virginia Sandifur, and Marti Rolph as Buddy, Ben, Phyllis, and Sally, thirty-two years after they had shown up on West Nineteenth Street to create the youthful ghost counterparts. And the Shubert Theater in Los Angeles, whose gala opening had been the West Coast importation of the entire Broadway production and cast, was itself closed for good in 2001. A local group established to perform concert stagings of musicals thought it would be appropriate to present *Follies* as the final production in the theater. The landlord wasn't interested.

Today, *Follies* is rarely performed twice in exactly the same version. James Goldman's widow made the observation that the show has morphed throughout its entire life. By the time rehearsals for the original production began, it had already gone through many more versions than most musicals. There had been well over five drafts, two titles, plot changes, characters written in and written out and renamed, over twenty songs, and endless small revisions. As the preceding pages attest, changes continued to be made right up until the Broadway opening, including the shifting of the order of scenes, the changing of tone of dialogue, and the creating and dropping of songs and musical arrangements. Shortly after the Broadway opening both the libretto and vocal score were published, documenting, at least, the text and score of the show that played on Broadway. The London production had new songs and dialogue. The Paper Mill Playhouse production used some elements from London but stayed close to the original. The 2001 Roundabout Broadway revival, the first major production following Goldman's death in 1998, was again a combination of previous versions.

It's tempting to wonder whether there ever was a version that both Sondheim and Goldman felt was definitive. *Follies* had come a long way from *The Girls Upstairs*. Was there a place along its history that both authors could point to and say: "That's the show we wanted to create"? Why did they agree to the constant requests to change the show? Did they feel the show wasn't finished? Did they keep trying to

"get it right"? Were they just cooperative collaborators trying to encourage any production the show would get?

A great deal of scholarly discourse has been focused on the show over the years. Every book published on the musical theater since the mid-1970s includes a mention of the show, and every book published on Stephen Sondheim—there are many—includes at least a chapter on *Follies*. Bold theories about the show's true meaning have ranged from "a searing commentary on the American experience in the middle of the twentieth century . . . [with] parallels between Nixon, as the symbol of the deterioration of faith in pervasive American myths, and the lives of the *Follies* characters . . ." (James Fisher) to "a lament for the lost age of female star glamour, an examination of failed heterosexual romance set in juxtaposition to a youthful romantic fantasy, all laden with the sort of irony that was central to gay culture of the time . . . show queens read their own show and their own lives into *Follies*" (John Crum). The British musicologist Stephen Banfield wrote that "*Follies*, like the world of the theater and our participation in it as spectators, operates between the tragedy and cruelty of self-delusion, Erasmus's 'sagging, withered breasts' and 'little love-letters,' and the exhilaration of self-preservation and celebration, for, as Erasmus's Folly acknowledges, 'Self-love . . . is so prompt to take my place on all occasions that she is rightly called my sister.' "

Theatrical historians take a more practical approach. In a piece written for the *New York Times* prior to the 2001 Broadway revival, Ethan Mordden, who was one of the first to describe the show as being "one of American music drama's few epics" in 1976, wrote: "*Follies* recalls a time when musicals were the smartest invention of a smart culture. . . . It is a flashpoint for who owns the musical. Florenz Ziegfeld or the Disney company? . . . Yet it is a timeless piece, for in a democracy there are always new roads to not take and always ghosts of our former selves looking on." In program notes for the 1985 concert, Bert Fink wrote, "simply and unsentimentally, *Follies* suggests that the past belongs in the past. . . . [it] does not condemn the past. . . . it condemns our tendency to hide behind a false depiction of the past rather than let ourselves be confronted by the reality of the present." Joanne Gordon wrote: "*Follies* is *of* the musical theater and *about* the musical theater; yet it transcends the musical theater. Larger than life, it synthesizes the dreams of its audience, the illusions of its actors, the distorted memory of a youthful America of the past, and a harsh

perception of the contemporary disillusion." Mordden concluded his piece by saying, "It's a fine show for kids, because they all think they're Moss Hart, with every choice in the world and no penalty to pay. It's a rough show for their elders, who have learned how marvelously perilous free will can be."

"It's my favorite show, really, and the reason is it is the most flying blind I've ever done. It was all about instincts and feelings." That was Hal Prince, speaking in his Rockefeller Center office in 2002. In another interview he had offered this: "The point of the show was that you should *use* the past to look into the future." To a reporter, Sondheim said, "*Follies* was a retrospective of all the different streams that had made up the American musical, so in that sense it was the end of a certain era. But *Follies* also was enormously experimental and therefore was not really the end of something but in fact a beginning." In a mid-1970s interview he elaborated, "*Follies* represented a state of mind of America between the two World Wars. Up until 1945 America was the good guy . . . now the dream has collapsed, everything has turned to rubble underfoot and that's what the show is about. It's also about the collapse of a dream. It's how all your hopes tarnish and how if you live on regret and despair you might as well pick up, for to live in the past is foolish." On the night of the 1985 concert, Michael Bennett told Graciela Daniele that of all the shows he had been affiliated with, *Follies* was the show of which he was the most proud. By then, his *A Chorus Line* had become its own time-consuming industry. "So much of that show [*Follies*] was better than anything I've ever seen or anything I've ever done" is what he told an interviewer shortly before he died in 1987. James Goldman told Craig Zadan, "You want something to succeed for being as close to what you wanted it to be, not something else."

Confessing that she was "scared shitless when Hal insisted that I do the show," costume designer Flossie Klotz said that there was no way her original costumes could be re-created today. "Not only would they cost upwards of $2 million, but we used fabrics from England that aren't even made anymore." Lisa Aronson reported that Boris was as proud of his work on *Follies* as he was on any show he ever designed.

For the stars, *Follies* proved to be a career highlight. Unfortunately, none achieved or maintained a new higher status for long, if at all, in the years following. Only John McMartin, a Broadway regular in 1971, remains a Broadway regular. Never really a star, he is nonetheless one

of the few respected and reliable leading men today. In 2002 he opened in a revival of Sondheim's *Into the Woods*, a show whose original production postdated *Follies* by sixteen years. Gene Nelson returned to Hollywood and went back to his career as a television director and occasional actor. He directed for the stage as well, and in 1984 took on a production of *Follies*. He admitted to being a hard taskmaster: "I would not let them bend one word," he told Terri Roberts for an interview in *The Sondheim Review*. "I told them: This is the way we did it; this is the way you're going to do it. Don't talk to me about motivation or I'll hit you right between the eyes." He concluded that interview by proclaiming, "*Follies* was a helluva great show." Cancer took his life three months later, in September 1996.

Alexis Smith remained a Broadway star, but unfortunately none of her subsequent roles provided anywhere near the success of Phyllis. In 1978, hers was the only name above the title of a musical directed by Joe Layton called *Platinum* about a faded movie star who attempts a comeback through the recording industry. It bombed. She went back to Los Angeles and made guest appearances on television shows and in small roles in movies. Dorothy Collins continued to perform for several years after *Follies*, but gradually withdrew into early retirement due primarily to the asthma that had hindered her career for years. (Few actually knew that she had needed to use an inhaler during the original run.) Both were invited to Houston in 1985 when a producer mounted a production of *Follies* to open a new theater. He seated them together. At the end of the first act—yes, by then the show most often played with an intermission—Alexis grabbed Dorothy by the arm and pulled her out of her seat, out of the auditorium, into some out-of-the-way place where they could be alone. A stall in a ladies room was the most expedient choice, and once they were out of sight and out of earshot, Alexis turned and looked straight at her co-star, the early favorite who ended up being overshadowed by the tall, willowy beauty from Hollywood. "Dorothy," she said, "I have to apologize. Seeing this show tonight, I realize—I had no idea how good you were."

Alexis died of cancer in 1993, in Los Angeles. Dorothy died at home in Florida in 1994. Many of the older actors didn't survive long after the original run ended. First to go was Ethel Shutta in 1976, followed by Ethel Barrymore Colt in 1977. Mary McCarty died in 1980, and Fifi D'Orsay in 1983, having once again made it into a new edition of the book *Whatever Happened To?*

As for the rest of the performers, every one has about the same feeling, best summed up by an interview Harvey Evans gave in 1996. "I've done nineteen shows, and this is the show I'm recognized for. I like that. I wouldn't mind having on my tombstone: Here lies Harvey Evans. He was in *Follies*."

In 1982, Hal Prince was in Los Angeles working on a new musical entitled *A Doll's Life*. For a backstage scene, he wanted a few racks of miscellaneous costumes. His production manager called Western Costume, Hollywood's oldest and most established independent costume house, which housed many of the discards from the major studios. As two racks of costumes were pulled out onstage, Hal noticed the purple cape in which Alexis had made her first entrance in *Follies*. It had been ten years since *Follies* closed.

I made a tape recording of Steve playing the score for the cast on the first day of rehearsal. For one of my meetings with him about this book, I made a copy. I saw him a week later, and he said, "I can't believe how fast I played that score. Judy Prince has been telling me for years that I play my stuff too fast. Now I see what she means. But when I got to the end of the tape, I thought, 'My God. *That* is all of the score I had on the first day of rehearsal?' "

And I thought—yes, Steve, that is all there was. And I have a story to tell.

Acknowledgments

Since I was never sure I'd actually get around to writing this book, I must thank those who made it happen. First, Eden Ross Lipson. I was introduced to her at a party, and as our conversation got around to Sondheim—she's a big fan—I told her about my *Follies* experience. She looked me in the eye and told me I *had* to write the book, and *now*. She pointed me in the direction of Sarah Lazin, who taught me how book publishing works and steered the project to Robert Gottlieb, who has been an inspirational and patient editor. For a first-timer, I struck gold. I know it and am most grateful.

Thanks, of course, to the two major creators of *Follies* who are still around: Stephen Sondheim and Harold Prince. I asked them both if they were okay with the idea of this book before I began. They were supportive and enthusiastic, agreeing to sit for interviews along the way. They read the manuscript and offered amazingly helpful corrections and suggestions. Thanks to Bob Avian, ace assistant to Michael Bennett, who offered perceptive and helpful comments, and special thanks to Bobby Goldman, keeper of the James Goldman flame and new friend. And to Lisa Aronson, widow of designer Boris Aronson, my deepest thanks. When Lisa presented me with a ¼-inch scale model of the set as a gift following our lunch at her home, I was speechless. I still am.

Thanks to Frank Rich, whose agreement to provide a foreword, long before word one had been put down on paper, was an early sign of faith. We have always had *Follies* at the Colonial Theatre in common, and it's been great having an opportunity to share it. For your kind words, your eloquence, and for the years of friendship, thank you.

I am indebted to the photographers who documented *Follies*, both

behind the scenes and in production, and who made their photographs available for this book with amazingly good cheer: Bill Yoscary, Van Williams, and Martha Swope. Thanks also to Robert Galbraith for his photos and to Margo Feiden for the Hirschfeld drawing.

From the original production of *Follies*, my thanks go to those I either ran into or sought out, all of whom were helpful: David E. Byrd, Larry Cohen, Graciele Daniele, Mary Jane Houdina, Florence Klotz, Dick Latessa, John McMartin, Joanna Merlin, Terry Marone, Spencer Mosse, Kurt Peterson, Marti Rolph, Virginia Sandifur, and Jonathan Tunick. And a special thank you to Harvey Evans. His being in the 2002 Broadway production of *Oklahoma!* made him the most accessible of the group, and he had wonderful stories to tell.

Thanks also to the various people who provided counsel, insight, thoughts, and/or paraphernalia through the years: Bill Ankenbrock, John Breglio, Barry Brown, Paula Cianci, Steve Clar, Pat Collins, Dr. Susan Corso, Osborn Elliott, Arlene Graston, Jane-Howard Hammerstein, Judy Haring, Jerome Leonard Isaacs, Robert Lo Biando, Donna McKechnie, Judith Maidenbaum, Stuart Ostrow, Alice Playten, Roger Puckett, Marilyn Rennegal, Paul Salsini, Steven Suskin, Jack Viertel, Joshua White, and Frank M. Young. And thanks to Bill Rosenfield, who loaned me the copy of the Boston poster that he had gotten signed by the company—by waiting, as a teenage fan, outside the stage door in both Boston and New York.

Special thanks to Dory Langdon, whose precise comments helped clarify moments in the text that needed help.

Thanks to those at Connecticut College who were supportive of my *Follies* notion way back when: Robley Evans, Jane Bredeson, Jan Hersey, and the late Rita Barnard.

To my colleagues at the Rodgers & Hammerstein Organization, my deepest thanks. Wayne Blood, Carol Cornicelli, Mike Dvorchak, Nicole Harman, and Victoria Traube helped in a variety of ways. Mike Hidalgo and Maxyne Lang were both helpful by reading the manuscript. Special thanks to Bert Fink, whose enthusiastic and consistent encouragement, as well as smarts, is deeply appreciated, and to Bruce Pomahac, who was indirectly responsible for my working on *Follies* in the first place and whose support, guidance, and friendship has been more important than he knows.

I owe a great deal to Mary Rodgers Guettel and Hank Guettel. As they made their brief but important appearances in this story, who

knew how important they would become to me? Were it not for the friendship between the Guettels and the Chapins, I have no idea what my professional life would be today. It was Mary who phoned me one day in 1981 and said, "What are you doing? I think they could use you at the Rodgers & Hammerstein office." How often does a thirty-second phone call lead to a career? And in this instance, it couldn't have happened without the support of the brothers Hammerstein, Bill and Jamie. I miss them and am sorry not to be able to share this book with them both. They would have gotten a kick out of it.

And my family: To my wife, JoAnna, and daughters Anika and Zoë, I owe an enormous debt. It was their time I stole to write this book. And to my parents, Betty and Schuyler Chapin, who invited my brothers and me into their world of the arts in the most gracious ways imaginable, and to Catia, who, following the death of my mother, came into the Chapin life at just the right moment. Sincerest thanks to you all.

Index

Index

Index

Variety, 185, 207, 297, 308, 310
Viertel, John, 306
Village Voice, 300, 301
Vineberg, Steve, 192
Vivian Beaumont Theater (New York), xix
Voelpel, Fred, xvii
Vogue magazine, 221

Wainwright, Loudon, 137
"Waiting for the Girls Upstairs," 14, 25–6, 46, 47, 53–5, 60, 66, 107, 113, 134, 138, 158, 169, 179, 180, 202, 212, 214, 216–17, 239, 257–8, 261, 306
Walker, Peter, 98, 130, 224, 231
Warner Brothers, 10
Watt, Douglas, 299
Weaver, Fritz, xxii
Webb, Ruth, 188
Weill, Kurt, xxiii
Weismuller, Don, 50, 86, 97–8, 274
Welch, Charles, 31, 64, 78–9, 96, 256, 309
Western Costumes, 316
West Side Story (musical), xix, xxi, 34
WGBH television station, 126
"When I'm Drunk I'm Beautiful," 232
White, George, xxv, 10
"Who's That Woman?," 6, 8, 10, 16, 30, 37, 39, 47, 50, 53, 62, 64–6, 70, 71, 86, 88, illus. 105, 107, 123, 138, illus. 139, 140, 152, 153, 162, 169, illus. 171, 172, 179, 182, 184, illus. 201, 201–2, 213, 221, 224, 231, 239, 251, 271, 275–6, 284

Whoopee! (musical), 49
Wilbur Theater (Boston), 126, 127, 240
Williams, Van, 270, 286
Williamson Music, Inc., 295
Wilson, Earl, 297
Winter Garden Theater (New York), 20, 44, 77, 99, 119, 131, 199, 260, 264–71, illus. 265, 299, 302; opening night at, 289–95; previews at, 271–87; run of Follies at, 307–9
Wiswell, Andy, 306
Wittop, Freddy, 19
Wolf, David, 71
"World's Full of Boys, The," 18, 24, 58, 61
"World's Full of Girls, The," 14
Wright, Carole, xxv
Wyman, Jane, 31

Yerma (Lorca), 98
Yoscary, Bill, 87, 144, 161
You're a Good Man, Charlie Brown (musical), xx
"You're Gonna Love Tomorrow," 15, 71, 84, 156, 259
"You're Just in Love," 126
Your Hit Parade (television show), 12

Zadan, Craig, 301
Ziegfeld, Florenz, 183, 313
Ziegfeld Follies, xx, 7, 8, 18, 19, 22, 23, 49, 50, 79, 82, 111, 144, 239, 253
Zindel, Paul, 127
Zorbá (musical), xxiii, 254

Photographic Credits

Photos in text:

© Martha Swope: xiv, 12, 29, 32, 36, 38, 132, 139, 143 (top and bottom), 145, 156 (top), 171 (bottom), 173 (all four), 174, 178, 183, 199, 201, 203, 219, 225, 229, 291, 303 (top and bottom)

Courtesy Bill Yoscary: 17, 53, 68, 75, 87, 91, 93, 103, 105, 110, 113, 117, 139, 148, 151, 154, 177, 187, 189, 197, 206 (top and center), 243, 255

© Robert Galbraith, photographer: 22, 310

© Van Williams: 42, 209, 265, 294

Copyright 2002 by Daily News L.P.: 60, 206 (bottom)

Photos in color insert:

Page 1: Eliot Elisofon/Timepix

Page 2: © Lawrence Fried (top), Ormond Gigli/Timepix (bottom)

Page 3: David Edward Byrd © 1971 (top), Reprinted by Permission of Forbes Magazine © 2003 Forbes, Inc. (bottom)

Page 4: [Time] Ormand Gigli/Timepix, [Newsweek] - © Lawrence Fried; © 2003 Newsweek, Inc. All rights reserved. Reprinted by permission.

Page 5: Courtesy Bill Yoscary

Page 6: Courtesy Bill Yoscary

Page 7: Bill Pierce/Timepix

Page 8: Ormand Gigli/Timepix

A NOTE ABOUT THE AUTHOR

Ted Chapin is president and executive director of the Rodgers & Hammerstein Organization in New York. His early career in the theater included production assistant or directorial assistant on the Broadway productions of *The Sunshine Boys*, *The Rothschilds*, *The Unknown Soldier and His Wife*, and, of course, *Follies*. During his time working with Alan Arkin he was a coproducer of the Broadway-bound play *The Soft Touch*. He was also producer of the Musical Theater Lab at the Kennedy Center and musical director of the National Theatre of the Deaf. He has been the chairman of the Advisory Committee for New York City Center's "Encores!" since its inception, and sits on the board of several arts organizations.

A NOTE ON THE TYPE

This book was set in Janson, a typeface long thought to have been made by the Dutchman Anton Janson, who was a practicing typefounder in Leipzig during the years 1668–1687. However, it has been conclusively demonstrated that these types are actually the work of Nicholas Kis (1650–1702), a Hungarian, who most probably learned his trade from the master Dutch typefounder Dirk Voskens. The type is an excellent example of the influential and sturdy Dutch types that prevailed in England up to the time William Caslon (1692–1766) developed his own incomparable designs from them.

Composed by North Market Street Graphics,
Lancaster, Pennsylvania
Printed and bound by Berryville Graphics,
Berryville, Virginia
Designed by Virginia Tan